Seguin's

COMPUTER
Concepts

Second Edition

Denise Seguin
Fanshawe College, London, Ontario

PARADIGM
EDUCATION SOLUTIONS

St. Paul

Senior Vice President	Linda Hein
Editor in Chief	Christine Hurney
Senior Editor	Cheryl Drivdahl
Developmental Editor, Digital and Print	Tamborah Moore
Assistant Developmental Editors	Mamie Clark and Katie Werdick
Contributing Writer	Janet Blum
Tester	Jeff Johnson
Director of Production	Timothy W. Larson
Production Editors	Rachel Kats and Carrie Rogers
Cover and Text Designer, Senior Production Specialist	Jaana Bykonich
Copy Editor	Heidi Hogg
Indexer	Terry Casey
Vice President Sales and Marketing	Scott Burns
Director of Marketing	Lara Weber McLellan
Vice President Information Technology	Chuck Bratton
Digital Projects Manager	Tom Modl
Digital Learning Manager	Troy Weets
Digital Production Manager	Aaron Esnough
Senior Digital Production Specialist	Julie Johnston
Web Developer	Blue Earth Interactive
Video Producer	Hurix Systems

Care has been taken to verify the accuracy of information presented in this book. However, the authors, editors, and publisher cannot accept responsibility for Web, e-mail, newsgroup, or chat room subject matter or content, or for consequences from application of the information in this book, and make no warranty, expressed or implied, with respect to its content.

Trademarks: Microsoft is a trademark or registered trademark of Microsoft Corporation in the United States and/or other countries. Some of the product names and company names included in this book have been used for identification purposes only and may be trademarks or registered trade names of their respective manufacturers and sellers. The authors, editors, and publisher disclaim any affiliation, association, or connection with, or sponsorship or endorsement by, such owners.

Image Credits: See page 245

We have made every effort to trace the ownership of all copyrighted material and to secure permission from copyright holders. In the event of any question arising as to the use of any material, we will be pleased to make the necessary corrections in future printings. Thanks are due to the aforementioned authors, publishers, and agents for permission to use the materials indicated.

Paradigm Publishing, Inc., is independent from Microsoft Corporation and not affiliated with Microsoft in any manner.

ISBN 978-0-76386-884-0 (print)
ISBN 978-0-76386-887-1 (digital)

© 2017 by Paradigm Publishing, Inc.
875 Montreal Way
St. Paul, MN 55102
Email: educate@emcp.com
Website: www.emcp.com

Printed in the United States of America

25 24 23 22 21 20 19 18 17 16   1 2 3 4 5 6 7 8 9 10

Contents

Preface

Course Overview

Today's students have grown up with technology all around them and are more connected to the Internet with more devices than any generation before them. They have always had the Internet as a source of information, entertainment, and communication. Students in the classroom today likely started using the Internet and a word processor before entering grade school. Some students never turn off their smartphones, even when they go to bed at night. For many, the cell phone or smartphone is integral to daily life. Being in constant touch with friends, family, and others (including classmates, teammates, colleagues, and social media followers) is a normal way of life.

So what can a textbook on introductory computer concepts provide as value to this technology-driven audience? Knowing how to type an essay in a word processor and look up information for a history course on the Internet is not all there is to this digital world in which we live. To be successful in any career, we need an understanding of how technology is put together and how the tools at our disposal can be used effectively. In the pages that follow, you will learn about all the equipment and programs that combine to provide you with technology applications for communicating and performing tasks in your personal and professional life. You will also learn about tools and practices for using technology safely and securely and for being mindful of privacy issues.

Along with well-designed textbook pedagogy, practice and problem solving will help you learn and apply computer concepts and skills. Technology provides opportunities for interactive learning as well as excellent ways to quickly and accurately assess student performance. To this end, this textbook is supported by SNAP, Paradigm Education Solution's web-based training and assessment learning management system. Details about SNAP as well as additional student and instructor resources appear on pages vii–viii.

Course Goals

Seguin's COMPUTER Concepts Second Edition, provides instruction in achieving a basic understanding of the components that comprise computer hardware, system software, application software, Internet connectivity and resources, social media, and the security and privacy issues related to technology. No prior experience with computer concepts is required. Even those with some technological savvy can benefit from completing the course by digging deeper into topics of interest with the instructor's guidance. After completing a course that uses this textbook, you will be able:

- to identify various types of computers; explain how data is converted into information; and understand technological convergence, cloud computing, green computing, and ergonomics.
- to identify hardware and software needed to connect to the Internet; explain broadband connectivity options; recognize popular web browsers, plug-ins, and players; search the web effectively; and distinguish various online services.
- to recognize and explain the components in a system unit, input devices, output devices, and network adapters; understand how data is represented on a computer; and distinguish various options for storage and storage capacity.
- to list the major functions of operating system software and recognize popular operating systems used for computing devices; explain the purpose of embedded and cloud operating systems; describe commonly used utility programs for maintaining a computer; and use troubleshooting tools in system software for solving computer issues.
- to identify productivity and multimedia applications used in workplaces and by individuals; differentiate web-based and open source applications; explain the process to acquire, install, uninstall, and upgrade software; and provide examples of mobile apps.
- to describe popular social networking, social bookmarking, media sharing, blogging, and wiki websites; and provide examples of how businesses are using social media strategies to connect and communicate with consumers.

- to explain various risks to security and privacy encountered by connected individuals, and describe strategies for protecting against security and privacy intrusions from unwanted sources.

Textbook Organization and Methodology

This textbook is divided into seven chapters, which can be done in any order. Some instructors will follow the chapter sequence as written; however, others may assign the chapters in a different order. For example, your instructor may prefer that you study the social media content before you learn about hardware.

Each chapter opens with a brief overview, including a list of the objectives covered and a Precheck quiz that allows you to quickly discover how much you already know about the topics. All the chapter content is presented in short topics with many visual aids to minimize reading time; you will learn just what you need to know to succeed. You want to spend your time doing something—not just reading. With that in mind, at the end of each topic is a hands-on activity. Your instructor will assign this activity if he or she wants you to dig deeper into the topic you've just read. Some activities involve getting out and asking classmates, friends, or family what they do with technology; other activities have you try out the technology yourself; and some activities require investigative research on your own. Learning by discovery can be the most rewarding learning of all.

At the end of each chapter, you will have a chance to review a summary of the topics, and then take a Recheck quiz to see how much you have learned and which topics require more attention. The student ebook accompanying this textbook includes workbook pages that offer additional study tools and interactive review exercises that will reinforce and expand the knowledge you've gained. Each chapter in the workbook section concludes with seven to ten assessments, some of which are to be done individually, in pairs, or within a team. Your instructor will assign assessments based on his or her goals for your level of learning. Each chapter includes an assessment on green computing and an assessment on computer-related ethics so you can engage in meaningful discussions with your classmates about issues that face everyone in this digital world.

Course Features

The following guide shows how this textbook and its digital resources use a visual approach combined with hands-on activities to help you learn and master key concepts and topics in computer technology.

SNAP Resources

SNAP icons in the margins of the textbook are accompanied by blue text listing exercises and assessments that are available in SNAP. If you are a SNAP user, go to your SNAP Assignments page to complete the activities.

Interactive Resources

Arrow icons in the margins of the textbook indicate interactive resources that are available through the links menu in your student ebook and, in some cases, in SNAP.

- **Precheck quizzes** test your knowledge of the chapter content before you study the material. Use the results to help focus your study on the topics you need to learn. SNAP users should go to their SNAP Assignments page to complete these quizzes.
- **Tutorials** expand on interesting tech topics. Each tutorial ends with a brief quiz. SNAP users should go to their SNAP Assignments page to complete these tutorials.
- **Recheck quizzes** at the end of each chapter enable you to recheck your understanding of the chapter content. You may recheck your understanding at any time and as many times as you wish. SNAP users should go to their SNAP Assignments page to complete these quizzes.
- The **Workbook** sections of the student ebook provide study resources, review exercises, and assessments to help you reinforce and demonstrate your understanding of the topics covered in each chapter.

Textbook Elements

The following elements provide clear information to help you master the key computer concepts taught in this course.

Check This Out features provide links to websites at which you can explore more information.

> **Check This Out** ✓
>
> http://CC2.Paradigm College.net/Green Button
>
> Go here to read about the US Green Button

Good to Know features highlight interesting or fun facts or trivia about the topic.

> **Good to Know** 🎓
>
> Devices that consume power when turned off or in standby mode are called energy vampires. The Department of

Blog Topic boxes offer a chance for you to write about your experience or opinions on the topic.

> **Blog Topic   Are You Green?**
>
> Do you practice green computing? If yes, are there ways you can improve your green computing practices? If no, which green computing strategies can you start to use? Have you purchased a new PC or mobile device within the last year? If yes, how did you dispose of your older equipment?

Career Connection boxes give job information to spark interest and invite exploration of computer-related careers.

> **Career Connection** | **IT Jobs in Demand**
>
> If you enjoy working with computers, consider an IT career. The 2015 Forecast survey conducted by *Computerworld* revealed that the 10 most in-demand IT jobs were as follows, ranked from most to

Security Alert boxes offer tips for security and privacy to help you learn safe computing practices.

> **Security Alert   Protect, Track, and Back Up Your Mobile Device**
>
> Notebook and tablet theft is on the rise. In some areas, organized criminals use people to distract you while another person steals your device. Be aware of your surroundings and use anti-theft and tracking software and devices. Always have backups just in case!

Tables organize information in a streamlined format to minimize your reading load.

> **Table 1.2**
>
> Symptoms Associated with RSI Injuries from Computer Use

Symptoms of Tendonitis	Symptoms of CTS
Tingling or numbness in the fingers	Numbness and tingling in the thumb and the first two fingers especially at night (can cause sleep disruptions)
Pain in the forearm and wrist	Burning sensation when the nerve is compressed

An **Explore Further** activity at the end of each topic invites you to dig deeper into the topic by interviewing others, trying out the technology yourself, and researching related topics.

> **Explore Further   Finding a Cloud Service Provider for Storing Pictur**
>
> A popular use of cloud computing is to upload photos from your PC to a cloud storage provider so you can them on a social media website, access them from multiple devices, or have a backup if something happen mobile device.
>
> 1. Research two free cloud storage providers. Find out the amount of free storage space and look for restrictions on the file sizes that can be uploaded.
> 3. Save the document as **CloudFil**
> 4. Submit the document to your ins has requested.

A **Topics Review** chart at the end of each chapter summarizes the main chapter content and key words learned.

> **Topics Review**

Topic	Key Concepts	Key Terms
1.1 Personal Computers	An understanding of computers, computer terminology, and how computers work is computer literacy.	computer literacy
		digital literacy
	Digital literacy means the ability to use various computer devices, communication technologies, and the Internet to find, assess, use, create, and share content appropriately.	computer
		hardware
	A computer is an electronic device programmed to process, store, and output data that has been accepted as input.	software
		personal computer (PC)

Workbook Elements

The workbook sections of the student ebook provide a variety of materials you can use to review, reinforce, and demonstrate your understanding of the concepts and topics covered in the textbook. For each chapter, you will find the following workbook elements.

Interactive **study tools**, including a presentation with audio support, help reinforce your understanding of the topics. These resources are accessed from the links menu.

Interactive **review exercises**, including multiple-choice, matching, and completion questions, give you an opportunity to practice and review your understanding of the concepts. These resources are accessed from the links menu and are also available in SNAP. SNAP users should go to their SNAP Assignments page to complete these exercises.

Seven to ten **assessments** of varying complexity provide opportunities to work individually, in pairs, or in teams to produce documents, presentations, blogs, videos, and podcasts that demonstrate your understanding of topics and how they apply to the workplace or an individual application.

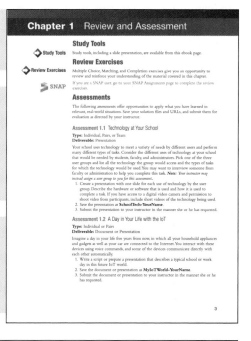

A **Green Computing assessment** prompts exploration of ways to protect the environment and make good use of its resources.

An **Ethics Discussion assessment** engages you and your classmates in a meaningful discussion about issues that face everyone in this digital world.

Course Components

The *Seguin's COMPUTER Concepts*, Second Edition, textbook contains the essential content you will need to master the key concepts and topics covered. Additional resources are provided by the following digital components.

SNAP Web-Based Training and Assessment for Microsoft® Office 2016

SNAP is a web-based training and assessment program and learning management system (LMS) for computer concepts and Microsoft Office 2016. SNAP offers rich content, a sophisticated grade book, and robust scheduling and analytics tools. SNAP courseware expands on the *Seguin's COMPUTER Concepts* text with tutorials accompanied by short quizzes. SNAP includes a quiz and exam for each chapter, plus an item bank that can be used to create custom assessments. SNAP provides automatic scoring and detailed feedback on the program's many exercises and assessments to help identify areas where additional support is needed—evaluating student performance at both the individual level and the course level. The *Seguin's COMPUTER Concepts* SNAP course content is also available to export into any LMS system that supports LTI tools. Paradigm Education Solutions provides technical support for SNAP through 24-7 chat at ParadigmCollege.com. In addition, an online user guide and other training tools for SNAP are available.

Student eBook

The student ebook provides access to all program content from any device (desktop, tablet, and smartphone) anywhere, through a live Internet connection. The versatile ebook platform features dynamic navigation tools including a linked table of contents and the ability to jump to specific pages, search for terms, bookmark, highlight, and take notes. The student ebook offers live links to the interactive content and resources that support the textbook, including the Precheck and Recheck quizzes, the tutorials with quizzes, and the workbook section.

Integrated into the student ebook, the workbook sections include access to study tools such as chapter-based presentations with audio support, interactive end-of-chapter review exercises, and end-of-chapter assessments. The student ebook is accessed through SNAP or online at Paradigm.bookshelf.emcp.com.

SNAP users should go to their SNAP Assignments page to complete all interactive quizzes, tutorials, and exercises in the student ebook.

Instructor eResources

All instructor resources are available through a web-based ebook at Paradigm.bookshelf.emcp.com. The materials are organized by type and can be previewed from the ebook or downloaded. The instructor materials include the following items:

- Grading rubrics for evaluating responses to chapter assessments
- Lesson blueprints with teaching hints, lecture tips, and discussion questions
- Syllabus suggestions and course planning resources
- Chapter-based PowerPoint presentations with lecture notes
- Chapter-based quizzes and exams

Acknowledgments

The author and editors would like to thank the following contributors and reviewers for their involvement in this project: Karen J. Allen, Assistant Professor, Community College of Rhode Island; Lenny E. Andrews, CIT/NT Program Head, Montgomery Community College, Iowa; Janet Blum, Professor, Fanshawe College, London, Ontario; Sharon R. Campbell, M.Ed., Pima Community College, Tucson, Arizona; Scott Cline, Southwestern Community College, Iowa; Cheryl Ann Farrell, Lecturer, Kauai Community College, Hawaii; Denise Gauthier, Lakehead University, Thunder Bay, Ontario; Keith Hare, Computer Instructor, Career/College Prep Program, St. Lawrence College, Kingston, Ontario; Prof. Lorraine Mastracchio, Senior Chairperson, Faculty/Curricula, Chair Office Technologies, The College of Westchester, White Plains, New York; Barbara Shapiro, Adjunct Professor, Pima Community College; Billie Terao, Kauai Community College.

About the Author

Denise Seguin has served on the Faculty of Business at Fanshawe College of Applied Arts and Technology in London, Ontario, from 1986 until her retirement from full-time teaching in December 2012. She developed curriculum and taught a variety of office technology, software applications, and accounting courses to students in postsecondary Information Technology diploma programs and Continuing Education courses. Seguin served as Program Coordinator for Computer Systems Technician, Computer Systems Technology, Office Administration, and Law Clerk programs and was acting Chair of the School of Information Technology in 2001. Along with authoring *Seguin's COMPUTER Concepts*, First and Second Editions, and *Seguin's COMPUTER Applications with Microsoft® Office 2013*, First Edition, and *with Microsoft® Office 2016*, Second Edition, has also authored Paradigm Education Solution's *Microsoft Outlook 2000 to 2016* editions and co-authored *Our Digital World* First, Second, and Third Editions, *Benchmark Series Microsoft® Excel®*, 2007, 2010, and 2013, *Benchmark Series Microsoft® Access®* 2007, 2010, and 2013, *Marquee Series Microsoft® Office*, 2000 to 2013, and *Using Computers in the Medical Office*, 2003 to 2010.

In 2007, Seguin earned her Masters in Business Administration specializing in Technology Management, choosing to take her degree at an online university. She has an appreciation for those who are juggling work and life responsibilities while furthering their education, and she has taken her online student experiences into account when designing instruction and assessment activities for this textbook.

Seguin's
COMPUTER
Concepts

Second Edition

Chapter 1

Living in a Digital World

 Precheck
Check your understanding of the topics covered in this chapter.

ndividuals and businesses interact with computers in numerous ways every day in our digital world. Some of your own interactions occur while you are at home, at work, or at school using a laptop, smartphone, or tablet. Many times you are interacting with a computing device while shopping, dining, or traveling. Consider the number of times you withdraw money from an ATM, gas up your car, swipe a debit or credit card to complete a purchase, use a self-checkout at the grocery store, or program your GPS to find a location. Many times throughout the day you are interacting with a computer without thinking about it.

To be successful in today's world, you need to use a computer independently and efficiently—which in turn requires that you have a basic understanding of computers, computer terminology, and how a computer works. These essential computer skills are often referred to as **computer literacy**. More recently the term **digital literacy** has become more widely used and is considered as important as computer literacy. To be digitally literate means that you can use various computer devices, communication technologies, and the Internet to find, assess, use, create, and share content appropriately with others.

In this chapter, you will begin your introduction to computer literacy and digital literacy by learning to distinguish the various types of computers, recognize the impact of computer innovation and convergence in our lives, explain how data is transformed into useful information, and identify trends and issues such as cloud computing, green computing, and ergonomics. This chapter is an introduction to the terminology and concepts you will explore in more detail in the chapters that follow.

 SNAP If you are a SNAP user, go to your SNAP Assignments page to complete the Precheck, Tutorials, and Recheck.

Learning Objectives

1.1 Define *computer* and identify the various types of personal computers

1.2 List various mobile devices and describe wearable and embedded computers

1.3 Differentiate servers, mainframes, and supercomputers

1.4 Define *Internet of Things* and give examples of ubiquitous computing and technological convergence

1.5 Define *information technology* and explain the four operations of information processing: input, processing, output, and storage

1.6 Explain cloud computing and list its advantages and disadvantages

1.7 Describe the goals of green computing and list ways to practice this trend

1.8 Recognize ways to use computing devices that conform to good ergonomic design

1.1 Personal Computers

A **computer** is an electronic device that has been programmed to process, store, and output data that has been accepted as input. Computers come in many sizes and shapes to meet a variety of computing needs. Most people are familiar with a desktop, laptop, or tablet and recognize it as a computer. Other electronic devices that contain programmed chips—such as digital cameras, game consoles, GPSs, or even some children's toys—also have computer capabilities designed to perform limited functions.

A computer needs both **hardware** (physical components and devices) and **software** (instructions that tell the computer what to do) to be useful. You will learn about hardware in Chapter 3, operating system programs in Chapter 4, and productivity software applications in Chapter 5.

Personal Computers

A **personal computer (PC)** is a computer in which the input, processing, storage, and output are self-contained. A PC is generally used by one person at a time, although PCs can be connected to a network where other people can access PC resources, such as a file on a storage medium. A PC is sometimes referred to as a *microcomputer*.

A **desktop computer** is a PC in which the processor, memory, and main storage device are housed within a horizontal or vertical case called the **system unit**. A vertical case is sometimes referred to as a *tower*. A separate monitor, keyboard, and mouse sit alongside or near the system unit as shown in Figure 1.1. An all-in-one case integrates the system unit and monitor into one device as shown in Figure 1.2.

Figure 1.1

A desktop computer may have a vertical system unit, which is sometimes called a *tower*.

Figure 1.2

The Apple iMac sports an all-in-one case where the monitor, processor, memory, and storage media are housed in one unit.

Mobile Computers

A **mobile computer** is a PC that can be moved from place to place. Mobile computers come in a number of configurations that vary in size, shape, and weight. A **laptop computer** fits comfortably on a person's lap and is also referred to as a **notebook**. These PCs often replace desktops for today's mobile workers and for home users who want the ability to move easily from room to room with their PCs. A typical notebook (Figure 1.3) has a clamshell-style design. When the notebook is opened, the monitor swivels up to reveal a keyboard. The processor, memory, storage media, and battery are housed below the keyboard.

Figure 1.3

Laptops, also referred to as *notebooks*, have a clamshell design in which the monitor opens up to reveal the system unit.

A type of notebook that is thinner, lighter in weight, but just as powerful as a traditional notebook is called an **ultrabook**. Ultrabooks were originally named by Intel (a company that manufactures computer chips) to differentiate the new slim, lightweight notebook design that aims to achieve faster processing and storage while extending battery life. Most ultrabooks are only 0.6 to 0.7 inches thick and weigh an average of 2.5 pounds. Apple's MacBook Air, shown in Figure 1.4, is a popular ultrabook; however, all the other major hardware manufacturers also have ultrabooks.

A **netbook** is a low-cost, smaller notebook designed for people who primarily only need access to web-based applications. These notebooks contain limited software applications. Netbooks have mostly been replaced by tablets and ultrabooks.

A **tablet** (also called a *tablet PC*) is a lightweight notebook with a small screen that you interact with using touch gestures or a special pen called a *stylus*. Slate tablets have an on-screen keyboard only, while other tablets come with a keyboard that pivots or plugs in so that the tablet acts more like a traditional notebook. Figure 1.5 shows the popular Apple iPad. A laptop that can be used like a tablet by swiveling the screen and/or folding down the screen (Figure 1.6) is called a **convertible laptop** or **hybrid laptop**.

Figure 1.4

Ultrabooks such as The Apple MacBook Air are slim and lightweight, yet powerful.

Figure 1.5

The Apple iPad is a popular tablet.

Figure 1.6

A convertible (hybrid) laptop can be used as a tablet.

Security Alert | **Protect, Track, and Back Up Your Mobile Device**

Notebook and tablet theft is on the rise. In some areas, organized criminals use people to distract you while another person steals your device. Be aware of your surroundings and use anti-theft and tracking software and devices. Always have backups just in case!

Blog Topic | **Is the PC Dead?**

Smartphones and tablets are increasingly powerful, with many of the same tools offered on a notebook. Desktop sales have been steadily decreasing. Some people argue that smartphones and tablets are simply supplementing the traditional desktop and notebook and that sales data are misleading since desktops and notebooks last longer.

1. Write and post a blog entry with a paragraph that describes the number of computing devices you own and how you use them. State your response to the blog topic question *Is the PC dead?* and provide your rationale.

2. Read at least two of your classmates' blog entries and post one comment to each.

3. Submit your blog URL and the URLs of the two classmates' blogs to your instructor in the manner she or he has requested.

Explore Further | **Comparing Ultrabooks with Tablets**

Assume the manager at the office where you intern is interested in buying a new mobile computer. The manager is not sure whether an ultrabook or a tablet is the better choice.

1. Research the similarities and differences between ultrabooks and tablets. Choose one model of each for your comparison. Specifically, find out the physical characteristics of each (weight and screen size), connectivity options (ports, wireless, Bluetooth options), input options (keyboard, touchscreen), storage options, and processor speeds.

2. Create a document or spreadsheet to present the comparison of an ultrabook to a tablet by each criterion. Clearly identify the

model of each device you are presenting and include the URLs of the websites from which you obtained the specifications.

3. Save the document or spreadsheet as **UltrabookvsTablet-YourName**.

4. Submit the document or spreadsheet to your instructor in the manner she or he has requested.

1.2 Mobile Devices, Wearable Computers, and Embedded Computers

A handheld computing device smaller than a notebook is referred to as a **mobile device**. Mobile devices have smaller screens and store programs and data within the unit or on a memory card. Some mobile devices rely entirely on touch-based input while others have a built-in or slide-out keyboard. Wearable computers are devices that can be worn on the body by attaching to an arm, a belt, a helmet, eyeglasses, or clothing. These computers are used to perform special functions such as health monitoring and to assist with other hands-free work. Embedded computers reside within electronic devices—such as household appliances and gadgets—that are designed to perform specific tasks.

Mobile Devices

Increasingly, mobile devices are expanding computer use outside our homes and offices. Examples of these mobile devices are shown in Figure 1.7:

- A **smartphone** is a cell phone with a built-in camera that offers software applications (called *apps*), web-browsing, and messaging capabilities via cellular or other wireless networks. A smartphone that has a screen size larger than 5.25 inches but that is not as large as a typical tablet is called a **phablet** (meaning the combination of *phone* and *tablet*).
- A **portable media player** is a device used to play music, watch videos, view photos, play games, and/or read electronic books.
- An **ebook reader** (also called an *ereader*) is a device sized larger than a smartphone but smaller than a tablet and used to read electronic versions of books (called *ebooks*), newspapers, magazines, or other digital media.

Figure 1.7

A smartphone, portable media player, and ebook reader are popular mobile devices.

Wearable Computers

A computing device that can be worn on the body and functions while the individual is walking or otherwise moving around is called a **wearable computer**. These devices are usually always on, include sensors for various purposes, and provide for hands-free use with communications capability. They may allow input with voice commands, hand movements, joysticks, buttons, or touch. Wearable computers are used to assist or monitor individuals with health conditions, track items, provide real-time information, access documentation, or engage in virtual reality simulations. For example, the Department of Defense helped develop wearable computers for soldiers that monitor the battlefield environment.

Google's Project Glass eyeglasses use a heads-up virtual display that interacts with the wearer to provide information and communication technologies without the wearer having to use a smartphone. A limited number of Google Glasses were available for purchase in 2013, but in January 2015 Google announced a halt to production while it brought the project in-house for more development. Google Glass 2 was in development at the time of writing, with reports indicating the Google team is working on improvements to battery life and performance for the next generation of the wearable device.

The launch in April 2015 of Apple's smartwatch, named Apple Watch, brought digital wristwatches (Figure 1.8) to the public eye—although these products had been available for several years prior. These wearable devices connect to your smartphone and provide you with apps to manage calls, messages, appointments, alerts, and other data from your wrist.

Figure 1.8

According to a 2014 study by Acquity Group (a digital marketing company), 23 percent of participants interviewed plan to buy a smartwatch by 2019.

Embedded Computers

Numerous household appliances and consumer electronics incorporate an **embedded computer** that has a processor programmed to perform a particular task (Figure 1.9). Often, this type of device is referred to as a **smart device**. Examples can include a microwave oven that calculates defrost time depending on weight, a refrigerator that sounds an alarm when the inside temperature becomes problematic, and a washer that connects to your smartphone, allowing you to change options or start a wash cycle remotely.

Digital cameras, game consoles, electronic thermostats, electronic alarm monitoring systems, ATMs, and car navigation consoles are just a few other examples of devices with embedded systems. Digital devices are everywhere and so prevalent that many times you may not be aware you are using a computer!

Figure 1.9

Electronic devices with embedded systems—such as this handheld game console, digital camera, and electronic thermostat—are each designed to perform a specific task.

Explore Further   Favorite Computing Devices

Have you ever wondered what mobile devices the people you know most like to use? There's one way to find out....

1. Conduct a survey with at least 10 relatives, friends, neighbors, or classmates to find out each person's favorite mobile device, wearable gadget, or smart household device.

2. Compile the results of your informal survey and create a document, spreadsheet, or presentation that presents the results.

3. Save the document, spreadsheet, or presentation as **DeviceSurvey-YourName**.

4. Submit the document, spreadsheet, or presentation to your instructor in the manner she or he has requested.

1.3 Computers for Connecting Multiple Users and Specialized Processing

Larger, more powerful computers are used by organizations that need to connect many people to resources and store and process large amounts of data. Individuals use PCs to connect via a network to these larger computers for access to programs, processing, and storage resources. A high-end computer with multiple processors, large amounts of memory, and a large storage capacity can function as a server in a small network. Larger organizations purchase midrange servers and mainframes when hundreds or thousands of users need to process transactions simultaneously. Supercomputers are used when massive computing power is needed to perform advanced calculations.

Servers

A **server** is a computer with hardware and software that allows it to link together other computers to provide services such as Internet access and to share resources such as programs, data, printers, and storage. A computer that connects to a server is called a **client**. Servers are high-performance computers often stacked in racks (Figure 1.10) and stored in a **server room** that is maintained to avoid heat, humidity, and dust.

Figure 1.10

Servers mounted in racks are stored in a separate room protected from excessive heat, humidity, and dust.

Good to Know

Midrange servers used to be known as *minicomputers*.

A **midrange server** is used in small and medium-sized organizations that need to connect hundreds of client computers at the same time. Midrange servers are more powerful than a PC but not as powerful as a mainframe.

A computer connected to a network that does not store any data or software on the local PC is called a **thin client**. Some companies use thin clients to reduce costs and/or maintain tighter security on software licensing and data.

A type of thin client called a virtual desktop infrastructure (VDI) allows a computer user to access a virtual desktop from any device connected to the Internet, including a smartphone or tablet. VDI software is installed on each device, and the user's operating system, applications, and files are all stored on a central server that can be accessed from anywhere in the world.

Mainframes

A large, powerful, and expensive computer used by governments and large organizations—such as banks, insurance companies, and other corporations—to connect hundreds or thousands of users simultaneously is known as a **mainframe** (Figure 1.11). These computers have specialized hardware and software capable of processing millions of transactions and retaining massive volumes of data.

Figure 1.11

Mainframe computers connect thousands of computers simultaneously and process and store millions of transactions.

Supercomputers

The fastest, most expensive, and most powerful of all computers is a **supercomputer**. A supercomputer is capable of performing trillions of calculations per second. These massive computers are usually designed for a specific task, such as performing the complex mathematical calculations needed for weather forecasting, nuclear research, oil exploration, or scientific research analysis.

Supercomputing speed is expressed in petaflops. A **petaflop** (a measurement used in scientific calculations) represents a quadrillion floating point operations per second. Figure 1.12 shows the Stratus supercomputer installed at the National Oceanic and Atmospheric Administration agency. According to the TOP500 project, which tracks supercomputers, the United States has more of the top 500 supercomputers than any other country in the world, but China was home to the world's most powerful supercomputer in 2015.

Figure 1.12

Stratus, a supercomputer installed at the National Oceanic and Atmospheric Administration, performs 69.7 trillion calculations per second, allowing meteorologists to rapidly update severe weather forecasts. The microprocessors inside Stratus contain 2,000 miles of copper wiring, enough to stretch from Washington, DC, to the Grand Canyon.

Good to Know 🎓

The United States has set 2023 as the target date for the next leap in supercomputing development. The Department of Energy announced plans to develop an exascale system with IBM. One exaflop in this system equals one quintillion (1 followed by 18 zeros) calculations per second! Top researchers say the technical challenges involved in developing software for such a system may require international cooperation.

Explore Further   A History of Computing Time Line

The Computer History Museum located in Mountain View, California, offers information about the most influential people, technology, and events in computing history. Its online exhibit Timeline of Computer History offers an interactive exploration into the origins of computers.

1. Go to **http://CC2.ParadigmCollege.net/ComputerHistory** to view the online Timeline of Computer History exhibit.

2. Pick five consecutive years in the time line that are of interest to you, click the year, and read the information presented in the online exhibit. *Note: Your instructor may instead choose to assign you a time period so that a complete time line is presented to the class.*

3. Create a presentation with one slide per year and provide a brief summary in your own words that describes the significant people, technology, or event shown in the time line.

4. Save the presentation as **ComputerTimeLine-YourName**.

5. Submit the presentation to your instructor in the manner she or he has requested.

1.4 Computer Innovations and Trends

Technology is constantly evolving, meaning there will always be change in the devices and methods that we use for completing tasks at home, at work, and at school. Technologies are also converging, meaning that a device that originally was designed for one purpose, such as a cell phone designed only to make voice calls, is now capable of performing multiple functions, such as browsing the web, taking photos, sending and receiving email, and creating documents. The Internet of Things will change the way we work and play by connecting everyday objects to a network and enabling them to communicate directly with one another.

Ubiquitous Computing

Dictionary.com defines *ubiquitous* as an adjective that means "existing or being everywhere, especially at the same time; omnipresent." **Ubiquitous computing** means that computing technology is everywhere within our environment and used all of the time. Effectively, the technology mostly fades into the background and users become unaware of the technology as they focus on the task at hand. Ubiquitous computing will become even more prevalent to all of us when the Internet of Things starts connecting everyday objects (such as your coffee maker) to the Internet. Consider these four examples of computer innovations in various industries:

Travel Starwood Hotels & Resorts is one of many companies that have developed a travel app for the Apple Watch, released in April 2015. With the SPG app on an Apple Watch, travelers can unlock the door to their rooms from their wrists. No room key is needed and the guest does not have to fumble around to point his or her smartphone at the lock. The app can also be used to view directions to the hotel and check in without having to visit the front desk.

Use your Apple Watch to view directions to your hotel, check in as you enter the lobby, and unlock your door.

Restaurant In 2015, McDonald's introduced self-serve kiosks at select locations. At these kiosks, customers use a tablet-style touchscreen to place an order and complete payment. They can also use the system to customize an item, including choosing from a selection of buns and toppings. At other McDonald's locations, customers are served at a table by a waiter using a tablet. Other fast-food or "fast casual" restaurants that have implemented self-serve kiosks or tablet ordering at the table include Chili's, Applebee's, and Taco Bell, to name a few.

Providing self-serve kiosks is just one way McDonald's is using new technology.

Law Enforcement Police officers are using wearable technology to provide better service and help with securing convictions. Some forces in Georgia supply officers with Google Glass eyeglasses to record everything and send information back to the station in real time. In other jurisdictions, wristwatch computers allow officers to receive information via text message or other type of alert, which can help officers in hostile situations or places where accessing a radio or smartphone will slow down or otherwise compromise their efforts and safety. Within the next decade, a Wi-Fi–enabled uniform that has a textile waveguide antenna sewn into the fabric will track a police officer's movements and remotely monitor his or her vital signs while maintaining constant communication.

Medicine In 2015, at Strong Memorial Hospital, a team of heart specialists used a 3-D printed model of a patient's heart to plan a less invasive heart valve replacement surgery for a high-risk patient. 3-D printing is also used to create custom prosthetic hands and arms for a lower cost than traditional prostheses. In March 2015, Robert Downey Jr. surprised a seven-year-old with a 3-D printed prosthetic arm that looks like the arm Downey wears as Iron Man.

A team of volunteer engineers at Limbitless Solutions created this "Iron Man" prosthetic arm for a seven-year-old boy using 3-D printing technology.

Convergence

Technological convergence, where innovation merges several technologies into a single device, is not just about cell phones becoming multipurpose smartphones. Game consoles used to be used only to play video games, but today's multipurpose consoles are also used to play movies from Blu-ray or DVD and to stream content via the web. You can also surf the web, browse photos, and play music on newer systems.

The Internet of Things

An emerging trend, called the **Internet of Things (IoT)**, describes situations where everyday objects contain embedded processors and are connected to a network, allowing devices to interact with the owner and/ or other connected "things." Imagine a world where every product—for example, alarm clocks, coffee makers, refrigerators, stoves, dishwashers, washing machines, clothes dryers, door locks, thermostats, and entertainment systems—can communicate via the Internet. In this connected world, imagine your day begins with the alarm clock awakening you with current weather and traffic conditions, reminding you about a meeting, adjusting the room temperature, and starting the coffee maker. This is just how your day begins! The possibilities for other interactions throughout the day are numerous. Since some of the interactions between connected devices occur without human intervention, this trend is also sometimes referred to as **machine-to-machine communications** or *M2M communications*.

Tutorial
What Is the Internet of Things?

Market research firm International Data Corporation (IDC) has forecasted that the global market for IoT devices and services will exceed $7 trillion by 2020.

Explore Further | What New Technology Innovation Is Occurring in Your Field of Study?

Technological innovation occurs every day, and a computer innovation will likely occur in your field of study while you are still in school.

1. Either by searching the web or by interviewing someone who works in your field of study, investigate a technology innovation that is occurring in your field or that will occur by the time you graduate.

2. Create a document with a brief description of the innovation you learned about and the impact the innovation is expected to have

within the industry. At the end of the document, include the URLs of websites you used or a reference for the person you interviewed.

3. Save the document as **ComputerInnovation-YourName**.

4. Submit the document to your instructor in the manner she or he has requested.

1.5 Information Technology and the Information Processing Cycle

Tutorial
What Makes Up a
Computer System?

Information technology (IT) refers to the use of computers, software, networks, and other communication systems and processes to store, retrieve, send, process, and protect information. The IT department in an organization is tasked with managing the hardware, software, networks, and other systems that form the information infrastructure. IT specialists are involved with designing, developing, implementing, and maintaining information systems.

Characters that are typed or otherwise entered into a computer are **raw data** or **data**. At the entry stage, the data is not meaningful as it is just a string of characters. Software programs provide the instructions for the computer to process and organize the data into meaningful and useful **information**. The **information processing cycle** includes the operations that transform data into information: input, processing, output, and storage, as shown in Figure 1.13 and described next. The terminology and hardware introduced in this topic will be explored in more detail in Chapter 3.

Figure 1.13

The information processing cycle includes four operations to transform raw data into useful information.

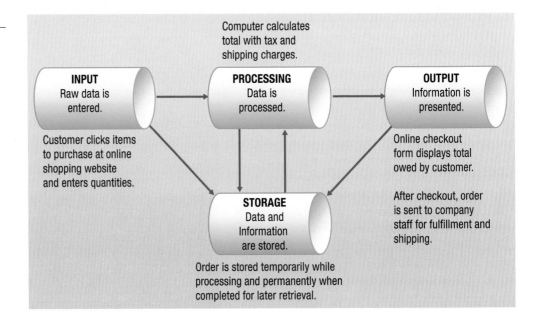

INPUT
Raw data is entered.

PROCESSING
Data is processed.

OUTPUT
Information is presented.

STORAGE
Data and Information are stored.

Computer calculates total with tax and shipping charges.

Customer clicks items to purchase at online shopping website and enters quantities.

Online checkout form displays total owed by customer.

After checkout, order is sent to company staff for fulfillment and shipping.

Order is stored temporarily while processing and permanently when completed for later retrieval.

Input

Any device used to enter raw data or communicate instructions to the computer is an **input device**. Commonly used devices include a keyboard, mouse, and touchscreen similar to the ones shown in Figure 1.14. A touchpad, scanner, bar code reader, digital camera, digital pen, webcam, and microphone are just a few other examples of input devices.

Figure 1.14

A keyboard, mouse, and touchscreen are common devices used to enter input.

Processing

A computer chip called the **central processing unit (CPU)** carries out the instructions given by the software to perform the **processing** cycle. Think of the CPU as the brain of the computer. A CPU is a silicon chip referred to as the **microprocessor** and is housed on the computer motherboard (printed circuit board that contains the main computer components). Microprocessors today are typically manufactured with multiple cores, which are independent units on the same chip that can process data simultaneously. A **multicore processor** significantly increases speed and performance. Intel is a leading designer and manufacturer of microprocessors (Figure 1.15).

Figure 1.15

In September 2015, Intel announced its sixth-generation family of Core processors. These are designed to enhance performance at the lowest power levels ever and will be available for a wide range of devices, from high-end desktops to the smallest IoT gadgets.

Output

Anything used to view the information processed and organized by the computer is an **output device**. Typically, you view information on a monitor and/or print it on a printer similar to the ones shown in Figure 1.16. Other output devices include speakers and screens such as those on mobile devices and televisions.

Figure 1.16

A monitor or embedded screen, and a printer are commonly used to view information processed by the computer. The speakers and screens on mobile devices such as a smartphone or tablet can also be considered output devices.

Storage

While processing, instructions and data are temporarily stored in a holding area called **random access memory (RAM)**. RAM is also housed on the computer motherboard. RAM is temporary storage that is cleared when power to the computer is lost.

Cache memory is located either on the CPU chip or on a separate chip between the CPU and RAM and is used to store frequently used data. Speed and performance are increased with cache memory since the CPU checks cache memory first before checking RAM. The faster retrieval of frequently used data saves the processor time.

Permanent storage (Figure 1.17) is any device or location that saves data and information for later use; this type of device is referred to as a **storage medium**. Several storage media, some portable and some housed inside the system unit, are available in various capacities. An internal hard disk drive is housed inside the system unit, while USB flash drives (also called *memory sticks*), external hard drives, and optical discs such as CDs, DVDs, and Blu-ray are portable (can be easily removed from the computer). You may also connect via a network to a hard drive on another computer for storage.

Figure 1.17

Permanent storage is available in media with various capacities such as an internal hard disk drive (shown with the top metal cover removed), a USB flash drive, an external hard disk drive, and optical discs.

An increasingly popular trend is to store information using **cloud storage**, where you log in to a website and copy documents, photos, or other information to a web service. Cloud storage services such as Flickr (a website used to store photos) and Dropbox (a website where you can store any type of file) have become popular since they offer free online storage that can be shared easily or accessed anywhere you can connect to the Internet. You will learn more about cloud computing in the next topic.

Communications

In today's highly connected world, a fifth operation called *communications* is often added to the information processing cycle. Computers accept input from and send output to other computers via various wired and wireless communication channels, such as cable, telephone line, satellite, cellular, microwave, and Bluetooth transmission media. A **communications device** is any component used to facilitate the transmission of data, such as a cable modem, DSL modem, or router (Figure 1.18).

An integrated modem and wireless router are used to connect the computer devices on the home network to the Internet.

Figure 1.18
Computers connect to other computers to receive input and send output using communications devices such as the integrated modem and wireless router shown.

Career Connection

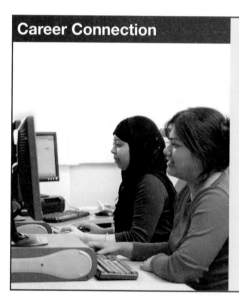

IT Jobs in Demand

If you enjoy working with computers, consider an IT career. The 2016 Forecast survey conducted by *Computerworld* revealed that the 10 most in-demand IT jobs were as follows, ranked from most to least: IT architecture, programming and application development, project management, big data, business intelligence and analytics, help desk and technical support, database administration, security and compliance administration, cloud computing, and web development. If any of these careers are of interest to you, look at courses offered in postsecondary programs in computer engineering, computer science, computer systems technician, information systems, information technology, and software engineering.

Explore Further   IT Job Profile

You have read in the Career Connection for this topic that IT jobs are in demand. You are interested in working with computers but want to learn more about specific job openings to find out what employers are looking for in new employees.

1. Using a job search website such as Monster.com, locate a current ad for an IT job that interests you within your area. *Hint: Use titles from the Career Connection.*

2. Create a document that describes the job opportunity in your own words, including the job title, the company offering the job, the duties involved in the job, and the qualifications required. Include

information on compensation if the ad lists a salary range. At the end of the document, provide the URL for the job ad.

3. Save the document as **ITJobAd-YourName**.

4. Submit the document to your instructor in the manner she or he has requested.

1.6 Cloud Computing

Tutorial
How Can Cloud Computing Save Businesses Money?

Individuals and businesses are turning to providers of software and computing services that are accessed entirely on the Internet. This delivery model of software and services is called **cloud computing**. With cloud computing, all you need to get your work done is a computer with a web browser, since all the software and files are stored online.

Cloud computing got its name because the Internet has always been identified with a cloud in technology documentation. Cloud computing places the processing and storage operations of the information processing cycle at an online service provider's server and/or data center, rather than on the hardware and software of your own PC or mobile device (Figure 1.19). You can use some cloud computing services for free. For example, at Google Drive, 15 GB of cloud storage is free (with an option to pay a fee for more storage space).

Figure 1.19

Cloud computing means that your software applications and/or data are launched from a web browser and stored on the service provider's equipment. The software and data are accessible from any PC or mobile device.

The delivery of software via the Internet is referred to as **Software as a Service (SaaS)**. Advantages and disadvantages of cloud computing are listed in Table 1.1.

If you open your web browser to check email, create documents, or upload photos, music, videos, or other files to store and share with others, then you are already using SaaS services. A few popular cloud computing services

Table 1.1

Advantages and Disadvantages of Cloud Computing

Advantages	Disadvantages
Applications and data are available at any time from any place since all you need is an Internet connection.	You are totally dependent on your Internet connection; if the service goes down, you cannot access your programs or files.
Updates to software are automatic and immediately available.	You do not have control over changes made to software—upgrading is not at your discretion.
The service provider makes continual investment in hardware and software. You pay only the subscription fees after you have purchased your computer and Internet connectivity.	Over a long period, monthly subscription fees could end up costing more than the initial outlay of cash for hardware and software and ongoing Internet connectivity.
Web applications are generally easy to use and navigate.	Web applications may be too limiting to meet your needs.
Web-based applications are generally compatible with PCs, Macs, and mobile devices—you can use any device.	Some businesses may have compatibility issues with exchanging data with legacy systems or infrastructure.
Documents, photos, music, videos, and other files are stored off-site. If you experience equipment malfunction, theft, or some other disaster, all that is lost is the physical equipment, which is easily replaced.	Large cloud computing vendors have reliable and secure storage; however, there is a risk that personal and/or sensitive data could be accessed by unauthorized users. Also be mindful of who actually owns the data you are storing online—is it you or the provider?

include Google Drive, Dropbox, iCloud, and OneDrive. Many more cloud computing service providers exist to meet the growing market for web applications.

Figure 1.20 illustrates a simple three-slide presentation created in Google Slides. If you are familiar with presentation software, creating a presentation in the Google Slides web-based application will be easy since the program contains tools similar to what you would find in other presentation programs. Google Slides is just one application in the free productivity suite offered by Google. Other applications include Google Docs, Google Sheets, Google Forms, and Google Drawings.

Microsoft offers a similar suite of free web-based applications called Office Online from which you can open Word Online, Excel Online, PowerPoint Online, and OneNote Online. To start any of these applications requires that you sign up for a Microsoft account, which can be any email address you want to use as your user name. A Hotmail or Live email address is automatically a Microsoft account and means that you do not need to sign up to use the Office Online applications.

Free productivity suites in the cloud are ideal options for anyone with a need to create a simple document, presentation, or worksheet. However, web-based applications have limited features—complex work most likely requires a traditional desktop software application.

Check This Out ✓

http://CC2.Paradigm College.net/Office Online

Go here to start a document, presentation, worksheet, or notebook using Microsoft's web-based Office Online suite. You will need to sign in with a valid Microsoft, work, or school email address to use the free software.

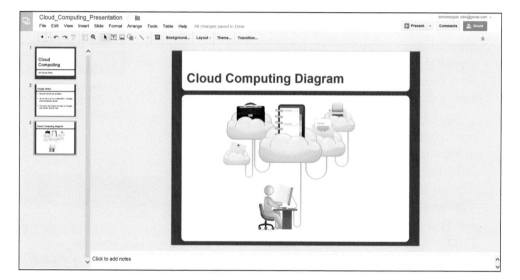

Figure 1.20

Sign in with a Gmail [ac]count at the Google home p[age] to access Google Drive a[nd] then start Google Slides to c[rea]te a presentation similar to [the] one shown here using free w[eb]-based software.

Security Alert   **Minimize Your Risks with Cloud Storage**

Data stored in the cloud is at risk of loss, theft, or breach by a hacker. One cloud security company predicts that 21 percent of data uploaded to a cloud storage provider by employees contains confidential data including a company's intellectual property. Protect against these risks by (1) never storing in the cloud a file with personal or otherwise sensitive information, (2) making sure your cloud provider encrypts data (that is, stores the file in a format unrecognizable to unauthorized users), and (3) saving a backup somewhere else just in case.

Explore Further   **Finding a Cloud Service Provider for Storing Pictures**

A popular use of cloud computing is to upload photos from your PC to a cloud storage provider so you can share them without posting them on a social media website, access them from multiple devices, or have a backup if something happens to the pictures on your PC or mobile device.

1. Research two free cloud storage providers. Find out the amount of free storage space and look for restrictions on the file sizes that can be uploaded.

2. Create a document that compares the two cloud providers.

3. Save the document as **CloudFileStorage-YourName**.

4. Submit the document to your instructor in the manner she or he has requested.

1.7 Green Computing

Green computing refers to the use of computers and other electronic devices in an environmentally responsible manner. Green computing can encompass new or modified computing practices, policies, and procedures. The green computing trend is growing, with more individuals and businesses adopting green strategies every year. Green strategies include reducing the energy consumption of computers and other devices; reducing the use of paper, ink, and toner; and reusing, recycling, or properly disposing of electronic waste (referred to as **e-waste** or *e-trash*).

In addition to changes in computing practices, manufacturers are working to produce electronics that are more energy efficient, reduce the amount of toxic chemicals used in computers, and incorporate more recyclable components and packaging. Finally, governments and industries are making available more recycling programs to reuse or properly dispose of electronics.

Five Ways to Go Green

1. Make sure you use Energy Star–certified devices.

   The Energy Star label on a device means the manufacturer has reached or exceeded the minimum federal standards for reduced energy consumption.

This label identifies a device as being Energy Star compliant.

2. Turn off devices when you are not using them and unplug them if you will not be using them for an extended period of time. Even better—use smart power strips that automatically reduce the power to devices when not in use.

   The US Department of Energy set new standards for microwave ovens manufactured on or after June 17, 2016, that reduce standby energy use. The department estimates that over a 30-year period, this change will be equivalent to removing 12 million new cars from the roads for one year! The savings over time with lower energy bills will also be a bonus for consumers.

A smart power strip reduces energy consumption by controlling the flow of power to peripheral devices when the main device is not in use or is in standby mode.

3. Reduce printing to only those documents, messages, or photos that absolutely must be in paper copy and make sure what you print uses the least amount of paper.

   Make it a policy to distribute PDF copies of documents and messages and to share photos online with friends and relatives. When you must print, consider using both sides of the paper and/or using narrower margins so you can fit more on a page. The cost savings from reduced paper consumption, toner, and ink cartridges is significant. Consider also that fewer print cartridges will end up in the landfills.

Reduce printing—only print what you absolutely must have a paper copy.

4. Modify the default power options on your computer to conserve more energy.

   Most Windows-based desktop and notebook computers default to a balanced power plan, which aims to balance performance with energy conservation. You can adjust the sleep and display settings to turn off power sooner than the default times. Choose *Power Options* in the Hardware and Sound category of the Control Panel on a Windows PC.

   On Mac computers, adjust the energy features using the Energy Saver pane in System Preferences.

5. Consider reselling or donating equipment you no longer need.

   Computers, cell phones, and electronics that are still in working order can be sold or donated to schools, churches, or nonprofit groups. If you must dispose of electronics, try to drop off the e-waste at an electronics recycling facility.

   In the United States, approximately 3.4 million tons of e-waste is thrown away each year. Most of this discarded electronic equipment ends up in landfills or is exported to countries such as China and India.

Modify power options on your PC to conserve more energy.

Whenever possible, divert e-waste from landfills.

Good to Know

According to estimates by the Environmental Protection Agency, only 27 percent of e-waste is recycled.

Blog Topic   Are You Green?

Do you practice green computing? If yes, are there ways you can improve your green computing practices? If no, which green computing strategies can you start to use? Have you purchased a new PC or mobile device within the last year? If yes, how did you dispose of your older equipment?

1. Write and post a blog entry that provides your answers to the questions.

2. Read at least two of your classmates' blogs and post one comment to each.

3. Submit your blog URL and the URLs of the two classmates' blogs to your instructor in the manner she or he has requested.

Explore Further   Locating Electronic Recycling Services in Your Area

Approximately 130 million cell phones were replaced last year in the United States. If only 27 percent of those phones were recycled, then almost 95 million cell phones ended up in landfills. This does not take into account other electronics such as game consoles, tablets, laptops, desktops, and televisions. Assume you decide to gather up some old electronics for disposal. Do you know where to take e-waste in your area?

1. Find out the nearest electronic waste drop-off location in your area. Determine the hours of operation, the items accepted for recycling, and items that are not accepted, if any.

2. Create a document that could be used as a flyer to advertise the service in your neighborhood and that contains all the information you found.

3. Save the document as **eWasteRecycling-YourName**.

4. Submit the document to your instructor in the manner she or he has requested.

1.8 Computers and Your Health

Frequent use of computing devices can adversely affect your health if you don't use proper care and preventive strategies. Physical ailments that can occur include fatigue, eyestrain, blurred vision, backaches, wrist and forearm pain, finger numbness or pain, and neck and shoulder pain. A leading job-related illness and injury in North America is **repetitive-strain injury (RSI)**. RSI is an injury or disorder of the joints, nerves, muscles, ligaments, or tendons.

Two common computer-related RSI injuries are **tendonitis** and **carpal tunnel syndrome (CTS)**. Tendonitis occurs when a tendon in your wrist becomes inflamed. CTS occurs when the nerve that connects the forearm to the palm of the hand becomes inflamed. Both conditions are caused by excessive typing, mouse scrolling, mouse clicking, and thumb typing/movements on mobile devices. Symptoms of tendonitis and CTS are listed in Table 1.2.

Carpal tunnel syndrome is a common RSI injury from computer use that causes pain in the hand and wrist.

Table 1.2

Symptoms Associated with RSI Injuries from Computer Use

Symptoms of Tendonitis	Symptoms of CTS
Tingling or numbness in the fingers	Numbness and tingling in the thumb and the first two fingers especially at night (can cause sleep disruptions)
Pain in the forearm and wrist	Burning sensation when the nerve is compressed
Decreased mobility of the wrist or fingers	Decreased grip strength leading the user to drop objects
Loss of strength in the hand	Loss of strength in the hand

Computer Vision Syndrome

Computer vision syndrome (CVS) is a temporary condition caused by prolonged computer use that involves eye strain; weak, itchy, burning, or dry eyes; blurred or double vision; difficulty with focus; sensitivity to light; headaches; and neck pain. According to the American Optometric Association, 50 to 90 percent of computer workers will experience some CVS symptoms.

CVS affects 50 to 90 percent of computer users.

Posture-Related Injuries

Pain in the lower back, neck, shoulders, and arms are common complaints from computer workers. Sitting for long periods of time in the same position causes fatigue and reduces circulation to muscles and tendons, which can lead to stiffness and soreness.

Neck pain is a common complaint among computer workers.

Prevention Strategies to Reduce Risk of RSI, CVS, and Muscular Pain

Knowing the three primary risk factors for developing health issues when using a computer is key to identifying strategies to reduce risk of injury: poor posture, poor technique, and excessive use. Prevention strategies are listed in Table 1.3. Many of these strategies involve the use of **ergonomics** to improve the computer workspace design. Ergonomics involves the design of equipment and a person's workspace to promote safe and comfortable operation of the equipment by the individual. In other words, good ergonomic design fits the computer equipment to the worker by adjusting components to the optimal height, distance, and angles (see Figure 1.21).

Figure 1.21
An ergonomically correct computer workspace helps prevent RSI injuries.

Table 1.3

Preventive Strategies for Avoiding Computer-Related Illness

Take frequent breaks. Get up out of the chair and walk around, stretch, and do another activity for a few moments.
Maintain good posture by sitting up straight with feet flat on the floor, shoulders relaxed, head and neck balanced and in line with torso, and your lower back supported by your chair or a rolled towel. If the desk height is not adjustable, use a foot rest.
Sit in a chair that has five legs for stability and allows adjustments to height and angle of backrest, seat, and arm rests.
When typing, the keyboard should be at elbow level with the elbows close to your body and supported by your chair. Wrists and hands should be positioned in line with forearms. If using a notebook computer, consider plugging in an external keyboard so that you can adjust the height and position.
The top of the computer screen should be at or slightly below your eye level. If using a notebook computer, consider using an external monitor that you can adjust to the correct height. Optimal viewing distance is 20 to 40 inches. Increase font size in documents and browsers if necessary to avoid eye strain.
Remember to blink—studies have shown computer users tend to blink about five times less than normal. Also minimize glare and use ambient lighting rather than overhead fluorescents if possible.
Look away from the computer screen once in a while and spend a few moments focusing on something that is off in the distance. For example, look out the window at something outside.

Check This Out ✔

http://CC2.Paradigm College.net/Work station

Go here for an interactive e-tool to learn more about proper workstation setup, or view setup checklists.

Explore Further | Notebook, Texting, and Smartphone Ergonomics

Good ergonomic workspace design for a notebook PC involves some factors not discussed in Table 1.3. Increased smartphone use can become a risk for some people. For example, the term BlackBerry thumb was devised to describe pain that developed from excessive texting.

1. Research ergonomics for laptops and smartphones. Specifically, find at least two articles that address the unique needs of mobile computing device users.

2. Create a document with a checklist that includes ergonomically correct usage of mobile devices. Include the URLs of the articles you used at the end of the document.

3. Save the document as **MobileErgonomics-YourName**.

4. Submit the document to your instructor in the manner she or he has requested.

Topics Review

Topic	Key Concepts	Key Terms
1.1 Personal Computers	An understanding of computers, computer terminology, and how computers work is computer literacy. Digital literacy means the ability to use various computer devices, communication technologies, and the Internet to find, assess, use, create, and share content appropriately. A computer is an electronic device programmed to process, store, and output data that has been accepted as input. A computer needs both hardware and software to work. A PC is a self-contained computer with input, processing, storage, and output resources. A desktop computer includes a system unit (a case that houses the memory, processing, and storage resources) and a separate monitor, keyboard, and mouse. A mobile computer is a computer that can be moved around. A typical laptop (also called a *notebook*) has a monitor that when swiveled up reveals a keyboard with the remaining components housed below. Ultrabooks are thinner, lighter, and more powerful notebooks. A netbook is a small notebook designed primarily for using web-based applications. A tablet is a lightweight notebook with a smaller screen that you interact with using touch or a digital pen. A laptop that can be converted into a tablet is called a *convertible laptop* or a *hybrid laptop*.	computer literacy digital literacy computer hardware software personal computer (PC) desktop computer system unit mobile computer laptop computer notebook ultrabook netbook tablet convertible laptop hybrid laptop
1.2 Mobile Devices, Wearable Computers, and Embedded Computers	A mobile device is a handheld computing device with a small screen and with programs and data stored within the unit. A smartphone is a cell phone with a built-in camera, apps, and web-browsing and messaging capabilities. A phablet is a device that is larger than a smartphone but smaller than a tablet. A portable media player is used to play games or other media, while an ebook reader is used primarily to read ebooks. A wearable computer contains sensors that are always on and provides for hands-free communications. An embedded computer is an appliance or other gadget that has a processor built-in and is designed to perform a specific task; an embedded computer is sometimes referred to as a *smart device*.	mobile device smartphone phablet portable media player ebook reader wearable computer embedded computer smart device

continued…

Topic	Key Concepts	Key Terms
1.3 Computers for Connecting Multiple Users and Specialized Processing	A server is a high-end computer that connects other computers and is stored in a specially maintained server room (a room equipped to avoid heat, humidity, and dust). A computer that connects to a server is called a *client*. Midrange servers are used to connect hundreds of clients at the same time. A computer that relies on the server for all programs and data is called a *thin client*. Mainframes are large, powerful, and expensive computers that are capable of handling hundreds or thousands of users. A supercomputer is the fastest, most expensive computer, capable of processing trillions of calculations per second. Supercomputing speed is measured in petaflops; one petaflop is a quadrillion floating point operations per second.	server client server room midrange server thin client mainframe supercomputer petaflop
1.4 Computer Innovations and Trends	Ubiquitous computing means that computing technology is everywhere within our environment and used all of the time. An Apple Watch with the Starwood Hotels & Resorts app can be used to locate a venue, check in, and unlock the door. McDonald's restaurants is one of the fast food companies that have installed self-serve kiosks and table service using tablets. Law enforcement officers use wearable technology such as Google Glass and smartwatches to improve service and help secure convictions. WiFi-enabled uniforms are expected within the next decade. 3-D printing is being used in medicine to plan difficult surgeries and make prostheses. Technological convergence involves the blending or merging of multiple technologies into a single device such as a smartphone or game console. The IoT is a trend where everyday objects are connected to a network and can interact with each other or other connected objects (referred to as *machine-to-machine communications*).	ubiquitous computing technological convergence Internet of Things (IoT) machine-to-machine communications

continued…

Topic	Key Concepts	Key Terms
1.5 Information Technology and the Information Processing Cycle	IT involves the use of technology to store, retrieve, send, process, and protect information. IT specialists are involved with designing, developing, implementing, and maintaining information systems. Raw data (or data) are characters entered into a computer that software turns into meaningful information. The Information Processing Cycle includes four operations: input, processing, output, and storage. A device used to enter raw data is an input device. The operation where instructions tell the computer what to do with the data is called *processing* and is carried out by the CPU, also called a *microprocessor*. A multicore processor has an independent unit on the same chip that allow multiple simultaneous processes. A device used to view processed and organized data or information is an output device. RAM is temporary storage used to hold data while processing. Cache memory is where frequently used data is stored. A permanent storage medium such as a hard disk drive, USB flash drive, optical disc, or cloud storage (storage at web servers) is where data is saved for later use. A communications device such as a cable modem or router transmits data to/from computers.	information technology (IT) raw data data information information processing cycle input device central processing unit (CPU) processing microprocessor multicore processor output device random access memory (RAM) cache memory storage medium cloud storage communications device
1.6 Cloud Computing	Cloud computing is a delivery model where software and computing services are accessed entirely from the web. Software over the Internet is called *SaaS*. Cloud computing places the processing and storage operations in the web. Some cloud services, such as Google Drive and OneDrive, are free. Several advantages and disadvantages of cloud computing must be considered before signing up for a cloud service. A few popular cloud computing services are Google Drive, Dropbox, iCloud, and OneDrive. Google and Microsoft both offer free web-based productivity software suites.	cloud computing Software as a Service (SaaS)

continued…

Topic	Key Concepts	Key Terms
1.7 Green Computing	Using computers and other electronic devices in an environmentally responsible manner is known as *green computing*. Green computing practices, policies, and procedures strive to reduce energy consumption; reduce use of paper and paper supplies; and reuse, recycle, or properly dispose of electronic waste (e-waste). Five ways to practice green computing are to use Energy Star rated devices, turn off or unplug devices when not in use, reduce printing of documents, modify power options on your computers, and resell or donate old equipment.	green computing e-waste
1.8 Computers and Your Health	RSI is the leading cause of job-related injury in North America and involves a disorder of the joints, nerves, muscles, ligaments, or tendons. Tendonitis occurs when a tendon in your wrist becomes inflamed. CTS occurs when the nerve that connects the forearm to the palm becomes inflamed. Both tendonitis and CTS are caused by computer overuse. Symptoms of tendonitis and CTS include pain, numbness, tingling, decreased mobility and decreased strength in the hand. CVS is temporary problems with your eyes caused by prolonged computer use. Ergonomic design involves adjusting components to optimal height, distance, and angles to prevent computer-related injury.	repetitive-strain injury (RSI) tendonitis carpal tunnel syndrome (CTS) computer vision syndrome (CVS) ergonomics

 Recheck
Recheck your understanding of the topics covered in this chapter.

 Workbook
Chapter review and assessment resources are available in the *Workbook* ebook.

Chapter 2

Exploring the World Using the Internet

 Precheck

Check your understanding of the topics covered in this chapter.

Chances are you have used the Internet today at home, at school, or at work to search for information, access study notes, play games, watch videos or movies, update your status, upload photos, or post a comment on a social media site. For many people reading this book, the Internet has always been available to accomplish these tasks, and the ability to connect and share information online with anyone in the world is taken for granted. Society has been shaped in many ways by the proliferation of the Internet and the World Wide Web over the last 25 years. In the next few years, the emergence of Internet of Things devices into our homes and vehicles will bring even more innovation to our lives.

Today, consumers and workers need to be network and web savvy. Knowing how to find the right information quickly, connect with others, and communicate professionally are essential skills for personal and professional success. In this chapter you will learn the difference between the Internet and the World Wide Web, study the equipment options used for Internet connectivity, review the most popular web browsers, search and evaluate web content, understand how multimedia pages access plug-ins and players, and identify the various services available to you in the online world.

Following this introduction to the Internet, you will learn to communicate and connect with others using social media and web publishing options in Chapter 6.

 SNAP If you are a SNAP user, go to your SNAP Assignments page to complete the Precheck, Tutorials, and Recheck.

Learning Objectives

2.1 Distinguish a network, the Internet, and the World Wide Web

2.2 Identify the hardware and various types of connectivity options for Internet service

2.3 Recognize the popular web browsers used to view online content

2.4 Describe parts of a URL and browse to web pages via web addresses and links

2.5 Locate content using a search engine, narrow a search using search tools, and describe content aggregators

2.6 Evaluate the accuracy and timeliness of web content

2.7 Recognize plug-ins and players used on web pages for viewing multimedia

2.8 Explain online services such as e-commerce, email, and VoIP

2.1 Networks, the Internet, and the World Wide Web

A **network** is two or more computers or other devices (such as a printer) that are linked together to share resources and communicate with each other. Computers are linked by a communications medium, such as a wireless signal or a cable that physically connects each device. You may have a small home network to share Internet access among a desktop, laptop, tablet, or smartphone. Often, home networks also share a printer.

Networks in business, government, and other organizations exist in a variety of sizes and types for sharing and communicating among workers. These larger networks share software, storage space, printers, copiers, and other devices in addition to Internet access. Businesses typically use the network for centralized data storage and for controlling access to computers and other equipment.

The Internet

The **Internet** or **net** is a global network that links together other networks, such as government departments, businesses, nonprofit organizations, educational and research institutions, and individuals. Think of the Internet as the physical pathway made up of thousands of other connected networks to make a worldwide network. For this network to transmit data around the world, special high-speed communications and networking equipment is needed to provide the pathway on which the data travels. For example, an email message you send to someone in another country travels through several networks, including telephone, cable, or satellite networks to reach its destination. This collection of networks is the Internet.

You connect your personal computer (PC) or mobile device to the Internet by subscribing to Internet service through an **Internet service provider (ISP)**, a company that provides access to the Internet infrastructure for a fee. You will learn about connecting to the Internet in the next topic.

Good to Know

The term *information superhighway* was made popular in the 1990s by former Vice President Al Gore, who recognized early the importance of building the Internet infrastructure and making it available to everyone. In recognition of his work, the Internet Society inducted him into the Internet Hall of Fame in April of 2012.

Check This Out ✓

http://CC2.Paradigm College.net/Usage Statistics

Go here for Internet usage statistics. Check the latest Internet usage and population by country or region. For example, in June 2015, 87.9 percent of North Americans were Internet users.

The Internet is a global network connecting thousands of other networks, providing the pathway for data to travel the world.

The World Wide Web

The global collection of electronic documents circulated on the Internet in the form of web pages make up the **World Wide Web** or **web**. A **web page** is a document that contains text and multimedia content, such as images, video, sound, and animation. Web pages are usually linked to other pages so that a person can start at one page and click links to several other related pages. Web pages are stored in a format that is read and interpreted for display within a **web browser** (a software program used to view web pages). A **website** is a collection of related web pages for one organization or individual. For example, all the web pages about your school that are available for viewing on the Internet make up your school's website. All the web pages and resources such as photos, videos, sounds, and animations that make the website work are stored on a special server called a **web server**. Web servers are connected to the Internet continuously so that anyone can access them at any time from any place.

While the Internet provides the path on which a web page is transmitted, web pages are just one type of data that uses the Internet. Other services that use the same network include email messages, instant messages, Voice over Internet Protocol services (telephone services via the Internet), and file transfer services. Figure 2.1 illustrates how the Internet delivers the web content to you at your PC or mobile device, and Figure 2.2 on page 30 provides an example of web pages with multimedia.

Figure 2.1

A web page travels along a collection of Internet networking equipment and telecommunications systems to your PC or mobile device.

The starting page for a website is called the *home page*.

A website includes a navigation area with the main headings or topics for the site. In these pages, the navigation area is at the top.

Web pages contain text and multimedia content such as video, sound, images, and animations. Related web pages are linked together.

Figure 2.2
Web pages can contain text, images, video, sound, and animation. A website is a collection of related web pages such as these from the US Navy.

Tutorial
How Is Web 2.0 Changing Our World?

Web 2.0 Initially, web pages mostly were a one-way communication medium where the organization or individual controlled the content and used the web simply as a means to provide information. Over time, a second generation of two-way communication web pages became available that allowed people to interact with the organization or with one another by sharing ideas, feedback, content, and multimedia. These websites that encourage and facilitate collaboration and sharing and allow users to add or edit content became known as **Web 2.0**.

Web 3.0 The next generation of the web is just starting to emerge and is known as **Web 3.0**. In this generation, meaningful connections between data and web pages will exist, allowing you to find personalized complex information more easily and quickly. Web 3.0 will use automated agents or intelligent agents, machines that will adapt and learn the type of content to show you based on previous searches and browsing you have done. Imagine starting a search with *Where is a good place to eat out tonight?* and the browser responds with a list of restaurants for the type of food you have searched for in the past within a few miles of your current location. Experts differ on the exact meaning of Web 3.0, and some even disagree with the name, preferring to call this evolution the Semantic Web. Elements of Web 3.0 already exist today. For example, the Google Now app uses predictive cards that provide you with information before you request it, such as driving directions to an upcoming appointment.

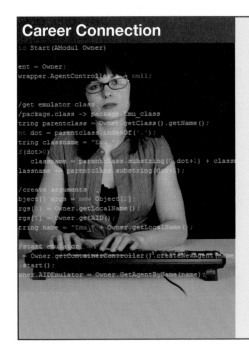

Career Connection

Careers for the Web

Web designers create the look, feel, and function of a website, while web developers program the website. Both specialists work together to create a dynamic and interactive site to support an organization's brand. Web designers and web developers that specialize in *responsive web design* are in demand. In this specialty, the website is programmed to query the device from which a request has been made to learn the screen size of the device and then adjust content for optimal viewing. For example, it will ensure that a restaurant menu is just as readable on a 5-inch smartphone screen as on a 27-inch desktop monitor. Other companies may design a separate set of web pages for smaller, mobile devices. Look up ads for web designers and web developers to see what training and experience you need if these professions are of interest to you.

Explore Further   What Is Internet2?

If the Internet is the world's largest network of networks, what is Internet2? What is the purpose of Internet2, how is it managed, and what benefits will be gained?

1. Search the web to locate answers to the above questions.
2. Create a document with a summary of your findings in your own words. Include the URLs of the web pages you used to create your summary.
3. Save the document as **Internet2-YourName**.
4. Submit the document to your instructor in the manner she or he requested.

2.2 Connecting to the Internet

At work or school, you connect to the Internet using the high-speed service installed on the organization's network. After logging in to a PC or other device by providing your user name and password, you can immediately launch a web browser and start searching the web. The networks you use in these settings are designed to handle more functions beyond sharing Internet access, such as providing access to shared software and centralized management of other resources. In this topic, you will learn about Internet connectivity options for a small home network.

Components Needed for Internet Access

Computers and mobile devices sold today are already equipped with the hardware needed to connect to a network. For example, a notebook may be sold equipped with a **network interface card (NIC)**, often referred to in computer ads as an **Ethernet port**. With this type of hardware, you plug one end of an Ethernet cable (a twisted-pair cable similar to a telephone cable but larger) into the notebook and the other end into a device that connects to the Internet. Newer PCs and all mobile devices come equipped with a built-in **wireless interface card** that allows you to connect to a network using wireless technology. Newer notebooks and mobile devices also integrate **Bluetooth** connectivity, which offers the ability to connect to another Bluetooth-enabled device, such as your smartphone.

In addition to your network-enabled PC, notebook, or mobile device, you will also need the following account service, hardware, and software to connect to the Internet and browse the web:

- an account with an ISP
- networking equipment (usually provided by your ISP), such as a cable modem, DSL modem, wireless modem, or satellite modem
- a router if you will be connecting multiple devices (however, newer modems integrate a wireless router within the same equipment)
- a web browser, such as Internet Explorer, Microsoft Edge, Firefox, Chrome, or Safari (you will learn about these software programs in the next topic)

ISPs

ISPs are companies that sell Internet access by providing the equipment and servers that allow your PC or mobile device to connect to the Internet backbone (main data routes). Typically, you contract with a telephone or cellular provider, cable company, satellite company, or dedicated Internet access company such as EarthLink.

Fees for Internet access vary and usually are based on the connection speed that you want. High-speed access costs more than a slower connection and is usually priced at various speed levels. Also be aware of download limits (called *data caps*) in your contract. Some ISPs attach a data cap to a service, and if you exceed the cap, additional fees may be charged.

Your choice of connection speed is usually based on your anticipated usage of the Internet. If you primarily only use email and browse web pages, you can get by with a slower speed than someone who wants to play online games or stream movies, music, or radio programs.

Search at your school or library to find the best deal for ISPs in your area if you need new service. Along with Internet access, you also receive multiple email accounts and security tools to keep your PC or mobile device virus- and spam-free.

Good to Know

A principle called *net neutrality* was in the news in February 2015 when the Federal Trade Commission passed new rules aimed to protect the flow of content. Net neutrality refers to the idea that ISPs should give consumers access to Internet content on an equal basis—without favoring one website or blocking another. The FTC's rules are meant to prevent ISPs from slowing down delivery speed for some content providers or creating a fast lane for other content providers that have paid a fee.

High-Speed Internet Connectivity

High-speed Internet access is called **broadband** and includes any always-on connection capable of carrying a large amount of data at a fast speed. Speed for broadband connectivity is expressed as **megabits per second (Mbps)**, meaning data transfers at the rate of 1 million bits per second. See Table 2.1 for a list of typical connection speeds by type of connection. When you evaluate ISP contracts, a higher Mbps value means a higher subscription fee. Be aware that speeds are faster for downloading content than for uploading content. Upload speeds are slower, and some ISPs restrict upload speeds. Figure 2.3 puts meaningful context to connection speed by comparing the number of photos and songs that can be downloaded at four speed levels. Typical broadband options are described next.

Table 2.1

Average Internet Connection Speeds

Type of Internet Connectivity	Average Speed
Cable	20 to 250 Mbps
Digital subscriber line (DSL)	6 to 20 Mbps
Fiber-optic	50 to 300 Mbps, with 500 and 1,000 Mbps in some areas
Satellite	1.5 to 15 Mbps

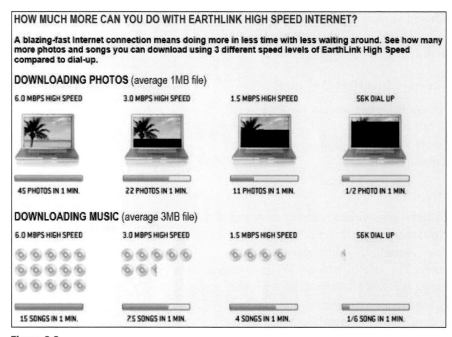

HOW MUCH MORE CAN YOU DO WITH EARTHLINK HIGH SPEED INTERNET?

A blazing-fast Internet connection means doing more in less time with less waiting around. See how many more photos and songs you can download using 3 different speed levels of EarthLink High Speed compared to dial-up.

DOWNLOADING PHOTOS (average 1MB file)

6.0 MBPS HIGH SPEED	3.0 MBPS HIGH SPEED	1.5 MBPS HIGH SPEED	56K DIAL UP
45 PHOTOS IN 1 MIN.	22 PHOTOS IN 1 MIN.	11 PHOTOS IN 1 MIN.	1/2 PHOTO IN 1 MIN.

DOWNLOADING MUSIC (average 3MB file)

6.0 MBPS HIGH SPEED	3.0 MBPS HIGH SPEED	1.5 MBPS HIGH SPEED	56K DIAL UP
15 SONGS IN 1 MIN.	7.5 SONGS IN 1 MIN.	4 SONGS IN 1 MIN.	1/6 SONG IN 1 MIN.

Figure 2.3

ISP EarthLink provides this chart at its website that compares the number of photos and songs that can be downloaded at various connection speeds.

Cable Internet Access

Cable Internet access is provided by the same cable company with which you subscribe for television service. A cable modem connects to your cable network outlet using a coaxial cable (Figure 2.4). From the cable modem, you use a twisted-pair cable to plug into your computer or wireless router to enable Internet access. Cable connections are very fast; however, you share the connection with others in your neighborhood so performance can vary.

Good to Know

Actual connection speed will vary due to factors such as distance from ISP, time of day (congestion slows down networks), and the web activities of others sharing the connection.

Check This Out ✓

http://CC2.Paradigm College.net/SpeedTest

Go here to perform a speed test from your PC or mobile device. Compare speed results at different times of the day until you find when speed is fastest.

Check This Out ✓

http://CC2.Paradigm College.net/Provider Stats

Go here, type in your address, and click Find Broadband to view statistics about broadband providers in your area.

Figure 2.4

A cable modem is connected to the cable company network using coaxial cable.

Figure 2.5

A DSL modem is connected to the telephone company network using twisted-pair cable.

Tutorial

Why Choose One Internet Connection Method over Another?

Digital Subscriber Line Internet Access

A **digital subscriber line (DSL)** provided by your telephone company connects using telephone lines (Figure 2.5). A DSL modem uses twisted-pair cable to plug into your telephone jack and your computer or wireless router. With DSL, your telephone line is not tied up while you are using the Internet.

Fiber to the Premises Internet Access

Fiber to the premises (FTTP), also referred to as *fiber to the home (FTTH)* or *fiber-optic service (FiOS)* involves the ISP running a fiber-optic cable directly to your home or business (Figure 2.6). This is the most expensive option and not widely available. A piece of networking equipment is installed to convert optical signals transmitted over fiber-optic cable to and from the electrical signals transmitted by your computer devices.

Satellite Internet Access

Satellite Internet access is an option in rural areas where cable or DSL is not available (Figure 2.7). Satellite requires the installation of a satellite dish and satellite modem. Access is slower and more expensive although newer services offer higher speeds using geostationary satellites.

Fixed Wireless Internet Access

Fixed wireless Internet access involves installing an antenna outside your home to send and receive radio signals. A wireless modem is used to connect to your computer or router.

Wi-Fi Hotspots

In a **Wi-Fi network**, wireless access points and radio signals transmit data (Figure 2.8). Wi-Fi networks are common in public spaces for free Internet access. The area in which a Wi-Fi network is within range is called a **hotspot**. Wi-Fi is also commonly used in homes, schools, and workplaces to provide connectivity to notebooks and mobile devices. A Wi-Fi hotspot encompasses a short distance, making it a good option for homeowners to connect their mobile devices via a wireless router from their cable or DSL modem.

Depending on the Wi-Fi equipment being used, connection speeds fall within the range of 6 to 8 Mbps for older equipment, 25 to 30 Mbps for midrange equipment, and 150 to 1,000 Mbps for newer devices. Devices capable of transferring data at 1,000 Mbps or more express speed in **gigabits per second (Gbps)**, which is 1 billion bits per second.

Figure 2.6

Fiber-optic networks transmit beams of light capable of speeds measuring in the billions of bits per second.

Figure 2.7

Satellite Internet is used in rural areas where cable and DSL are not available.

Figure 2.8

A wireless access point is used in a Wi-Fi network to provide connectivity to wireless users.

Mobile Broadband Sticks

A **mobile broadband stick** (also called an *Internet dongle*) is a portable modem that plugs into a USB port on your mobile device and connects via a cellular network (Figure 2.9). The advantage to a mobile broadband stick is that you can carry your Internet connection with you.

3G and 4G Cellular Communications

Today, smartphones are either **3G** (third generation) or **4G** (fourth generation) devices that provide Internet access through cell towers. Average speed for a 3G connection is around 1 Mbps; however, performance varies depending on location. Average speed for 4G devices is often advertised as 10 times faster than 3G, and the network connecting them is often described as a 4G **LTE** (Long-Term Evolution) **network**, which is the fastest network for mobile devices. These networks use the 4G technology standard with advanced design to improve speed. Devices have to be able to send and receive using 4G technology to take advantage of the higher speed.

In April 2015, Google announced Project Fi, a new wireless service that offers subscribers a network in which their device will automatically switch to free Wi-Fi or the fastest LTE network in the partnership as the subscriber moves around. The device intelligently moves to another network without the user's intervention. Project Fi is bound to have a positive impact for consumers, though we do not yet know how it will affect wireless service and contracts in general.

In some communities, broadband Internet access may not be available, or the cost may be too high for some people. A low-cost way of connecting to the Internet is to use **dial-up**, in which you connect your PC to your telephone system via a modem built into your PC. The ISP provides you with a local telephone number that the computer dials to get on the Internet. The disadvantages to dial-up are the slow speed and the inability to use your telephone while online.

The ISP provides you with instructions to connect to the ISP network. Generally, the installation requires that you plug in the modem and run a software program. See Appendix B for help setting up a wireless network in your home.

Once you've established connectivity to your ISP service, you are ready to explore the web using a web browser.

Figure 2.9

A mobile broadband stick is a portable modem that you plug into a USB port.

At the time of writing, a 4G LTE device on an LTE network experienced the fastest speed for a smartphone or tablet user.

Good to Know

5G is on its way! The wireless industry is working on 5G standards with deployments expected in 2020 and a goal to deliver 1 gigabit per second (Gbps) speed to mobile devices.

Explore Further   What Is Tethering?

Assume you are planning a vacation in a cabin where there is no Internet access. You are bringing your smartphone and notebook with you to the cabin. Your smartphone plan includes Internet access. You decide to investigate tethering as a means to get Internet access on your notebook.

1. Search for information on tethering. Specifically, find out how a cell phone can be used as a modem for another device such as a notebook or tablet. How does it work? What do you need to do to connect the two devices? Are there any issues with tethering of which you should be aware?

2. Create a document that summarizes your answers to the questions in your own words. At the end of the document, include the URLs of the main articles you used for this topic.

3. Save the document as **Tethering-YourName**.

4. Submit the document to your instructor in the manner she or he has requested.

2.3 Popular Web Browsers

Tutorial

How Is HTML 5
Transforming the Web?

Once you are connected to the Internet, you are ready to start browsing, shopping, watching videos, playing games, or checking out what your friends and family are posting at social media websites. Web pages are viewed using browser software. A web browser is a program that locates a web page on the Internet and interprets the code in which the web page has been stored to compose the page as text and multimedia. Many web pages are created using a markup language called **HTML**, which stands for **Hypertext Markup Language**. A markup language uses tags to describe page content.

In this topic you will review the most popular web browsers for PCs: Internet Explorer, Microsoft Edge, Firefox, Chrome, and Safari. You will also be introduced to the unique needs of mobile web browsers.

Internet Explorer and Microsoft Edge

Internet Explorer (IE) is the web browser included with Microsoft Windows for editions prior to Windows 10. With the release of Windows 10 in 2015, Microsoft replaced IE with a new web browser called **Microsoft Edge**. Figure 2.10 shows the desktop version of IE version 11 (included with Windows 8.1) on the left and Microsoft Edge (included with Windows 10) on the right.

Microsoft Edge provides faster searches than IE with a cleaner and clearer reading experience. Pages can be saved to a reading list. You can highlight text, draw, or write notes on a web page, and those notations can be saved and shared. Cortana, a digital assistant, searches and helps you do things online faster. For example, while viewing a restaurant page, Cortana will pop up with the phone number, directions, and hours of operation. The Hub, a pane that you open at the right side of the screen, collects your favorites, downloads, history, and reading list in one place accessible across all devices.

Chrome

Google **Chrome** is a free web browser that runs on PCs and mobile devices, including Apple desktops, tablets, and smartphones. The browser was initially released in 2008 with features that included fast page loading and the ability to navigate and search within the Address bar. Signing in with a Google account while using Chrome allows you to sync open tabs, bookmarks, history, and saved passwords with your

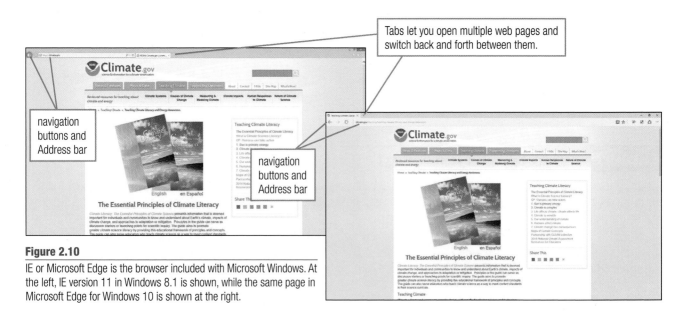

Figure 2.10

IE or Microsoft Edge is the browser included with Microsoft Windows. At the left, IE version 11 in Windows 8.1 is shown, while the same page in Microsoft Edge for Windows 10 is shown at the right.

other devices. In Figure 2.11, Chrome is shown with the web page for Grand Canyon National Park.

StatCounter, a company that measures Internet usage, reported Chrome was the browser preferred by 53 percent of web users worldwide in September 2015. Web surfers report a preference for Chrome's fast page loading, minimalist design, and synchronized searches across all devices.

Firefox

Firefox is a free web browser offered by the Mozilla Foundation. The browser runs on PCs, Macs, and mobile devices. Since the initial release of Firefox version 1 in 2004, the browser has enjoyed a steadfast fan base. Figure 2.12 shows Firefox with a web page about the history of the library from the Library of Congress website.

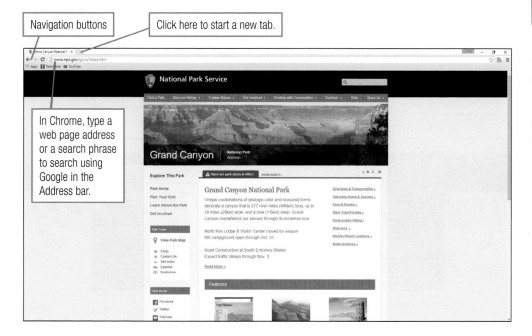

Navigation buttons

Click here to start a new tab.

In Chrome, type a web page address or a search phrase to search using Google in the Address bar.

Figure 2.11

Google Chrome browser is frequently updated; version 42 is shown here. The browser is popular with people who want fast page loading within a streamlined window.

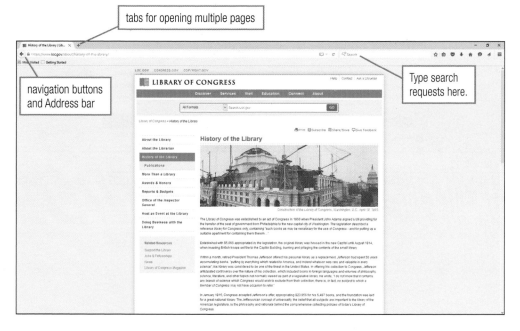

tabs for opening multiple pages

navigation buttons and Address bar

Type search requests here.

Figure 2.12

Mozilla Firefox is a free open-source browser. Version 37 is shown here.

You will notice similarities between Firefox and Chrome with the placement of the navigation buttons, Address bar, and tabs for browsing multiple pages. Firefox differs from Chrome with the search text box at the right of the Address bar. Fans of Firefox indicate they favor the browser's speed in loading web pages and believe it has better privacy and security features than IE or Chrome.

Safari

Apple **Safari** browser (Figure 2.13) is used on Mac and Apple mobile devices, such as iPads and iPhones. The browser is also available as a free download for a PC. Safari stores passwords, bookmarks, history, and the reading list in iCloud so that the information is available across all devices. Apple claims that Safari version 9 for Mac OS X El Capitan has optimized browsing to allow you to browse for up to two hours longer or watch videos for up to four hours longer than with Firefox or Chrome.

Type a web address or a search phrase in the Address and search bar, and Safari searches using Google.

Click here to open a new tab. A tab bar opens below the Address and search bar when multiple pages are open, and you can use this bar to switch pages.

window and navigation buttons

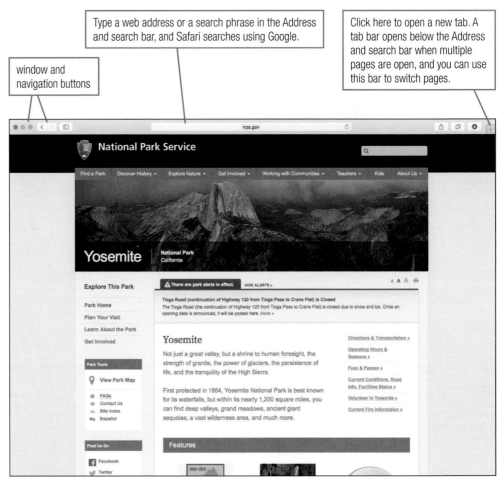

Figure 2.13

Safari for Mac OS is the browser supplied on Mac PCs and notebooks. A version of Safari for iOS on iPads and iPhones works similarly.

Mobile Browsers

A **mobile web browser** is designed to quickly display web pages optimized for the smaller screens on devices such as tablets and smartphones. The challenge for mobile browsers is that web pages designed for larger screens have to be readable in a smaller viewing area. Mobile browsers incorporate text wrapping and try to avoid the user having to scroll sideways. Mobile versions of IE, Microsoft Edge, Chrome, Firefox, and Safari are available in addition to numerous other browser apps for Android and Apple smartphones and tablets (Figure 2.14).

Figure 2.14

Google Chrome (left) and Apple Safari (right) have mobile versions for tablets and smartphones.

Blog Topic   **Which Browser(s) Do You Favor?**

Which browser do you use? Have you tried one of the other browsers mentioned in this topic? Do you use multiple browsers? If yes, why? If you could develop your dream browser, what would it do differently than what you use now?

1. Write and post a blog entry that answers the above questions.

2. Read at least two of your classmates' blogs and post one comment to each.

3. Submit your blog URL and the URLs of the two classmates' blogs to your instructor in the manner she or he requested.

Explore Further   **What Other Web Browsers Are Available?**

Other web browsers are available for PCs and Macs in addition to the ones mentioned in this topic. Each of these other web browsers is designed to be different in various ways from IE, Microsoft Edge, Chrome, Firefox, and Safari.

1. Research other web browsers for a PC or a Mac. Pick one alternative web browser and learn more about what it does and why people use it.

2. Create a document that describes the alternative web browser in your own words. At the end of the document, include the URLs of the articles you used.

3. Save the document as **AlternativeBrowser-YourName**.

4. Submit the document to your instructor in the manner she or he has requested.

2.4 Understanding Internet and Web Addresses, and Navigating Web Pages

All the popular web browsers share similar features and navigation options designed to assist with finding and viewing web pages. Regardless of the browser you use, web addressing and search techniques (discussed in the next topic) are universal.

If you are invited to visit a friend at his house, you need to know the address so you know where to go to find his home. Similarly, on the Internet, you locate a connected device (PC, smartwatch, tablet, smart appliance, and so on) by using an address. When a computing device is connected to the Internet, it is assigned a unique address called an **Internet Protocol (IP) address** so that the device can send and receive data. Two addressing systems are in use for the Internet. In Figure 2.15, the two addresses for a web server installed for the National Oceanic and Atmospheric Administration (NOAA) are shown. The **Internet Corporation for Assigned Names and Numbers (ICANN)** is a nonprofit organization that is in charge of keeping track of the Internet addresses and names all around the world.

A system of addressing that uses four groups of numbers from 0 to 255 separated by periods is referred to as *IPv4*. A new system called *IPv6* was launched in 2012 because the number of unique IPv4 addresses was running out. IPv6 uses eight groups of characters separated by colons, where a character can be a number 0 through 9 or a letter *a* through *f*. Methods are available to abbreviate the full IPv6 address. With IPv6 there will be enough IP addresses for years to come. For now, both IPv4 and IPv6 coexist since some equipment and software connected to the Internet cannot handle IPv6 addressing.

Figure 2.15

A URL contains a domain name that allows you to locate a website using a text-based name rather than the numeric IP address.

Web Addresses

If you know the numeric address for a computer on the Internet, you can navigate to the site by typing it in the browser's Address bar. For example, typing 209.46.18.200 in the Address bar will bring you to the EMC Publishing, LLC, website. (EMC is a sister company to the publisher of this textbook.) However, using complicated numeric addresses to find a website is not feasible. Instead, we use a **web address**, which is a text-based address. A web address is also called a **uniform resource locator (URL)**. Figure 2.15 shows that the URL for NOAA is http://www.climate.gov. The four parts of this URL are explained in Table 2.2 (page 41). The parts of a URL are separated by punctuation consisting of a colon (:), one slash (/) or two slashes (//), and a period (.), referred to as a *dot*. When telling someone the NOAA URL, you would say "climate dot gov."

When you type a URL, a server locates the IP address for the domain name to transmit data to the correct computer. A server that holds this directory is called a **Domain Name System (DNS) server** and is owned by a business or an ISP.

Navigating Web Pages

Most people browse the web in one of two ways: by typing the web address of a company or organization to go directly to a website (Figure 2.16) or by typing a search phrase into a search engine website such as Google or Bing to search for information (Figure 2.17, page 42). In the next topic you will learn about using search engines to find information.

Table 2.2

The Parts of a URL

Part of URL	What It Represents	Examples	
http	The protocol for the page. A protocol is a set of rules for transmitting data.	http ftp https	Hypertext transfer protocol File transfer protocol Hypertext transfer protocol secure
www	World Wide Web server.		
climate	The organization's **domain name**, also referred to as a *second-level domain name*. Domain names are the text-based version of the IP address and are usually the name of the owner, an abbreviation of a company or organization, or an alias associated with the owner.	nytimes google navy loc	New York Times domain name Google Inc. domain name US Navy domain name Library of Congress domain name
gov	The part of the domain name that identifies the **top-level domain (TLD)**. TLDs identify the type of organization associated with the domain name. Several TLDs with three or more characters are known as **generic top-level domains (gTLDs)**. ICANN is expanding the number of approved gTLDs. Watch for websites in the future with domain names such as myroadsideinn.*hotel* or mylawfirm.*legal*. A two-character TLD is a country code called a **ccTLD**.	com edu gov mil net org biz ca	Commercial organizations Educational institution Government website Military site Network providers such as ISPs Nonprofit organizations Business Canada

2. Click a hyperlink to a topic that interests you.

3. Continue clicking hyperlinks until you find what you need.

1. Type the web address into the Address bar of the browser. For example, typing *http://www.nps.gov* in the Address bar and pressing Enter caused the home page for the National Park Service to appear.

Figure 2.16

Navigating the web starting from a web address

Figure 2.17

You can navigate the web using a search engine website such as Bing.

1. Type the web address for the search engine you like to use, such as http://www.google.com or http://www.bing.com.

2. Type a search phrase and then press Enter or click the Search button.

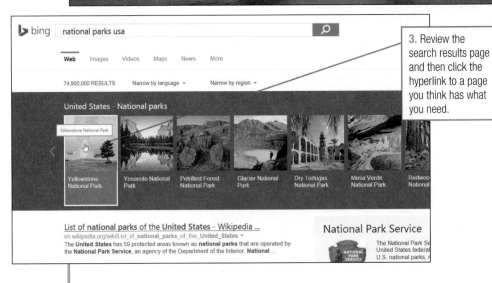

3. Review the search results page and then click the hyperlink to a page you think has what you need.

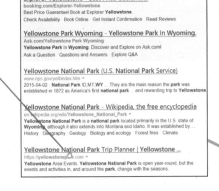

4. Continue clicking hyperlinks until you find what you need.

The first page of a website that displays when the web address is requested is called the **home page**. Main headings appear along the top or edges and are organized by topic to guide you to subpages within the site. Web pages contain hyperlinks (called *links* for short). A **hyperlink**, or **link** is any item on a web page that when clicked displays another page. For example, a title, word, phrase, photo, video, icon, button, or audio object may be a hyperlink. As you move a mouse pointer around a page, the white arrow pointer will change to a white hand with the index finger pointing upward when you are pointing at text or an object that is a hyperlink. Hyperlinked text is usually a different color, boldfaced, or underlined. Click when you see the icon change or click the text or object to move to the related web page.

You can also type the web address of a linked web page directly into the Address bar. For example, typing *http://www.nytimes.com/pages/todayspaper/index.html* takes you directly to "Today's Paper" at the *New York Times* website.

Blog Topic   **What Type of Web Activity Do You Do Most Often?**

A variety of tasks are performed on the Internet, but one or two types of activities generally predominate. In what activity do you spend most of your time on the web? Is it reading news or reading or writing blogs? Is it online shopping? Is it connecting with friends and family? Is it sharing photos, videos, or music? Is it looking for information for work, school, or personal interest? How many hours per week on average do you estimate you spend on each of these activities?

1. Write and post a blog entry that answers the above questions.

2. Read at least two of your classmates' blogs and post one comment to each.

3. Submit your blog URL and the URLs of the two classmates' blogs to your instructor in the manner she or he requested.

Explore Further   **How Do I Register a Domain Name?**

Assume you are planning to start a new business when you graduate. You know you will need to have a website but are not sure how to get a domain name for your organization.

1. Research online to find out how to check for an available domain name and how to register the name.

2. With millions of websites already in existence, the name you want to use may already be taken. Find out what alternatives you have if the domain name you want is already in use.

3. Create a document that summarizes in your own words what you learned about domain names in Steps 1 and 2. At the end of the document, include the URLs of the articles you used when researching this topic.

4. Save the document as **DomainNames-YourName**.

5. Submit the document to your instructor in the manner she or he has requested.

2.5 Searching the Web

A **search engine** is a company that searches web pages and indexes the pages by keywords or by subject. When you type a search phrase at a search engine website, a results list displays links to the web pages associated with the keywords used in the search phrase. To generate indexes, a search engine uses a program called a **spider** or **crawler** that reads web pages and other information to generate index entries. Generally, website owners submit information to search engines to make sure they are included in search results.

Some search engines display a subject directory that provides links to categories of information, such as *Music, News, Shopping,* or *Travel.* Clicking a category brings you to another page with subtopics for that category. In most cases, you can specify if you want search results to come from the entire web or from indexes associated with images, maps, news, shopping, or videos. Table 2.3 lists five popular search engines; however, be aware that many other search engines exist.

Table 2.3

Popular Search Engines

Search Engine	URL
Google	https://www.google.com/
Bing	http://www.bing.com/
Yahoo!	https://www.yahoo.com/
Ask	http://www.ask.com/
Dogpile	http://www.dogpile.com/

You will get different results from various search engines. Figure 2.18 displays the search results from the same search phrase *green computing* entered at two search engines, Bing and Ask. Differences in results can occur for a variety of reasons. For example, spider and index program parameters differ by search engine, some search engines locate and index new or updated pages at different speeds or times, and page relevance to the search phrase may be ranked differently.

Figure 2.18

Search engines provide different results for the same search phrase for many reasons, including the way in which spiders and indexers find and rank pages and keywords.

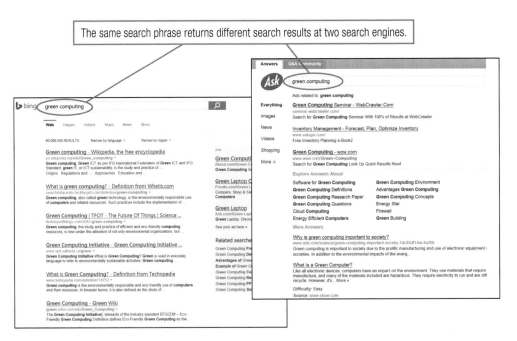

The same search phrase returns different search results at two search engines.

Fine-Tuning a Search

Regardless of the search engine you like to use, knowing how to fine-tune a search request will make your searching quicker and easier. With practice, you will develop a search technique that works best for you. Following are some guidelines for searching:

- A search phrase in quotation marks returns pages where the keywords are in the same sequence; otherwise, the search results may have the keywords in any order. For example, "endangered animals" returns pages with the word *endangered* immediately followed by the word *animals*.

- Type a minus symbol in front of a keyword to *exclude* the keyword from the search results; for example, "endangered animals" −africa returns pages about endangered animals in continents other than Africa.

- Rather than searching the entire web, consider using search engine categories, such as News, Images, or Videos, to restrict the search results to a specific type of page or object (Figure 2.19).

- Check out advanced search tools to further refine your search terms, domain, or region (Figure 2.19).

- Most search engines allow you to restrict searches to a specific time frame; for example, in the Google search tools, you can filter results by *Past hour*, *Past 24 hours*, *Past week*, *Past month*, *Past year*, or *Custom range* (Figure 2.19).

- Look for Help at the search engine website to learn more about how the search engine indexes pages and the recommendations for searching at its site.

Tutorial
How and Why Is the Deep Web Hidden from Us?

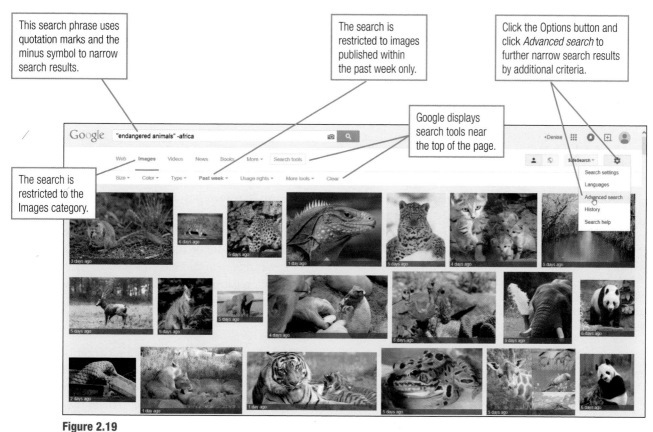

This search phrase uses quotation marks and the minus symbol to narrow search results.

The search is restricted to images published within the past week only.

Click the Options button and click *Advanced search* to further narrow search results by additional criteria.

Google displays search tools near the top of the page.

The search is restricted to the Images category.

Figure 2.19

Using the search tools offered by a search engine can help you narrow a search.

Some search engines are metasearch search engines. A **metasearch search engine** sends your search phrase to other search engines and then compiles the results in one list. Using a metasearch search engine allows you to type your search phrase once and access results from a wider group of search engines. Dogpile is an example of a metasearch search engine that provides search results in one place from Google, Bing, and Yahoo!, among others.

Some metasearch search engines specialize in one type of search service. For example, KAYAK (http://www.kayak.com/) specializes in searching travel websites to provide you with a comparison of flights, hotels, and car rentals in one place (Figure 2.20).

Figure 2.20

KAYAK, a metasearch search engine, specializes in searching travel websites.

Content Aggregators

Click the Feeds button at a web page to subscribe to the website's feed.

A **content aggregator** is an organization that searches the web for new content, and collects and organizes the content in one place. Some content aggregators send updates automatically to subscribers. Subscribers receive an update, sometimes referred to as a **web feed** or feed based on selections made for the type of information in which the subscriber is interested. For example, you can elect to receive new items related to news or music. Some content aggregators provide this service for free, while others charge a fee to send out updates to subscribers. The advantage to subscribers is that the content aggregator does the work of searching the web and organizing related information.

Really Simple Syndication (RSS) is a specification used by content aggregators to distribute feeds to subscribers. Feeds push content to the subscriber when something new is added to a website. An RSS reader program collects the feeds to which you subscribe and displays the headlines and/or articles. Most browsers incorporate the reader software automatically; however, several free reader apps are also available for PCs and mobile devices. **Atom** was developed as an alternative to RSS and is another specification used to distribute web feeds.

Popurls (http://popurls.com/) is a content aggregator that lists on one page all the latest headlines from the most popular sites on the Internet (Figure 2.21). Another aggregator, Techmeme (http://techmeme.com/), tracks changes to technology news and presents a summary each day.

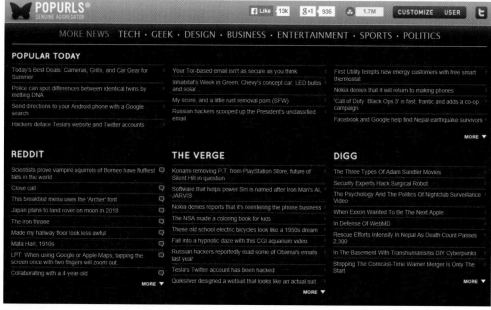

Figure 2.21

Popurls is a content aggregator that lists all the latest changes at popular websites.

Explore Further   Try Out Your Search Skills

Assume you are planning a vacation to celebrate the end of the school year, and you want to use the Internet to find information for your trip.

1. Choose a destination for your vacation—anywhere in the world!

2. Use your favorite search engine to conduct a search, using only the name of the destination as the search phrase. What search phrase did you use, and how many pages were in the search results list?

3. Next explore the search engine tools for conducting advanced searches and narrow your search results by further specifying criteria and/or excluding a topic in your search. How did you refine your search, and how many pages were in the revised search results list?

4. Follow one or two links in the search results and determine if the search refinements at Step 2 were enough to find useful information. If not, further refine the search parameters and explore new links.

5. Create a presentation that summarizes your search activities. Include a slide for each of your answers in Steps 1 and 2 and for your analysis of the search results at Step 3.

6. Save the presentation as **VacationSearch-YourName**.

7. Submit the presentation to your instructor in the manner she or he has requested.

2.6 Evaluating Web Content

Increasingly, the web is becoming the only resource people turn to when looking for information, news, shopping, connecting with others, and sharing media. Anyone with an Internet connection and space allocated on a web server can publish a page on the web. Many websites rely on users to generate the content that is posted. With thousands of new websites coming online every year, how can you be sure the information presented at a site is true, accurate, and timely?

Start at the Web Address

Look at the domain name in the web address. Is the site hosted by an organization you recognize and trust? For example, an article published at http://www.nytimes.com is associated with a highly recognizable media organization, the *New York Times*. Look for the domain names of print-based publishers with which you are familiar. For example, if you are familiar with *Psychology Today* magazine, then you will be comfortable reading content at https://www.psychologytoday.com (Figure 2.22). If you do not recognize the domain name in a web address, consider doing a search for the domain name owner and then searching the owner's name to find out whether the organization is reputable.

Next look at the TLD in the web address (the three characters after the period in the domain name). A TLD with .gov, .org, or .edu is, respectively, a government department or agency, a nonprofit organization, or an educational institution—all trusted sources.

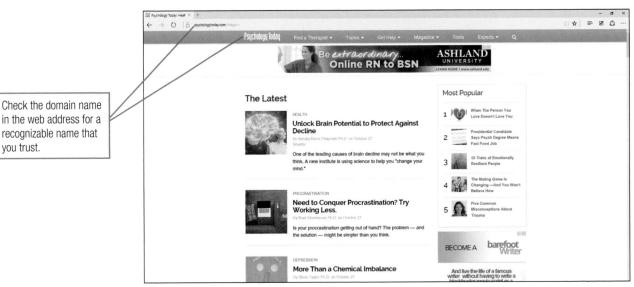

Check the domain name in the web address for a recognizable name that you trust.

Figure 2.22

Begin evaluating web content by looking in the web address for a domain name that is an organization you recognize and trust.

Look for an Author and the Author's Affiliation

Check for an author's name at the page. Is the author affiliated with the organization in the web address? Expert authors are often identified as such in the introduction, in other biographical information, or by credentials after their names.

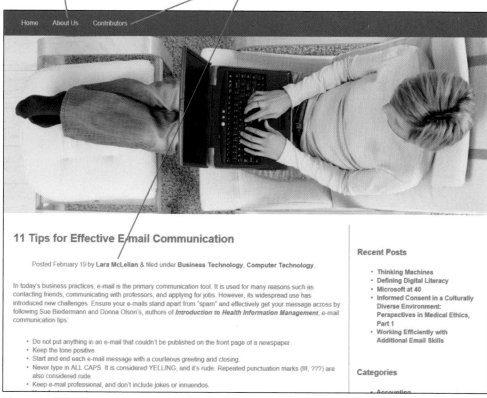

Try the <u>About Us</u> link to find out more about the organization publishing the content, especially when an author's name is not present or the name is not complete.

This page has an author name. Look for biographical information about the author or other ways to learn more about the author.

Figure 2.23

Check for an author's name on a web page; if the author has credentials or other biographical information, that helps you evaluate the validity of the content.

If no author name is shown, use other means to try to determine if the information is credible. For example, check for a link that describes the organization presenting the content. Most websites have an <u>About Us</u> or a <u>Contact Us</u> link (Figure 2.23). Check these sources to determine if a bias might exist for the information you are reading.

Check the Publication Date

In most cases, you want to find the most recent information about a topic. Look for the date of publication on the page (Figure 2.24, page 50). Use the search engine advanced search tool to filter your search results by a recent time frame and see if the page remains in the list. Sometimes the original publication date may be older, but a notation (usually near the top or bottom of the page) can provide a date the content was updated. Finally, a clue to the date of publication may appear in the web address. For example, a page may have an address similar to http://www .companyname.com/articles/2016/March/pagename.html.

If no date can be found, consider whether the content seems dated. For example, look for something in the article that may give a clue to the time frame it was published, such as a reference to an event. When in doubt, corroborate the content by finding another source that is published with a recent date.

Most pages have the publication date at the top or bottom of the page.

Figure 2.24

Always look for a publication date to evaluate if the content is current.

Purpose and Design of the Site

Finally, consider the purpose and design of the page you are reading. Is the publisher of the web page a business that markets products or services? If yes, the content may be biased toward convincing you to buy the company's goods.

Blog Topic   **Is *Wikipedia* a Valid Source of Information for a Research Paper?**

Wikis are websites where the page content is created by the user community. Generally, anyone can add content, and additions or changes that are wrong may be visible for a while before they are caught. The openness of wikis has led some in the academic world to discredit sources such as *Wikipedia* (the most popular encyclopedia with content developed by volunteers). What do you think?

1. Go to **http://CC2.ParadigmCollege.net /Wikipedia** and read the information on the "About Wikipedia" page.

2. Create and post a blog entry with your opinion on whether *Wikipedia* content is an acceptable source for a research paper and state your rationale.

3. Read at least two of your classmates' blogs and post one comment to each.

4. Submit your blog URL and the URLs of the two classmates' blogs to your instructor in the manner she or he has requested.

A web page design, spelling, and grammar will also indicate the credibility of that page. A professionally designed, well-written page will invite trust. The page shown in Figure 2.25 may indeed present accurate information on asteroids and meteors; however, the page design uses layout, colors, and organization typically not used by professionals, and links such as <u>ASK AN ALIEN!</u> are cause for further inspection.

A poorly designed web page that lacks a recognizable domain name, an author's name, and a recent publication date indicates a page that you need to be careful with. The information could be accurate and credible, but you should do some additional checking to be sure.

The link <u>ASK AN ALIEN!</u> may be just showing the author's sense of fun. However, the wording, page design, and lack of author or date all indicate that you should verify the content on this page with another source.

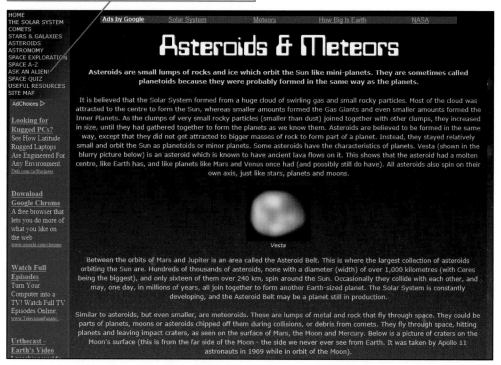

Figure 2.25

The design of a web page, including layout, organization, and choice of colors, provides clues as to whether the page was published by a professional organization.

Explore Further   Evaluate Information on Geocaching in Your Area

Geocaching is an outdoor activity where participants use a GPS or other mobile device to locate a container hidden by other participants. The container usually contains a logbook and may also have a prize of small value. When a participant finds the geocache, the participant updates the logbook and leaves a prize for the next person.

1. Find information on geocaching in your area. Pick a web page and evaluate the web page. Is the content accurate? Is the page from a credible source? Is the information current?

2. Create a document with a screen capture of the web page. Below the screen capture, list the elements that you used to evaluate the web page in Step 1. Provide the URL at the bottom of the document. ***Hint:*** *One way to make a screen capture of*

a web page is to display the desired web page, press the Print Screen key on your keyboard, and then use the Paste button in Word to paste the image into a document.

3. Save the document as **Geocaching-YourName**.

4. Submit the document to your instructor in the manner she or he has requested.

2.7 Popular Web Plug-ins and Players for Multimedia Content

Most web pages have some multimedia content, such as images, animations, audio, and video. This type of rich content enhances the experience. In order for some multimedia content to work, a **plug-in** (also referred to as an **add-on**) or **player** may need to be installed. Plug-ins, add-ons, and players are all the same type of program—a software program that allows the browser to display enhanced content that it cannot display on its own.

Some plug-ins and players are included in the browser (Adobe Reader) or with your operating system (Windows Media Player). However, you might encounter a web page with a message similar to the one shown in Figure 2.26, indicating that you need to install a plug-in or player to view the content. When you encounter a message like this, a link will be provided to the source program, which you can download for free. Instead of clicking the link, you may want to open a new tab and go directly to the company's URL (see the Security Alert on page 53). At the company's site, follow the instructions to download and install the software on your PC or other device (Figure 2.27). Read each prompt carefully so that you do not install other software unintentionally. After installing the player, you may see the desired content appear immediately in the web page that gave you the message, or you may need to close

Figure 2.26

A message such as this one will appear if you display a web page that requires a plug-in or player that is not installed.

A link will be provided to the plug-in or player that is needed. You can click the link to download and install the latest version from the software program website. In this example, the link connects you to the Adobe download page. Take care when clicking such a link; see the Security Alert on the next page.

Watch for messages that will add extra software or toolbars to your browser that you may not want. If necessary, deselect these options and then click the Install now button.

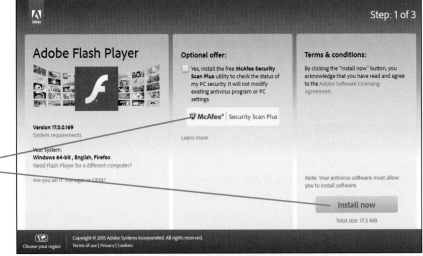

Figure 2.27

Install a plug-in or player by following the steps provided at the software program website.

and reopen the browser. Some older plug-ins or players that are no longer used much are Real Player for playing music and video; Microsoft Silverlight, which Microsoft stopped developing in 2013; and the Java plug-in, which has been associated with numerous security flaws. In most cases, these programs can be uninstalled or disabled in the browser if you find them on your PC or mobile device.

Popular plug-ins and players used on the web are listed in Table 2.4. With the release of HTML 5 in October 2014, technology writers expect that plug-ins and players will become obsolete in the near future because HTML 5 supports multimedia within the browser without a plug-in. In a few years, expect that it will be unnecessary to install or update Adobe Flash or QuickTime.

Plug-in and Player Updates

From time to time, you will be prompted to install an update to a plug-in or player. Generally, when these messages occur, you should install the updates so that web pages work as expected. Adobe Flash is frequently exploited by hackers to distribute malware. If you have Adobe Flash on your device, always update it when prompted, to make sure you have the latest patches that address security issues.

Table 2.4

Common Web Plug-ins and Players

Plug-in or Player Name	Description	URL
Adobe Reader	Used to view PDF documents. PDF documents are popular for exchanging richly formatted documents on the web. PDFs are formatted as they would look when printed without requiring the source program in which the document was created to view or print.	https://get.adobe.com/reader/otherversions/
Adobe Flash Player	Used often for animations on web pages with high-quality graphics, sound, and interactivity. Many browsers include the Flash Player since it is a popular plug-in.	https://get.adobe.com/flashplayer/
Adobe Shockwave Player	Used to play interactive games, including 3-D games; complete an online course that includes interactive simulations; and navigate interactive product catalogs.	https://get.adobe.com/shockwave/
QuickTime	A player from Apple and built into Mac computers and mobile devices. PCs will also need QuickTime if the web page has video or animation provided in the QuickTime format, such as trailers found on iTunes.	https://www.apple.com/quicktime/download/

Security Alert **Be Alert for Fake Plug-Ins and Players**

Some viruses appear on web pages as spoofs of popular plug-ins and players. These viruses look like the real player, but you can find clues that they are not real. Look for typos in the name of the player or linked web page. If in doubt, do not click the link. Instead, navigate to the website of the company that publishes the player and download the software from there.

Explore Further **Add-on Toolbars for Your Browser**

Some programs, such as many antivirus applications, install add-on toolbars to your browser automatically. As shown in Figure 2.27 on page 52, you may inadvertently install an add-on when you download a plug-in or player. Some browsers refer to add-ons as *extensions*.

1. Using your favorite browser, find out how to enable and disable add-ons/extensions.
2. Create a handout that specifies the browser and version, as well as provides step-by-step instructions on how to turn on or turn off additional toolbars in the browser.
3. Save the document as **AddOnToolbars-YourName**.
4. Submit the document to your instructor in the manner she or he has requested.

2.8 E-Commerce, Messaging, and Internet Telephone and Conferencing Options

The Internet is not just for connecting with others at social media websites or looking up information you need for work, school, or your personal life. Many people turn to the Internet for e-commerce (shopping), electronic mail (email), text and instant messaging, telephone calls, and conferencing services.

E-Commerce

E-commerce is the abbreviation for electronic commerce, which involves buying or selling over the Internet (Figure 2.28). Most software is now purchased directly via the Internet, where the link to download the program becomes available once the license fee is paid. Shopping online for music, videos, books, clothing, and other merchandise may require a credit card for payment. Increasingly, however, some merchants allow customers to pay directly from their bank accounts or through third-party payment services, such as PayPal or Google Wallet. With Google Wallet, a Gmail account can be linked to a credit or debit card, which can be used for purchases at websites. E-commerce on mobile devices is a fast-growing market, as consumers love to shop for favorite apps or music to use on smartphones or tablets. Table 2.5 on page 55 describes three categories of e-commerce.

Figure 2.28

The online shopping process for business-to-consumer (B2C) transactions involves the five steps illustrated here.

Step 1
Customer visits an electronic storefront and views the online catalog.

Step 2
Items are selected and placed into the shopping cart.

NAME: ********
ADDRESS: ********
CREDIT CARD: ********

Step 3
Customer accesses checkout and enters personal and financial data.

Step 5
Customer receives confirmation notice of the purchase.

bank's server

Step 4
E-tailer verifies shopper's financial data at a banking website.

e-tailer's secure server

Table 2.5

Types of E-Commerce Transactions

E-Commerce Activity	Description
Business-to-consumer (B2C)	B2C is a familiar category of e-commerce if you have ever bought music, software, or other merchandise on the web. A business, such as Amazon, sets up a website that allows any consumer to purchase merchandise or services. A business that sells online to consumers is often referred to as an **e-tailer** (short for electronic retailer). Figure 2.28 on page 54 illustrates the typical steps in a B2C transaction.
Business-to-business (B2B)	In B2B a business sells directly to other businesses using the web. In some cases, B2B transactions occur at websites used by consumers. For example, if you are on a website that shows ads and you click the ad, a payment is charged to the business that posted the ad. B2B website ads allow website owners to provide content free of charge to consumers.
Consumer-to-consumer (C2C)	C2C activity occurs at websites such as Craigslist or eBay, where transactions occur directly between two consumers. C2C websites generally also involve B2C or B2B transactions since the website owner that provides the service charges fees to advertisers and/or sellers to post ads.

Tutorial

What Are the Differences among the Three Kinds of E-commerce?

Security Alert | **Keep Your Personal Data Safe When Paying Online**

When paying online, make sure you are using a secure website before entering personal data, such as your credit card number. The web address should start with *https* (meaning the website is transferring data using encryption), and some browsers show an icon of a closed lock indicating your personal data is safe. You will learn about secure websites in Chapter 7.

Email

Electronic mail (**email**) is the sending and receiving of digital messages using the Internet, sometimes with documents or photos attached. Businesses were using the Internet for email long before consumers embraced the service when PCs became mainstream in the 1980s and 1990s. In today's workplaces, email is the standard communication medium and often is preferred over voice conversation, since email provides a written record of what has been agreed upon.

When you sign up for an account with an ISP, one or more email accounts are included with your Internet service. An **email address** is used to connect to your email account at the ISP server and is generated in the format *username@mailserver.com* or *username@mailserver.net*. Your ISP will provide the means for you to create your own user name to include before the @ symbol. The text after the @ symbol is the ISP server name. Once your email account is created, you can use a program called an **email client**, such as Microsoft Outlook or Apple Mail, to create, send, store, and receive messages.

Good to Know

In 1971 the first message was sent across a network with the @ symbol used to separate the user name from the computer name.

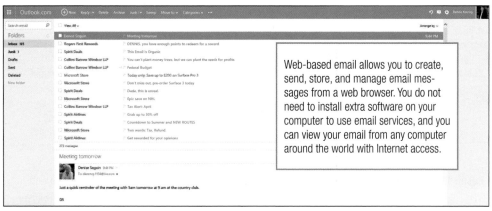

Figure 2.29

Microsoft Outlook.com is a popular choice for a web-based email service.

Web-based email allows you to create, send, store, and manage email messages from a web browser. You do not need to install extra software on your computer to use email services, and you can view your email from any computer around the world with Internet access.

Web-based email, such as Hotmail or Gmail, are popular among email users, since you do not need a separate email client program to send and receive messages. Outlook.com or Gmail users sign in from their browsers to access email. Once logged in, all messages are created, sent, stored, and otherwise managed from the browser window as shown in Figure 2.29.

Text and Instant Messaging

Messaging between mobile devices is often preferred over email since messages can be sent more quickly without a special email program. A **text message** is a short text exchange, referred to as **texting**, sent to another mobile device using a service called **short message service (SMS)**. Some mobile devices provide the ability to use **instant messaging** (exchanging text messages in real time) between other users of similar devices. Examples of instant messaging services on mobile devices are BlackBerry BBM and Apple iMessage.

Text or instant messaging from a mobile device is a popular method of communicating with others.

Voice Conversations

The ability to engage in a voice conversation using the Internet is called **Voice over Internet Protocol (VoIP)**. Skype is a popular service example and includes the ability to make video calls using web cameras to allow each party to see one another while chatting. FaceTime is a similar service used on Apple devices. Software and hardware on your PC or mobile device convert your voice and/or picture into digital signals that travel the Internet.

Check This Out ✓

http://CC2.Paradigm College.net/VoIP

Go here to learn more about Internet telephone service and compare plans.

Video calls using the Internet are a popular choice for staying in touch with long distance friends or relatives.

Web Conferencing

Web conferencing programs allow individuals to connect online to engage in a meeting. Web conferencing software similar to that shown in Figure 2.30 allows each participant to talk and share ideas and information using presentations or online whiteboards. A person's desktop can be shared so that other participants can watch a demonstration. Online meetings allow businesses to save on travel expenses.

Other services use the Internet, such as newsgroups, discussion boards, chat rooms, and remote access support providers. New applications for the Internet that will make creative use of text, video, and audio are sure to be invented.

Web conferencing programs provide the ability to talk and share documents or presentations with a group of individuals. Tools are included to annotate and mark up the online whiteboard during the conference.

Figure 2.30
Web conferencing software allows a group of individuals to connect and collaborate using the Internet.

Participants can pose and answer questions with the group in this window.

Explore Further   Netiquette Guidelines

With so much communication taking place over the Internet, rules for acceptable social interactions have been developed called *netiquette*, which is short for *Internet etiquette*. Without the visual cues that are present in face-to-face communication, messages can often be misunderstood. What are some common netiquette guidelines?

1. Research netiquette and pick what you think are the five most important rules.

2. Create a presentation with one rule per slide, and provide an example of appropriate and inappropriate netiquette to demonstrate the rule. Include a slide at the end with the URLs of the sites from which you obtained your rules.

3. Save the presentation as **Netiquette-YourName**.

4. Submit the presentation to your instructor in the manner she or he has requested.

Topics Review

Topic	Key Concepts	Key Terms
2.1 Networks, the Internet, and the World Wide Web	Networks link computers together to share resources. The Internet is the physical structure that represents a global network linking other networks from around the world. Connection to the Internet is provided by ISPs for a fee. Web pages circulated on the Internet make up the World Wide Web, sometimes referred to simply as the *web*. Web pages stored on web servers are viewed using a web browser. Websites are a collection of related web pages. Web 2.0 refers to websites that have two-way communication, sharing, and collaboration with users. Web 3.0 incorporates automated agents that will adapt and learn the type of content you want to see on the web. This evolution is sometimes called the *Semantic Web*.	network Internet or net Internet service provider (ISP) World Wide Web or web web page web browser website web server Web 2.0 Web 3.0
2.2 Connecting to the Internet	Computers sold today have an NIC (also called an *Ethernet port*) and/or a wireless interface card to facilitate connection to the Internet. Newer notebooks and mobile devices also integrate wireless Bluetooth connectivity. ISPs provide the equipment and servers to connect to the Internet backbone with fees based on connection speed. High-speed Internet access is referred to as *broadband* and is measured in Mbps, which is 1 million bits per second. Cable Internet access requires a cable modem that connects via coaxial cable to the cable company's network. With a DSL, your telephone company supplies a DSL modem that uses twisted-pair cable to connect into a telephone jack in your home. FTTP means a fiber-optic cable is installed directly to your home, and a piece of equipment converts optical signals to electrical signals for your computer. Satellite Internet access is found in rural areas and requires the installation of a satellite dish and satellite modem. Fixed wireless Internet access requires an antenna outside the home and a wireless modem to send/receive radio signals. A Wi-Fi network uses wireless access points and radio signals to transmit data. It is often used for public spaces and homes. A hotspot is an area in range of a Wi-Fi network. New connection devices capable of transferring data at 1,000 Mbps or more express speed in Gbps instead. Mobile broadband sticks are portable modems that connect to the Internet via a cellular network. Smartphones and tablets connect using a third-generation (3G) or fourth-generation (4G) network to cellular towers, with 4G LTE networks the fastest option for mobile devices. Dial-up uses a modem to connect via a telephone line.	network interface card (NIC) Ethernet port wireless interface card Bluetooth broadband megabits per second (Mbps) cable Internet access digital subscriber line (DSL) fiber to the premises (FTTP) satellite Internet access fixed wireless Internet access Wi-Fi network hotspot gigabits per second (Gbps) mobile broadband stick 3G 4G LTE network dial-up

continued…

Topic	Key Concepts	Key Terms
2.3 Popular Web Browsers	Web pages are viewed using web browser software that interprets the code the page is stored in as text and multimedia content. HTML is a markup language used in many web pages that describes page content using tags. IE is the browser included with Microsoft Windows for Windows 8.1 and earlier editions. Windows 10 in 2015 included a new browser named Microsoft Edge with faster page loads, a streamlined design, drawing ability, Cortana, a digital assistant, and a Hub, which stores favorites, history, and a reading list. Chrome, provided free by Google, runs on PCs and mobile devices. Chrome is popular due to its fast page loading, minimalist design, and synchronized searches. Firefox is a free browser for PCs, Macs, or mobile devices available from the Mozilla Foundation. Firefox has similarities with IE. Fans prefer its speed and security. Apple Safari is used on Mac and Apple mobile devices. Safari 8 uses battery power more efficiently. Mobile web browsers are designed to quickly display web pages optimized for much smaller screens.	Hypertext Markup Language (HTML) Internet Explorer (IE) Microsoft Edge Chrome Firefox Safari mobile web browser
2.4 Understanding Internet and Web Addresses, and Navigating Web Pages	Every computing device connected to the Internet is assigned an IP address. ICANN is a nonprofit organization in charge of keeping track of IP addresses around the world. An IP address with four groups of numbers from 0 to 255 separated by periods is known as *IPv4*. IPv6, developed when the number of unique IPv4 addresses was running out, uses eight sets of characters 0 through 9 or letters *a* through *f* separated by colons. A web address, also called a *URL*, is a text-based address used to navigate to a website. A DNS server holds the directory that associates an Internet address with a web address. The *http* in a URL refers to the Hypertext Transfer Protocol used for displaying pages. A domain name is the text-based name for an organization within the URL. The three- or four-character extension in a domain name is called the *TLD* and identifies the type of organization. For example, *.gov* means government. ICANN is expanding gTLDs. A two-character extension in a domain name is a country code called a *ccTLD*. For example, *.ca* means Canada. The first page you see when you visit a website is called the *home page*. Web pages contain hyperlinks (links) that take you to a related web page when clicked.	Internet Protocol (IP) address Internet Corporation for Assigned Names and Numbers (ICANN) web address uniform resource locator (URL) Domain Name System (DNS) server domain name top-level domain (TLD) generic top-level domain (gTLD) ccTLD home page hyperlink or link

continued…

Topic	Key Concepts	Key Terms
2.5 Searching the Web	Search engines read web pages and create indexes using keywords associated with the page. Spiders and crawlers are programs used by search engines to find and index web pages. Some search engines provide categories of topics and subtopics that you can use to narrow your search. You will get different results from different search engines using the same search phrase because spider and index programs vary, pages may be updated at different times, and rankings may differ. Use the advanced tools or options to fine-tune a search. A metasearch search engine compiles results from other search engines in one place. Content aggregators are websites that collect and organize web content. Subscribers can sign up for updates (called *web feeds*) that alert the subscriber when new content is added. RSS and Atom are two specifications used for collecting, organizing, and displaying web feeds.	search engine spider crawler metasearch search engine content aggregator web feed Really Simple Syndication (RSS) Atom
2.6 Evaluating Web Content	Domain names in the web address can provide clues to the authenticity or trustworthiness of a web page. Check a web page for an author's name and affiliation; if no name is present, try reading the <u>About Us</u> or <u>Contact</u> links. Look for dates to make sure the information you are reading is the most recent; if no date exists, look for clues in the content or web address. Evaluate the purpose of a website to help decide if a bias may exist in the information presented. A poorly designed website with errors in spelling and grammar should have its content corroborated by another source.	
2.7 Popular Web Plug-ins and Players for Multimedia Content	Plug-ins, players, and add-ons are all software programs needed by a browser to display multimedia content. Adobe Reader is a program used to view PDF documents. Adobe Flash Player and Shockwave Player are programs used to view animations with high-quality graphics, sound, and interactivity. QuickTime from Apple is used for videos or animations. Proceed with caution when downloading and installing a plug-in or player since some programs will add additional unwanted software to your system or may in fact be malware designed to look like the real player. When in doubt, navigate to the company website on your own to download the software instead of using links. Once installed, plug-ins and players will periodically require updating.	plug-in add-on player

continued...

Topic	Key Concepts	Key Terms
2.8 E-Commerce, Messaging, and Internet Telephone and Conferencing Options	E-commerce involves transactions online between businesses and consumers (B2C), businesses and other businesses (B2B), and consumers and other consumers (C2C). Businesses that sell online to consumers are referred to as *e-tailers*. Shopping online generally requires a credit card or account with a third-party payment service, such as PayPal or Google Wallet. Email is the sending and receiving of messages via the Internet. An email address connects you to the ISP mail server to send, receive, and store messages. An email client is a program installed on a PC that is used to create, send, receive, and manage email messages. Text messages are short messages sent via an SMS on your smartphone or tablet (referred to as *texting*). Instant messaging is exchanging messages with someone else in real time. VoIP is technology that allows users to make telephone calls via the Internet. Web conferencing software allows a group of individuals to engage in meetings online with shared documents. Netiquette is short for *Internet etiquette* and refers to rules for acceptable social interactions on the Internet.	e-commerce e-tailer business-to-consumer (B2C) business-to-business (B2B) consumer-to-consumer (C2C) email email address email client text message texting short message service (SMS) instant messaging Voice over Internet Protocol (VoIP) web conferencing

Recheck

Recheck your understanding of the topics covered in this chapter.

Workbook

Chapter review and assessment resources are available in the *Workbook* ebook.

Chapter 3

Computer Hardware

 Precheck

Check your understanding of the topics covered in this chapter.

As you learned in Chapter 1, computers come in all shapes and sizes. Whether you are working with a desktop or a notebook, ultrabook, tablet, or other mobile device, certain components are found in each one. All computers have a central processing unit (CPU), input device(s), output device(s), memory, connectivity adapters, and storage. These electronic and physical components found in a computing device are collectively known as *computer hardware*.

Some hardware is visible to you, such as the screen, keyboard, and mouse, while other hardware is housed inside the system, such as the CPU, memory, network adapter, and some storage. Hardware used for input, output, connectivity, or storage that you plug in or connect to your computer wirelessly, such as a USB storage medium or printer, is called a **peripheral**.

If you have looked at ads for computers, you know that a basic understanding of the terminology and hardware components is helpful to making a purchase decision. In Chapter 1, you were introduced to many of the hardware components found in a PC. In Chapter 2, you learned about hardware, such as cable modems and DSL modems, that provide connectivity to the Internet. In this chapter you will explore what's inside the system unit, input and output devices, network adapters, digital data representation, and storage options in more detail. Appendix A contains tips for buying a computer or mobile device.

Learning Objectives

3.1 Recognize the major components in a system unit and explain their purpose

3.2 List and recognize various types of input devices

3.3 List and recognize various types of output devices

3.4 Identify wired and wireless network adapters used for connectivity purposes

3.5 Explain how data is represented on a computer and describe typical speed and storage capacities

3.6 Describe various options for permanent storage and their corresponding storage capacities

 SNAP If you are a SNAP user, go to your SNAP Assignments page to complete the Precheck, Tutorials, and Recheck.

3.1 The System Unit

As stated in Chapter 1, the system unit is the horizontal or vertical (tower) case in which the computer microprocessor, memory, and storage are located. In a mobile device, such as a laptop, tablet, or smartphone, these components are inside the unit below the integrated keyboard and/or screen. In an all-in-one system, these components are mounted in the same case in which the monitor is housed. Regardless of the configuration, the main components in the system unit are the power supply with cooling fan, motherboard, ports for plugging in peripherals, and storage devices. Figure 3.1 shows the inside view of a notebook system unit.

In this topic you will learn about the power supply, motherboard components, and ports. In Topic 3.6 you will learn about storage.

Figure 3.1

Inside view of a notebook

optical disc drive
In many notebooks, this drive is omitted.

cooling fan
In 2015, Apple released the first MacBook without a cooling fan. Look for more notebooks in the future to be fanless.

hard drive

motherboard

heat sink

ports for plugging in peripherals

Power Supply

All computers operate with power. In a tower or desktop the power supply is at the back of the unit where you plug in the power cord. A notebook or tablet is powered by a charged battery or the power adapter when the power adapter is plugged into a power outlet (Figure 3.2). A cooling fan is located near a power supply to draw heat away from the CPU and prevent the CPU from overheating. A heat sink is also installed near a CPU to draw heat away from the processor.

With the ubiquity of mobile devices, accessories for charging batteries are plentiful. External battery chargers that charge multiple devices at once are popular. Charging mats let you charge multiple devices without connecting the devices to the mat via a cable.

Figure 3.2

Notebooks are powered by a charged battery (top) or by a power adapter (bottom) plugged into a power outlet.

Motherboard

The main circuit board in the computer is called the **motherboard**. All of the other devices plug directly into or communicate wirelessly with the motherboard. Figure 3.3 shows a typical motherboard you might find inside a desktop PC.

Figure 3.3

The motherboard is the hub that connects all the devices together and is designed to support a certain type of CPU.

The motherboard includes the CPU, memory, expansion slots, and circuitry attached to ports that are used to plug in external devices. Many computers integrate video and sound electronics into the main circuit board of the motherboard, while other computers may include one or more of these components as an **expansion card** that plugs into an expansion slot on the motherboard. Expansion slots are used to plug in additional circuit boards to your computer to either add or improve functionality. Another common use of an expansion card in a tower unit is to provide a network adapter into which a cable, called an Ethernet cable, is plugged for connectivity to a network. Notebook computers also have built-in card readers that allow you to insert a memory card from a digital camera or plug in a card used for wireless networking.

Data travels to the CPU and memory from the other components on the motherboard over wires called a **data bus**. Think of a data bus as a highway upon which data travels. The size and speed of a data bus affects performance since a data bus that carries more data to the CPU and memory faster performs better. Similarly, traveling by car on a four-lane highway at high speed means you arrive at a destination faster than if you traveled on a two-lane highway at a slower speed.

CPU As you learned in Chapter 1, the CPU performs the processing cycle and is often referred to as the *brain* of the computer. Today, computers do **parallel processing**, which involves having multiple microprocessor chips (more than one CPU chip on the motherboard), or a multicore processor (one CPU chip separated into independent processor cores). Parallel processing provides the ability to execute multiple instructions at the same time. Most notebooks are configured with a four-core microprocessor. Parallel processing has vastly improved system performance when combined with software written to take advantage of its capabilities.

Apple A9 Advanced RISC Machines (ARM) CPU is the processor in the 2015 edition of the popular iPhone. ARM processors use less energy than Intel processors, making them a popular choice for mobile devices.

A CPU goes through an **instruction cycle** that involves the CPU retrieving, decoding, executing, and storing an instruction. The speed at which a CPU operates is measured in the number of instruction cycles the CPU can process per second, referred to as **clock speed**. Clock speed is typically measured in **gigahertz (GHz)**, which is 1 billion cycles per second. A CPU in most notebooks and tablets sold today runs at speeds between 1 and 3 GHz.

In Chapter 1 you were introduced to cache memory, which is memory either built into the CPU or located next to the CPU on a separate chip on the motherboard and that is used for storing frequently used instructions and data. Cache memory located closest to the CPU is called **Level 1 (L1) cache**. L1 cache is memory built on the CPU chip and operates the fastest of all memory. Secondary cache memory may be either built on the CPU chip or located on the motherboard and is called **Level 2 (L2) cache**. L2 cache feeds the L1 cache. A third level of cache memory, called **Level 3 (L3) cache**, is usually located on the motherboard and feeds the L2 cache. The amount of L1, L2, and L3 cache affects performance since the CPU accesses cache memory faster than other memory.

Tutorial
What Are the Various
Types of RAM?

Memory   On the motherboard are two types of memory: **read-only memory (ROM)** and RAM. ROM is used for storing instructions that do not change. For example, the programming code with the instructions used when starting a computer is often stored on a ROM chip, which is called the **BIOS (basic input/output system)**, or **UEFI (Unified Extensible Firmware Interface)**. UEFI is expected to replace the older BIOS technology with a faster, more secure startup process.

Recall from Chapter 1 that RAM is temporary memory where data and instructions are stored while processing and is cleared when power is turned off. RAM is configured in modules that plug into slots on the motherboard (see Figure 3.3 on page 65). Since all software and data you are working with must reside in RAM to access the CPU, the size and type of RAM in a computer affect its performance.

A memory module like this one used in a notebook has chips on a smaller circuit board than one used in a desktop.

Desktop and notebook computers manufactured during or before 2015 have DDR3 SDRAM. DDR stands for Double Data Rate and refers to the ability to transfer data twice as often. The number after DDR represents the generation of DDR. For example, *DDR3* means third generation DDR, which is twice as fast as DDR2. SDRAM means Synchronous Dynamic Random Access Memory and refers to a type of RAM that operates at higher clock speeds than older RAM technologies. DDR4 RAM, engineered to use less power and transfer data at a faster rate, appeared in new PCs in 2015. Installing more RAM into an empty module slot can improve computer performance, extending the life of an older system.

Ports

A **port** is a connector located at the back, front, or side of a computer or mobile device. Ports are used to plug in external devices. The most common type of port is the **universal serial bus (USB) port**, which is used to connect an external device, such as a keyboard, mouse, printer, smartphone, or external storage medium. Most computers today provide several USB ports to accommodate multiple USB devices being used simultaneously. A USB hub can be used to increase the number of USB

Good to Know
A USB 3.0 device (known as a SuperSpeed USB device) can operate approximately 10 times faster than a USB 2.0 device and is easily recognizable by its blue plastic insert in the cable. In 2015, USB 3.1 Gen 2 (called SuperSpeed+) became available, and it can operate at double the USB 3.0 speed, to a maximum 10 Gbps.

ports if your computer does not provide enough to meet your needs (Figure 3.4).

A typical notebook also includes a port for plugging in an external monitor, a port for connecting to a network, and a high-definition multimedia interface (HDMI) port for connecting to a high-definition television (Figure 3.5). Ports will also be found on a notebook or other mobile device to plug in headphones, external speakers, or a microphone.

Figure 3.4

Plug in a USB hub to add more USB devices if you do not have enough USB ports.

In desktop PCs, the ports are often color coded to make it easy for someone to plug in a device with a similar end to the correct port. For example, on older desktop PCs the connectors are colored purple for the keyboard and green for the mouse so that the devices are not mixed up.

Motherboards also house other components, such as drive controllers and interfaces, to connect a hard drive or DVD drive to the motherboard via cables.

Video port

Network port, also called Ethernet port. In some newer laptops, this port is no longer included as manufacturers move to wireless-only interfaces.

USB port. The blue connector indicates the port is USB 3.0.

HDMI port

Figure 3.5

Ports at the sides, back, and sometimes front of a notebook are used to plug in external devices.

Blog Topic   **Are You a Techno Enthusiast?**

Manufacturers update hardware components as new developments in technology make it possible to produce faster, more energy efficient computers with expanded capabilities. How often do you update your computer hardware? Do you like to always have the latest equipment, or are you one to stick with a PC as long as possible? Do you consider yourself a technology enthusiast, or do you avoid new technology?

1. Write and post a blog entry that answers the above questions and gives your reasons.

2. Read at least two of your classmates' blogs and post one comment to each.

3. Submit your blog URL and the URLs of the two classmates' blogs to your instructor in the manner she or he requested.

Explore Further   **What Is USB Type-C?**

In 2015 Apple released a new MacBook with only one port—a USB Type-C port. This design created quite a stir in the technology community, which was used to multiple ports offered in notebooks. Just what is a USB Type-C port? How is USB Type-C different from the USB ports you use now? Will USB Type-C become the new standard on Windows-compatible PCs?

1. Go online and find out the answers to the questions posed.

2. Create a document that provides answers in your own words to the above questions. Include the URL(s) for the article(s) you read about the topic.

3. Save the document as **USB-TypeC-YourName**.

4. Submit the document to your instructor in the manner she or he has requested.

3.2 Input Devices

As stated in Chapter 1, any device used to enter raw data or communicate instructions to the computer is an input device. Several input devices exist, with the most common being a keyboard and mouse. Other devices used for input are also described in this topic.

Keyboards and Mice

While wired keyboards and mice were the standard for traditional desktop PCs, computer users prefer to be untethered. A wireless keyboard and/or mouse (Figure 3.6) can be used with any computer device. Wireless keyboards and mice use batteries as a source of power. A wireless receiver is plugged into a USB port and connects with the wireless keyboard and mouse. Electronic signals from the keyboard are interpreted by the keyboard device controller and sent to the computer operating system via the wireless receiver, which in turn sends the keystrokes to the active running program for display on the screen.

Figure 3.6

Wireless keyboards and mice are popular for traditional PCs and as peripherals for mobile devices.

A **keyboard** is a device used to type and input data into a computer. In addition to the alphabetic and numeric keys on a keyboard, special purpose keys (such as Esc, Insert, Delete, function keys labeled F1 through F12, the Start key on a Windows-compatible computer, and the command key on an Apple computer) allow commands to be sent to a program. Directional movement keys (such as the up, down, left, and right arrow keys, and the Home, End, Page Up, and Page Down keys) provide the ability to move around a screen. Finally, keys labeled Ctrl, Alt, and Shift allow you to use a combination of one or more of these keys with letters, numbers, and function keys to send instructions to the active program.

Notebooks include a built-in keyboard. Tablets and smartphones may or may not have integrated keyboards that are built in or slide out. Some tablets include a keyboard that you can use by plugging the tablet into a port on the top of the keyboard (called a *dock port*). Most tablets and smartphones come with touch-enabled screens that display a keyboard you use by tapping with your fingers or a stylus (Figure 3.7).

A **mouse** is a device used to point to, select, and manipulate objects on the screen. The mouse works by detecting its motion in relation to the surface beneath it and by the clicks of its buttons. Most mice in use today track the movement using light technology, while older mice used a trackball. As you move the mouse, the pointer on the screen moves in the same direction. Buttons on the mouse provide the ability to send a command when the pointer is resting on the target that you wish to manipulate. A wheel on the mouse facilitates scrolling.

Figure 3.7

Current tablets and smartphones offer on-screen keyboards, which you tap using your fingers or a stylus (digital pen).

On notebooks, a **touchpad** is located below the keyboard. This rectangular surface is used in place of a mouse to move the pointer on the screen and manipulate objects. The touchpad senses finger movement and taps much like a mouse senses movement and clicks. Depending on the touchpad device, multi-finger gestures and pinch and zoom movements can be used to scroll and zoom the display. Some notebooks and smartphones include a track pointer, which senses finger pressure for moving the pointer. Figure 3.8 shows a typical track pointer and touch pad.

Touchscreens

Mobile devices, such as tablets, smartphones, and some portable media players, include a touch-enabled display, called a **touchscreen**, for accepting input. Some laptops and monitors for desktop PCs and all-in-one PCs are also touch-enabled. A touch-enabled device has a layer of capacitive material below a protective screen. When you touch the screen with your finger or with a digital pen called a **stylus**, an electrical signal is sensed by the capacitive layer, which sends data about the location you touched and any gesture you used to the computer touch processor and software that interpret the gesture.

Self-serve kiosks, such as airline check-in stations and ATMs, use touchscreens in combination with other input devices, such as keypads, buttons, and magnetic strip readers, to accept input.

Figure 3.8

On a notebook, a touchpad and/or a track pointer (red button in middle of keyboard) moves the pointer on the screen using finger movements, while taps and buttons manipulate objects.

▶**Tutorial**
How Do Touchscreens Work?

Mobile devices and self-serve kiosks are touch-enabled or can be operated with a stylus.

Scanners and Readers

A **scanner** is a device that uses optical technology to analyze text and/or images and convert them into data that can be used by a computer. A scanner can be a separate input device, such as a flatbed scanner (a scanner that sits on a desk) or a handheld scanner. Many printers and photocopiers used today are multipurpose devices that also incorporate scanners.

A **bar code reader** optically scans bar codes to identify products in warehouses or at checkout counters. Even smartphones include the ability to scan a **QR (Quick Response) code**, a type of bar code that looks like a matrix of black square dots. The smartphone reads the QR code, which usually directs the device to display a website. A **magnetic strip reader** can read data from the magnetic strip on the backs of cards, such as debit cards, credit cards, or key cards used to open doors or parking gates. A **biometric device** identifies people by individual human characteristic, such as a fingerprint, iris, or voice pattern. Finally, a **radio frequency identification (RFID) reader** scans an embedded RFID tag to identify an object. RFID readers and tags use tiny chips with antennas that are readable when the reader and tag are within range of each other. Typically, RFID technology is used to read tags up to 300 feet away.

Many different types of scanners and readers are used to generate input from documents, images, bar codes, biometrics, or wireless tags.

Digital Cameras, Digital Camcorders, and Webcams

Digital cameras capture still images, while digital video cameras called *camcorders* capture live video and audio. Many of these devices are multipurpose, meaning some digital cameras could be used to capture short live-video segments, and some camcorders double as digital cameras.

A **webcam** is a video camera built into a video display screen (mounted at the top center of the screen edge) or plugged in as a peripheral and is used to provide images to the computer during live web conferencing or chatting using a program, such as Skype or FaceTime.

Smartphones and tablets have digital camera capabilities that allow you to snap pictures and record video and send them via messaging applications directly from the device.

Digital cameras, camcorders, and webcams are used to convert images and live video into a digital format.

Microphones and Voice Recognition

A **microphone** can be used in conjunction with software to create a digital audio file from voice input or other sounds captured by the device. You may also use a microphone to chat with someone online. Some games played online or with game systems accept voice commands. **Voice recognition technology** (also called *speech recognition technology*) is used to recognize voice commands as input for hands-free operation at work, with the navigation and communications system in your car, or with your mobile device. Siri on the Apple iPhone uses voice recognition to send messages, schedule meetings, or make a call. A program such as Dragon NaturallySpeaking converts input you speak into your microphone into text and commands in documents or messaging applications.

Microphones are built into notebooks and mobile devices. An external microphone or a headset with a microphone attached can also be plugged in as a peripheral (Figure 3.9).

Figure 3.9

A standalone microphone or headset microphone provides voice input during a conversation via a computer or for a voice recording.

Entertainment Controllers

Gaming systems accept input using a variety of methods, such as wired or wireless game controllers (Figure 3.10), joysticks, and motion sensors. Some games have specialized controllers, such as guitars, other musical instruments, or tennis rackets. Some exercise games use pressure sensitive mats or boards.

Other devices, such as keypads and magnetic ink character recognition systems, are used in specialized applications to provide input. Medical devices, such as heart rate monitors and blood glucose meters, send data to connected devices, such as smartphones, for health monitoring. Wearable keyboards and holographic inputs are no longer considered science fiction owing to new technology that works with GPS sensors to transmit location data. The Microsoft HoloLens, developed for use with Windows 10, accepts a gaze, gesture, or voice input from an untethered device for interaction with content (Figure 3.11). Imagine yourself in the future wearing your keyboard on your sleeve or responding to content via a hologram!

Figure 3.10

Game consoles and other entertainment systems use controllers such as the one shown here for input.

Figure 3.11

The Microsoft HoloLens is specialized hardware that lets you interact with holograms.

Explore Further | Virtual Reality Devices

Virtual reality devices are used with games and in commercial applications to train workers, such as simulating flights for pilots. Data input detectors may be worn on the body—for example, in headsets or gloves.

1. Research a virtual reality device for a game or training purpose.
2. Create a brief presentation that describes in your own words what you learned about the virtual reality device. Include a slide with a picture of the virtual reality device that you researched. Include the URLs of the sites from which you obtained information.
3. Save the presentation as **VirtualReality-YourName**.
4. Submit the presentation to your instructor in the manner she or he has requested.

3.3 Output Devices

In Chapter 1, you learned that devices used to view the information processed and organized by the computer are output devices. The most commonly used output device is a **monitor** or other type of screen or display in a mobile device. Computer output can also be connected to high-definition televisions, projectors, or interactive whiteboards. Other types of output devices explored in this topic include speakers, headsets, printers, and copiers.

Video Displays

An electronic device called a **video display** presents information from a computer visually. A desktop PC uses a device called a monitor to connect to the computer video port. Notebooks and other mobile devices have built-in video display screens.

Video displays come in many different sizes, which are measured by the diagonal length of the viewing area. For a mobile device, the size of the video display is constrained by the size of the notebook, tablet, or smartphone. Small notebooks may have screens as small as 11 inches, while large notebook screens can be as big as 18.4 inches. Tablet screens typically range from 7 to 11 inches. Smartphone screens can be as small as 2.5 inches, with newer phones breaking in near 5.5 inches.

Display screen size varies by device, with some smartphone screens as small as 2.5 inches and some notebooks as large as desktop monitors.

Notebooks are often connected to external video displays, such as a computer monitor or a high-definition television screen, to take advantage of larger viewing areas or to use two screens at the same time. Monitors are typically a wide-screen **liquid crystal display (LCD)** or **light-emitting diode (LED)**, both of which are flat-panel liquid crystal technology in various sizes upward from 20 inches. The difference between LCD and LED lies with the backlighting that allows light to pass through the panels. LCD screens use a type of fluorescent lamp whereas LEDs use smaller, more efficient light emitting diodes. The technology in LED screens means they consume less energy while displaying brighter, more vibrant colors than LCD screens.

Another flat-panel display screen is **plasma**. Plasma was popular with home theater enthusiasts for many years because of its truer color representation; however, LED technology has improved such that plasma is expected to eventually be obsolete.

A newer technology that is known as **organic light-emitting diode (OLED)** does not require backlighting like LCDs and LEDs, making the displays far more energy efficient for any device that runs off battery power. OLED

Connecting two display screens to a PC or notebook is becoming commonplace, as well as streaming movies or other Internet content on a high-definition television.

screens without backlighting are thinner and produce the best picture quality because each organic cell behind the panel creates its own light source, meaning no light spills over into other areas of the picture.

The video display **resolution** setting affects the quality of output on the display screen. Resolution refers to the number of picture elements, called *pixels*, that make up the image shown on the screen. A **pixel** is square with red, green, and blue color values (called *RGB*) that represent each color needed to form the image. Resolution is expressed as the number of horizontal pixels by the number of vertical pixels, such as 1920 x 1080 pixels for a 17-inch notebook display. The more pixels used to render the output, the sharper the image, as shown in Figure 3.12. Displays default to recommended settings, but operating system software can be used to change the resolution.

A newer display technology called **4K UHD** (ultra-high-definition) has found its way into display screens, such as those on monitors, televisions, and digital cameras. *4K* refers to the resolution of the display. A 4K UHD screen uses more than 4 times as many pixels as the standard high definition (HD) screen with which most of us are familiar (approximately 8 million pixels for a 4K UHD screen versus 2 million pixels for an HD screen). 5K displays are also in limited supply, and an 8K display is expected on a new iMac from Apple in 2016.

Figure 3.12

A character displayed at a low resolution using fewer pixels to form the character appears fuzzy (left) compared to the same character at a higher resolution using more pixels (right).

Video Display Projectors and Interactive Whiteboards

A **video display projector (VDP)** is used to project a computer output on a large screen when making presentations to groups (Figure 3.13). VDPs are often ceiling mounted in classrooms and boardrooms, while portable projectors are available for other venues. A notebook or other computer connects to the projector via a video output cable, or using wireless technology.

An **interactive whiteboard** displays a computer output on a large white surface. Special pens are used to annotate on the whiteboard while the image is displayed for making notes or to draw attention to objects on the display. In these instances, the whiteboard is acting as both an output device and an input device. The annotations can be saved with the images as electronic files for viewing later. Tools for touch gesture interaction with the computer while the display is being viewed are also included.

Figure 3.13

A computer image can be directed to display on a VDP (top) or an interactive whiteboard (bottom) when making presentations to groups.

Speakers and Headphones

Audio output from the computer, such as music, voice, or sound effects, is heard through internal speakers, external speakers, or headphones. PC monitors have built-in speakers. Notebooks and other mobile devices have integrated speakers. Plugging headphones or earbuds into the audio port of a computer or mobile device redirects the audio output to your headset. High-quality headphones reduce background noise improving the audio experience. External speakers can give home theater quality sound. A **Bluetooth headset** paired with a smartphone or other mobile device is used to listen to voice conversations. See Figure 3.14 for examples of these output devices.

Figure 3.14

External speakers, earbud headphones, and a Bluetooth headset are common ways to hear audio output from a computing device.

Printers and Copiers

Video displays provide output that is temporary. When the computer is turned off, the output disappears. Printed copies of computer output are called **hard copy**. Hard copy can be generated by a laser printer, inkjet printer, photo printer, thermal printer, plotter, or digital photocopier. 3-D printers manufacture objects on demand.

Figure 3.15
A laser printer is a popular choice for high volume output.

Laser Printers A **laser printer** is a popular choice for producing hard copy in offices and homes (Figure 3.15). A laser beam electrostatically charges a drum with the text and images sent for printing. A dry powder called *toner* sticks to the drum and is transferred to the paper as the paper passes through the printer. Paper feels warm when it comes out of a laser printer because heat is used to permanently adhere the toner to the paper. Color laser printers, once found only in business settings, are becoming popular with home users.

Inkjet Printers A common type of printer found in a home is an **inkjet printer** (Figure 3.16). These printers form text and images on the page by spraying drops of ink from one or more ink cartridges that move back and forth across the page. Inkjet printers allow home users to print in color relatively inexpensively.

Figure 3.16
Inkjet printers spray drops of ink on the page to form text and images.

Figure 3.17
Photo printers print directly from your camera or the memory card in your camera.

Photo Printers A **photo printer** generally connects directly to a digital camera to print high-quality photos on photo paper usually using inkjet technology (Figure 3.17). Professional photo-printing service companies use higher-end photo printers that produce a high-quality image on specially treated paper for prints that last longer than those produced by inkjet printers.

Thermal Printers Most of the receipts you receive from retail stores or services are printed on a **thermal printer** (Figure 3.18). Thermal printers produce output by heating coated paper as the paper passes over the print head. These printers produce receipts quickly; however, the image fades away over time.

Figure 3.18
Thermal printers are used to print receipts and barcode labels.

Figure 3.19
Plotters are used to print blueprints or other large technical drawings.

Plotters Blueprints, technical drawings, large drawings, and signs are often produced on a **plotter** (Figure 3.19). A plotter moves one or more pens across the surface of the paper to produce the drawing. Plotters are slow, as the movement of the pen or pens across the page takes time.

Digital Copiers A **digital copier** in an office can act as a traditional paper photocopier and, when connected to a network, accept output from computers for printing (Figure 3.20). Often these copiers are used to share color-printing capabilities in a workplace.

Figure 3.20
Digital copiers in modern offices are connected to a network to print computer output.

All-in-One Printers Many laser and inkjet printer models are multipurpose, meaning that in addition to printing, they can be used for scanning, photocopying, and sending/receiving faxes (Figure 3.21). Having a multipurpose printer saves desktop space, cuts down on multiple supply costs, and means you only have to learn to operate one device. The downside is that you cannot perform multiple functions at the same time. For example, you cannot copy a document while printing.

3-D Printers A **3-D printer** can produce anything from a replacement part for a coffee maker to an entire car (Figure 3.22). At the Detroit Auto Show in 2015, the Department of Energy displayed an electric car that was produced from 3-D printed carbon fiber–reinforced plastic. 3-D objects are designed using software in which the object is created, drawn, scanned, or otherwise generated with computer assistance. The object is then printed using a technique where consecutive layers of material are placed on top of one another precisely cut to build the object. The process is sometimes referred to as *additive manufacturing*.

The 3-D printing industry is expected to generate $5.2 billion in printers and associated materials in 2015, with growth forecasted to reach $20.2 billion by 2019 according to Canalys, a global technology research and consulting firm.

Other Output Devices

Special-purpose printers, such as label printers and portable printers, are used for carrying out specific tasks. Other output devices are available, such as a document camera that displays an image from hard copy on a video display. In addition, some virtual reality devices provide output.

Figure 3.21
All-in-one printers have multifunction capability for printing, copying, scanning, and faxing.

Figure 3.22
3-D printers are used to print on demand what businesses used to inventory, such as replacement parts.

Tutorial
How Does 3-D Printing Work?

In Chapter 1, you read that a 3-D printed replica of a patient's heart was used to plan surgery on a high-risk patient. Here you can see how the heart was generated using 3-D software and a 3-D printer.

Explore Further   **Laser or Inkjet—Which Printer Would You Buy?**

You are looking to buy a printer and are not sure whether to buy a laser printer or an inkjet printer. You also wonder if you should buy an all-in-one printer, since you occasionally like to make copies or scan photos or documents.

1. Research the advantages, disadvantages, and costs of a laser printer and an inkjet printer. Be sure to include the costs of replacement toner or ink cartridges for comparable printers in your research.

2. Decide whether you prefer laser or inkjet and if you would buy an all-in-one printer.

3. Create a document that summarizes in your own words what you learned, your decisions, the reasons for your decisions, and the URLs of the main sources for your information.

4. Save the document as **PrinterDecision-YourName**.

5. Submit the document to your instructor in the manner she or he has requested.

3.4 Network Adapters

Recall from Chapter 1 that the term *communications device* refers to any component or device used to facilitate the transmission of data. In Chapter 2, the various types of Internet connection options were explored, and you learned about hardware used for accessing the Internet, such as cable modems, DSL modems, and mobile broadband sticks. A communications device can be thought of as both an input device and an output device since it receives data (input) from and sends data (output) to the computing device and other computers via a network. In this topic, you will examine further the hardware provided in a desktop, notebook, tablet, or mobile device that enables connectivity to a network.

Network Adapters

Tutorial
What Devices Can Be Built into Your Computer to Enable Communications?

Any device used to connect a computer to a network is called a **network adapter** (also called a *network card*). The network adapter is the interface between your computer and the other networking equipment, such as the modem or router that provides the pathway for data to travel to/from the network. All pieces of networking equipment communicate with one another using a set of standards called *protocols*. A **protocol** can be thought of as a set of rules that define how data is exchanged between two devices. A network adapter has to use the same protocols as the modem or router with which the adapter is trying to communicate for each device to understand the other. This usually becomes a factor when trying to use an older wireless network adapter with a newer router that uses a faster data transfer protocol. In that case, you can purchase a newer adapter that supports the faster protocol.

Network Adapters for Wired Connectivity

A network adapter for a wired connection is called an Ethernet port (sometimes referred to as an RJ-45 port). One end of a network cable is plugged into the network port on the computer or mobile device, and the other end is plugged into a modem or router to provide the communications channel as shown in Figure 3.23.

Ethernet refers to the type of cable used to connect two devices and the data transfer speed that the media can support. Typical ads for a computer will state Ethernet 10/100 or 10/100/1000. The numbers after Ethernet refer to the data transfer speed the adapter can support with 10 indicating 10 Mbps, 100 indicating 100 Mbps, and 1000 indicating 1,000 Mbps (or 1 Gbps, called Gigabit Ethernet).

Figure 3.23

With a wired network adapter, a network cable connects two devices in a network.

With a wired network adapter, plug one end of a network cable into the network port of a computer and the other end into a modem or router to provide the communications pathway.

Network Adapters for Wireless Connectivity

Wireless connectivity is preferred by people who do not want their movements constrained by the length of a physical cable. At home, at work, or when you are on the go, a wireless network allows you the freedom to move around. Currently, computers come equipped with a wireless interface card that is integrated into the system unit as either Wi-Fi or Bluetooth.

Wi-Fi Adapters A **Wi-Fi adapter** communicates with a wireless access point or wireless router using radio frequencies to transfer data. Wi-Fi is often referred to as the **802.11 protocol**, which is the name of the standard developed to facilitate wireless communication among several hardware providers. As the protocol was improved to transmit data at faster rates, version letters were added to the 802.11 standards. At the time of writing, the latest Wi-Fi standard is 802.11ac. A computer ad may state that the integrated Wi-Fi adapter is 802.11 b/g/n/ac, which means the adapter can communicate with older Wi-Fi networks as well as the newer wireless networks.

If the integrated wireless adapter does not support a newer wireless network or you have a desktop PC that does not have a wireless interface, you can purchase an **external wireless adapter**. External wireless adapters have built-in radio transmitters and receivers to allow you to connect to a wireless modem or wireless router. The most common type of external wireless adapter is a **USB wireless adapter**, also referred to as a *USB dongle* or *USB mobile broadband stick*. A **wireless ExpressCard** adapter plugs into a narrow slot on a notebook or other mobile device. See Figure 3.24 for examples of these devices.

Figure 3.24

A USB wireless adapter or a wireless Express-Card is often used to provide wireless connectivity or upgrade an existing Wi-Fi adapter.

Connecting with Bluetooth Bluetooth is a communications technology for short-range distances. With Bluetooth, one Bluetooth-enabled device is paired to another that is usually within a 30-foot range (though some devices can connect at distances up to 300 feet). When the Bluetooth adapter on one of the devices is activated and the other Bluetooth device is turned on, the adapter detects the wireless signal and the two devices are paired, meaning they can exchange data. Bluetooth is a popular way of connecting a smartphone to a communications system inside a car. The technology is also used to provide network access on other mobile devices, such as a notebook or tablet. Newer notebooks and mobile devices include an integrated Bluetooth adapter. You can purchase a USB Bluetooth adapter to add Bluetooth to older devices (Figure 3.25).

Figure 3.25

A USB Bluetooth adapter can be used to provide connectivity with another Bluetooth device.

Good to Know

The name Bluetooth came from 10th century King Harold Bluetooth who was instrumental in uniting warring countries in Europe. Bluetooth seemed an appropriate name, as hardware competitors had to collaborate to make devices that work with each other.

Security Alert **Use Wireless Wisely**

Wi-Fi hotspots in public areas are not secure networks. Never enter personal data at a website, in a text, or in an email message sent from a public location. Do not perform any financial transactions while using a public Wi-Fi network. At home, make sure your wireless network identification name is not obvious to your household and is secured with a strong password.

Explore Further **What Wireless Technology Is Used by Google Wallet and Apple Pay?**

Mobile payment apps, such as Google Wallet and Apple Pay, let you pay for something by placing your smartphone or smartwatch in close proximity to a reader or tapping a device that reads your information for contactless payments. The wireless data transfer is quicker than paying with cash in many cases. But just how does mobile payment technology work?

1. Research near-field communication (NFC) and how it works. Be sure to find out the range that NFC-enabled devices must be within to transfer data.
2. Create a one-page document that explains NFC and how it can be used for payments. Assume the document will be given at

stores to their customers to encourage mobile payments.

3. Save the document as **MobilePaymentsNFC-YourName**.
4. Submit the document to your instructor in the manner she or he has requested.

3.5 Digital Data

Tutorial
How Does Your
Computer Translate Text
into Numbers?

When you type a document on a computing device, you see characters, numbers, and symbols as you type them displayed on the video display screen. However, the digital data temporarily stored in RAM, processed by the CPU, and eventually saved to permanent storage when you save the document exists as binary digits. In the **binary system**, only two possible values exist—0 and 1. Every document you save, picture on your camera, or message you send is really a series of 0s and 1s according to the computer. Understanding the way digital data is represented is helpful to put context to the speed of an Internet connection and the capacity of storage devices and memory.

Binary Bits and Bytes

The smallest unit for digital data in the binary system is called a **bit**. The name *bit* is derived from *bi*nary dig*it*. A bit is either 0 or 1. By itself, a single bit of 0 or 1 is not meaningful, because only two possibilities exist. However, by adding additional bits to form a group, more possibilities to represent data are available, because different combinations of 0s and 1s can be created to represent something. By grouping 8 bits together, 256 possibilities for combinations of 0s and 1s are created. This provides enough combinations to represent each letter of the alphabet in both uppercase and lowercase, each number, and symbols (such as $, ?, and !). Each group of 8 bits is called a **byte** and represents one character. When you type the letter *A* on the keyboard and see *A* appear on the screen, one byte of RAM memory is being used to store the letter. Table 3.1 illustrates the binary equivalents for the two forms of the letter *A*, the number 4, and the $ symbol.

Good to Know

A coding system called Unicode based on binary was developed to accommodate every letter in every language. More than 100,000 characters are represented in Unicode, with some requiring two 16-bit groups to represent a character! Unicode is the standard for programming characters in browsers and operating systems.

Table 3.1

Binary Equivalents for Letter a, Number 4, and Dollar Symbol

You type . . .	Computer stores in RAM . . .
a (lower case)	01100001
A (upper case)	01000001
4	01100100
$	00100100

Measuring Internet Speed and Data Caps

Bits are used to measure speed for transmitting data on the Internet. Recall in Chapter 2 when discussing broadband, average speeds were measured in mega*bits* per second (Mbps). One megabit was defined as 1 million bits. If it takes eight bits to represent one character, then one megabit transfers 125,000 characters. If your cable modem performs at an average speed of 20 Mbps, that means your cable modem is transmitting 2,500,000 characters per second.

Some Internet service providers (ISPs) put a limit on your monthly data transfer capacity. These limits are called *data caps* and are expressed in gigabytes. For example, a data cap of 100 GB means the ISP is limiting data transfer to 100 gigabytes in the billing period.

Measuring File Size and Storage Capacity

A document, such as an essay that you create in a program like Word, is simply a collection of characters (bytes). When saved, the collection of bytes that comprises the document is called a **file**. The unique name you assign to the document when you save it is called a **file name**, and it allows you to identify that particular file among others on your storage medium. A file could potentially hold several million characters. Similarly, memory, such as RAM, and a permanent storage medium, such as a hard disk drive, can store several billion characters.

An average speed of 20 Mbps means 2.5 million characters per second are being transmitted!

Prefixes added to the word *byte* describe progressively larger storage capacities. For example, adding *kilo* in front of *byte* creates the word **kilobyte (KB)**. One KB is 1,024 bytes, but people use the approximated value of 1,000 characters when calculating storage capacity. The next prefix is *mega*, creating the term **megabyte (MB)**. One MB is approximately 1,000,000 bytes. Table 3.2 summarizes storage units including **gigabyte (GB)** and **terabyte (TB)** with their corresponding abbreviations and capacities for the types of storage mediums you would encounter at home or at work.

Storage capacity for a USB flash drive is usually measured in GB although 1 TB flash drives are also available.

Table 3.2

Storage Units and Capacities in Bytes

Storage Unit	Abbreviation	Popular Reference	Approximate Capacity in Bytes
Kilobyte	KB	K	1,000 (one thousand)
Megabyte	MB	meg	1,000,000 (one million)
Gigabyte	GB	gig	1,000,000,000 (one billion)
Terabyte	TB	TByte	1,000,000,000,000 (one trillion)

Adding Context with Storage Capacity

Understanding that 1 MB is approximately 1,000,000 characters is more helpful to you if you can put this value into some meaningful context. According to eHow, 1 MB equals approximately 500 typed pages of text with no images. However, most documents created today have some images or other graphics added to the text to make the documents more appealing to read. The picture shown at the right of Balancing Rock uses 1.29 MB of storage space. One picture needs more digital storage space than 500 typed pages of text!

Many people like to download and store music and videos. It is not uncommon for one mp3 song to use more than 8 MB of storage and a movie file to require more than 4 GB. If you like to use your computer to store pictures, music, and movies you will need a storage medium with a large capacity.

This picture of Balancing Rock in Nova Scotia, Canada, uses 1.29 MB of storage space.

Good to Know 🎓

Big data is a term used to describe a vast amount of complex data that is analyzed for patterns or trends. The payoff to business for analyzing big data lies with better informed decisions.

Explore Further | Compressing Digital Photos

Picture files are large because of the number of bytes needed to digitize an image. Digital image sizes are measured in pixels. For example, a typical photo taken with a digital camera may be in the range of 3000 x 2000 pixels. Such a photo would be 6 million pixels, where each pixel has its own RGB color values. RGB color information uses 24 bits for each pixel (or 3 bytes). Therefore, the file size is 18 million bytes or 18 MB (6 million pixels times 3 bytes per pixel). However, if you were to look at the file size of the picture on your digital camera memory card, the file size would be much lower than 18 MB. This occurs because of the image file format compression scheme.

1. Find out about two methods of compression: lossy and lossless and the advantages and disadvantages of each method. Which method is used by JPEG (pronounced *jay-peg*), a format for digital cameras?

2. Create a document that describes in your own words the information you learned from Step 1. Include the URLs for the articles you read.

3. Save the document as **JPEG-YourName**.

4. Submit the document to your instructor in the manner she or he has requested.

3.6 Storage Options

Saving a document, spreadsheet, or presentation makes a permanent copy of the work in a file that is available after power to the computer is turned off. When saving, a **storage device** for the file is identified. A storage device is a piece of hardware with the means to write new data to and read existing data from storage media. A storage device is often referred to as a **drive**. Each drive is identified by a unique letter and label on a Windows-compatible computer (Figure 3.26). On a Mac computer, each storage device is assigned a name, such as Macintosh HD for the hard disk drive.

Several storage options for saving a permanent copy of a file are available, such as internal and external hard disk drives, solid-state drives, network storage, USB flash memory, optical discs, and flash memory cards. Cloud storage is another option for saving files when connected to the Internet. In this topic you will learn about each of these storage devices and the cloud storage option.

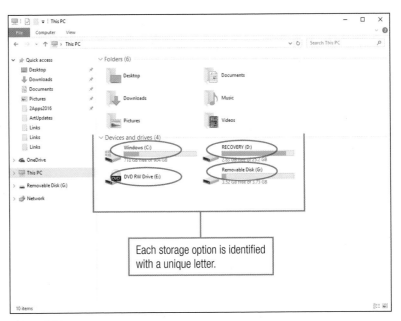

Each storage option is identified with a unique letter.

Figure 3.26

In a Windows-compatible computer, storage drives are identified with a letter.

Hard Disk Drives

Inside the system unit of a PC is an internal **hard disk**, also called *hard drive* and *hard disk drive (HDD)* (Figure 3.27). The internal HDD is usually the largest storage device on a standalone PC and is assigned drive letter *C* on Windows-compatible computers. This is the storage medium upon which the operating system and application software programs are stored as well as data files. Hard disks are round pieces of metal called *platters* stacked inside a sealed unit with a magnetic coating on their surface. The disks spin, and a read/write head moves across the surface of the disk, magnetizing the data to the surface.

Figure 3.27

Internal hard disk with top cover plate removed to show platters and read/write head; a read/write head for each surface moves over the disks together as the platters spin.

An external HDD is a storage device that you attach to the computer using a USB port (Figure 3.28). External HDDs are a popular option for extending the storage capacity of a PC and/or for backing up documents, photos, videos, music, and other files.

Storage capacities for HDDs vary but are typically in the range of several hundred GB with newer computers having HDDs in the range of one to three TB.

Figure 3.28

External HDDs are often used to back up an entire computer.

Solid-State Drives

Another type of drive technology called **solid-state drive (SSD)** is popular in mobile computers (Figure 3.29). SSDs use **flash memory**. Flash memory uses chips to store data electronically, instead of magnetically as on a traditional HDD. With chip-based flash memory, no mechanical parts are required inside the drive, making the device more durable. SSDs also weigh less than traditional HDDs, make no noise when operating, and require less power. Internal and external SDDs are available in storage capacities similar to those of traditional HDDs. A solid-state hybrid drive combines solid-state memory into a traditional HDD. The most frequently accessed data is stored in the solid-state area, with the rest on traditional hard disk platters.

Network Storage

In some workplaces, data is required to be stored on a network drive for security and cost reasons. Network drives are HDDs installed in a server made available to users with access rights to the server storage via their user name and password. A network drive often has a letter assigned that is higher in the alphabet, such as drive R or drive S. Networked storage is automatically backed up daily at the server. Centralizing network storage is considered more secure than leaving data on individual HDDs scattered about a workplace.

Home users can connect various storage devices to a single wireless media hub for storing and sharing data with multiple devices and people. Wireless media hubs are also battery powered Wi-Fi routers and charging stations.

USB Flash Drives

A **USB flash drive** is a portable storage device with flash memory inside the case. USB flash drives are popular because they are easy to use, small enough to carry easily, and inexpensive. The drive is powered through the USB port of the PC. When you plug in a USB flash drive, a drive letter is assigned—usually *E, F, G,* or a higher letter, depending on the number of ports and other devices.

USB flash drives are made in all kinds of shapes, sizes, and colors. Some are disguised inside toys or cartoon characters. Others are available as plastic wristbands. Storage capacities meet all needs; some store as little as 2 to 4 GB, and some store up to 512 GB. USB flash drives with 1 TB of storage are also now available. Many other names are used to refer to a USB flash drive, such as *thumb drive, memory stick, jump drive, key drive,* and *pen drive.*

Figure 3.29

SSDs are used in ultrabooks because they weigh less and use less power than traditional HDDs.

USB flash drives come in all shapes, sizes, colors, and capacities.

Optical Discs

An **optical disc** is a compact disc (CD), digital versatile disc / digital video disc (DVD), or Blu-ray disc (BD). Note that the spelling of this storage media is *disc* (not *disk*). An optical drive is internally mounted inside the system unit. Optical drives are usually used to play music CDs or watch movies on DVD or Blu-ray. Fewer and fewer PCs and notebooks are including optical drives because of the popularity of streaming media from the Internet and a preference to use USB drives. Netbooks and ultrabooks omit the optical drive to decrease weight and thickness and extend battery life. The optical drive is expected to become obsolete within the next few years. Optical drives are usually identified with the letter *E* or *F*, although this could vary depending on the number of other installed devices. A laser beam is used to read data from and write data to an optical disc. Recording to an optical disc is referred to as *burning a disc*.

Optical discs are sometimes used to back up important data or to make copies of music, pictures, or movies, since the removable media can be used in other devices and players and is relatively inexpensive. Optical disc types and storage capacities are listed in Table 3.3.

With Blu-ray's higher storage capacity and better quality video and audio, Blu-ray media has mostly replaced DVDs.

Table 3.3

Recordable Optical Discs and Storage Capacities

Type of Optical Disc	Media Options	Storage Capacity
CD	CD-R (write once) CD-RW (rewritable up to 1000 times)	700 MB
DVD	DVD +R or −R (write once) DVD +RW or −RW (rewriteable up to 1000 times)	4.7 GB for single-layer 8.5 GB for dual-layer
BD	BD −R (write once) BD −RE (erase and re-record multiple times)	25 GB for single-layer 50 GB for double-layer

Flash Memory Cards

Tutorial
How Can I Get More Storage on My Tablet or Smartphone?

The most common type of storage for a digital camera, smartphone, or other portable device is a **flash memory card** (Figure 3.30). A flash memory card is a small card that contains one or more flash memory chips (similar to SSDs and USB flash drives). Flash memory cards come in a variety of formats, such as Secure Digital (SD), CompactFlash (CF), and proprietary formats made by Sony and Olympus for their digital cameras. Capacities for flash memory cards can range from 1 GB to more than 60 GB. The type of flash memory card you would buy for a device depends on the formats the device can read.

Some computers and notebooks have a card reader built in for easy transfer of files stored on the flash memory card of a portable device (such as a digital camera) and the PC. Some USB hubs also contain readers.

Figure 3.30

Flash memory cards are used for storage in digital cameras, smartphones, and other portable devices.

Cloud Storage

Recall from Chapter 1 that cloud computing involves accessing software and storage services from the Internet. Some cloud computing providers offer a limited amount of free storage space to account holders, with subscription plans available for those who need a higher capacity. For example, both Google Drive and Microsoft OneDrive allow 15 GB free storage at the time of writing. Other popular cloud storage providers are Dropbox and Box.

The main advantage with storing documents, pictures, video, or music using a cloud provider is the ability to access the files using a web browser from any location with Internet connectivity. You can also sync documents between multiple devices and easily share files with others. Transferring files via the Internet is fast and easy, and you no longer need to buy, organize, and store media, such as USB flash drives, CDs, DVDs, or BDs.

Storage capacities continue to grow to meet demands by consumers and businesses to store increasing amounts of data. The typical storage capacities mentioned here are likely soon to be replaced by higher capacity drives or media.

Storing files using a cloud storage provider is one way to access documents from multiple devices and easily share pictures or other files.

Career Connection

Computer Technician

If you like hardware and are a good communicator, you may want to consider a career in computer hardware repair. Computer technicians troubleshoot and repair PCs and mobile devices. To succeed as a computer systems technician, you need to like working with customers as well as hardware. CompTIA's A+ certification validates entry-level knowledge and skills for computer support. Consider also enrolling in a program at a community college in PC/Desktop Support or PC Support Technician.

Explore Further   Comparing Cloud Storage Providers

Using a cloud storage provider to keep a copy of important documents or media files (such as pictures, music, and videos) has many advantages, but which provider offers the best deal?

1. Research three cloud storage providers other than Google and Microsoft. Find out how much, if any, free storage space is offered and the costs to purchase additional storage. Also learn the maximum file size that can be transferred to the provider's servers.

2. Create a presentation with one slide per provider. Describe the features, benefits, costs, and file-size limits for each provider.

Include the URLs of the providers' websites where you found the information described. Conclude the presentation with a slide that states your recommendation for a cloud storage provider and give your reasons.

3. Save the presentation as **CloudStorage-YourName**.

4. Submit the presentation to your instructor in the manner she or he has requested.

Topics Review

Topic	Key Concepts	Key Terms
3.1 The System Unit	A peripheral device is hardware plugged into the system used for input, output, connectivity, or storage. The power supply is where you plug in the power cord. A cooling fan near the CPU prevents the CPU from overheating. A motherboard is the main circuit board into which all other devices connect. Expansion cards are plugged into expansion slots on the motherboard to provide or improve functionality. Data travels between components on the motherboard and the CPU via data buses. Parallel processing means the CPU can execute multiple instructions simultaneously. The instruction cycle is the process the CPU carries out to retrieve, decode, execute, and store an instruction. Clock speed is the number of instruction cycles per second the CPU processes, measured in GHz (1 billion cycles per second). L1, L2, and L3 cache affect system performance, since the CPU accesses cache memory faster than RAM. ROM stores instructions that do not change, such as the BIOS or UEFI instructions used to start up a computer. RAM is configured in modules that plug into the motherboard. The size and type of RAM affects system performance. External devices plug into a port attached to the motherboard. USB ports are the most common type of port.	peripheral motherboard expansion card data bus parallel processing instruction cycle clock speed gigahertz (GHz) Level 1 (L1) cache Level 2 (L2) cache Level 3 (L3) cache read-only memory (ROM) BIOS (basic input/output system) UEFI (Unified Extensible Firmware Interface) port universal serial bus (USB) port
3.2 Input Devices	Wireless keyboards and mice communicate with a wireless receiver plugged into a USB port. Special purpose keys on the keyboard are used to send commands to the active program running on the computer. Tablets and smartphones usually display an on-screen keyboard. A mouse detects movement using light technology and moves the pointer in the same direction you move the mouse. Buttons and a scroll wheel on a mouse are used to manipulate objects or send commands. On notebooks, a touchpad or track pointer senses finger movement and taps or finger pressure in place of a mouse. A touchscreen accepts input from finger gestures or a stylus (digital pen). A scanner uses optical technology to convert text and images into data. Other readers used for input are bar code, QR code, magnetic strip, biometric device, and RFID reader. Digital cameras, camcorders, and webcams are input devices used to provide pictures or live video to the computer or mobile device. Microphones combined with voice recognition technology are used to create data from audio sources. Various game controllers provide a means to input commands to entertainment systems.	keyboard mouse touchpad touchscreen stylus scanner bar code reader QR (Quick Response) code magnetic strip reader biometric device radio frequency identification (RFID) reader webcam microphone voice recognition technology

continued...

Topic	Key Concepts	Key Terms
3.3 Output Devices	Video display screens connect to a video port on a PC or are integrated into a notebook or mobile device.	video display
	Newer monitors for PCs are wide-screen LCD or LED displays.	monitor
	A plasma display, often used for televisions, is expected to become obsolete due to advances in LED display technology.	liquid crystal display (LCD)
	OLED displays are thinner and provide the best video output.	light-emitting diode (LED)
	Resolution is the measurement of horizontal and vertical pixels (squares with red, green, and blue color values) used to render an image. Higher resolutions produce clearer images.	plasma
	4K UHD is a new display technology that uses four times the pixels as high definition.	organic light-emitting diode (OLED)
	VDPs and interactive whiteboards are used to display computer output on large screens.	resolution
	Audio output is heard from speakers, headphones, or headsets.	pixel
	A Bluetooth headset is used to hear audio during voice calls.	4K UHD
	Printed copy of computer output is called *hard copy*.	video display projector (VDP)
	A laser printer uses a laser beam to charge a drum, which causes toner to stick to the paper as it passes through the printer.	interactive whiteboard
	Inkjet printers form text and images by spraying drops of ink from ink cartridges onto a page.	Bluetooth headset
	Photo printers are used to print high-quality pictures from digital cameras.	hard copy
	Thermal printers heat coated paper and are often used to print receipts at retail stores.	laser printer
	Blueprints and technical drawings are printed on plotters that move a pen across the page.	inkjet printer
	Digital copiers connected to a network can be used to print output.	photo printer
	Multipurpose printers include printing, scanning, copying, and faxing capabilities in one device.	thermal printer
	A 3-D printer produces a 3-D object by precisely cutting successive layers of material on top of one another.	plotter
		digital copier
		3-D printer
3.4 Network Adapters	A network adapter is any device used to connect to a network.	network adapter
	The network adapter is the interface between a computer and a modem or router that allows data to be exchanged.	protocol
	Data is exchanged in a network using a system of rules called *protocols*.	Wi-Fi adapter
	A network connection for a wired connection is called an Ethernet port.	802.11 protocol
	Ethernet refers to the type of cable used for the connection.	external wireless adapter
	Wi-Fi adapters are used to communicate with a wireless network.	USB wireless adapter
	The 802.11 protocol is the name of the standard used for wireless communications in Wi-Fi networks.	wireless ExpressCard
	A USB wireless adapter and a wireless ExpressCard are external wireless adapters that can be purchased to connect to a wireless network.	
	A Bluetooth adapter is used to provide connectivity within short ranges to other Bluetooth-enabled devices.	

continued…

Topic	Key Concepts	Key Terms
3.5 Digital Data	Computers understand the binary system, which uses only 0s and 1s.	binary system
	The smallest unit in the binary system is a bit, which can have one of two values: either 0 or 1.	bit
	A group of 8 bits equals a byte and represents one character, number, or symbol.	byte
	Internet speed is measured in megabits per second, which is 1 million bits transferred per second.	file
	Files are permanent copies of documents, photos, or videos assigned a file name and measured in bytes.	file name
	A KB is approximately 1,000 bytes.	kilobyte (KB)
	An MB is approximately 1 million bytes.	megabyte (MB)
	A GB is approximately 1 billion bytes.	gigabyte (GB)
	A TB is approximately 1 trillion bytes.	terabyte (TB)
	One MB can store approximately 500 pages of text.	
	Images, music, and videos often require many MB of storage space.	
3.6 Storage Options	A storage device provides the means to read data from and write data to a permanent storage medium.	storage device
	Storage devices are referred to as *drives*.	drive
	An internal HDD is usually the largest storage device on a standalone PC.	hard disk
	Traditional HDDs are magnetic storage media.	solid-state drive (SSD)
	External HDDs are connected via a USB.	flash memory
	SSDs use chip-based flash memory to store data; they are also more durable and use less power than HDDs.	USB flash drive
	Some workplaces require data to be stored on network servers.	optical disc
	In homes, a wireless media hub lets you store and share data among multiple devices and with other people.	flash memory card
	USB flash drives are portable, easy to use, and come in all shapes, sizes, and storage capacities.	
	CDs, DVDs, and Blu-ray discs use optical technology to read and write data to recordable discs.	
	Flash memory cards are used in portable devices, such as digital cameras.	
	Some computers have a card reader built in for easy transfer of data from portable flash memory cards.	
	Cloud storage providers allow you to store and share files that are accessible from any device with an Internet connection.	
	Some cloud providers allow access to a limited amount of free storage space, with higher capacities available for a subscription fee.	

Recheck
Recheck your understanding of the topics covered in this chapter.

Workbook
Chapter review and assessment resources are available in the *Workbook* ebook.

Chapter 4

The Operating System and Utility Programs

A computing device needs to have software installed for the device to work. *Software* is the term that describes the set of programs that contain instructions to tell the computer what to do and how to perform each task. **System software** includes the operating system that is designed to work with the hardware that is present. It also includes a set of utility programs that are used to maintain the computer and its devices. The **operating system (OS)** program provides the user interface to work with the computer, manages all the hardware resources, and provides the platform for managing files and application programs (the programs you use to perform tasks). It is the most important software on your computer, because without an operating system, the hardware and other software programs would not work.

For example, most often you go to your computing device because you have a specific task you want to do. Assume you want to log in to Facebook to check for updates from your friends. To do this, you start your computer and connect to the Facebook website. The computer first has to start the OS before you see the interface that allows you to launch the Internet browser program, such as Microsoft Edge. Without the OS, the interface would not appear, and the browser would not be able to connect to the Internet to load the Facebook page.

In this chapter, you will learn the various OSs available for computers, the typical tasks that OSs perform, and how to use a few utility programs to maintain and troubleshoot your computer.

 SNAP If you are a SNAP user, go to your SNAP Assignments page to complete the Precheck, Tutorials, and Recheck.

Learning Objectives

4.1 List and describe the major functions of operating system software

4.2 Identify the operating systems in use for personal computers and describe characteristics that differentiate them from one another

4.3 Describe the functions of a mobile operating system and list the most common mobile operating systems

4.4 Explain the purpose of an embedded operating system and the purpose of a cloud operating system, and give an example of each

4.5 Describe common utility programs used to maintain a computer

4.6 Recognize and locate troubleshooting tools found in the operating system to solve computer problems

4.1 Introduction to the OS and OS Functions

The OS manages all the activities within the computer. The OS routes data between the hardware resources and the application programs as shown in Figure 4.1. The OS also starts the user interface and properly shuts down the hardware. Files that are stored on devices are managed by the OS. While you are working, the OS controls the flow of data between memory and the central processing unit (CPU). If you plug a new device into the computer, the OS looks for and installs the software that allows the device to work. Consider the OS as the conductor of a symphony; each instrument (hardware component and application program) needs the conductor (the OS) to direct when and how to play its individual piece so the song performs correctly.

Figure 4.1

The OS controls the flow of data and manages programs and memory.

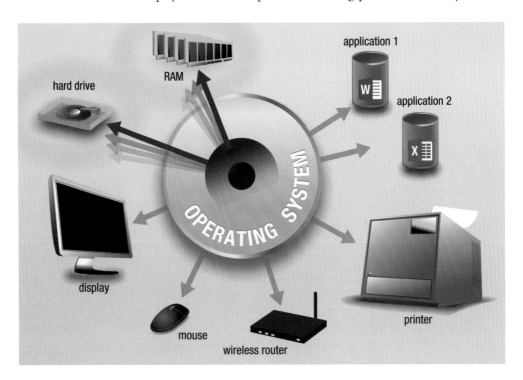

Starting and Shutting Down a Computer

Starting a computer is called **booting**. If you turn on a computer that has been shut off, you are doing a **cold boot**. If you restart a computer without turning off the power, you are doing a **warm boot**. The instructions for booting are stored on the basic input/output system (BIOS) or Unified Extensible Firmware Interface (UEFI) chip that resides on the motherboard. At startup the OS **kernel** is loaded into RAM where it remains until you power off the PC. The kernel is the core of the OS that manages memory, devices, and programs and assigns resources. Other parts of the OS are copied into RAM only when needed.

As the computer is booting, a series of messages may appear on the screen depending on the OS you use. When the boot process is complete, the screen will display the user interface, the lock screen, or a sign-in screen. For example, on a computer running the Microsoft Windows 10 OS, after the lock screen is cleared, users see a sign-in screen prompting them to sign in with a Microsoft account and password. Following the sign-in process, the desktop shown in Figure 4.2 on page 89 appears.

If you decide to turn off the power to your computer, you should always perform a shutdown command so that programs and files are properly closed. Depending on the OS, choose the **Shut Down** option, which turns the computer off, or choose a

Good to Know 🎓

The term *booting* is derived from the phrase "to pull oneself up by the bootstraps." The bootstrap program contains the instruction that tells the computer where to find the OS.

Figure 4.2
The Windows 10 desktop shown after booting and signing in to the system.

power-saving mode, such as Sleep, which saves open documents and programs while turning off unnecessary functions and devices.

Although different OSs are available for computers, most OSs perform similar functions. Most of these functions are performed automatically in the background, often without the user's awareness.

Providing a User Interface

The **user interface (UI)** is the means to interact with the computer. For example, in Windows 10, two methods can be used to launch an application program: (1) double-click a program icon on the desktop or (2) click the Start button and then click the program name or tile in the Start menu that opens. Most OSs provide the user with a **graphical user interface** (**GUI**, pronounced *gooey*) that presents visual images, such as tiles, icons, or buttons, that you click or double-click to tell the OS what you want to do.

Sometimes a **command-line interface** (see Figure 4.3) is used to interact with an OS. In a command-line interface, you type commands on the keyboard at a prompt to tell the OS what to do. Network specialists sometimes use a command-line interface to configure or troubleshoot a network device.

```
C:\WINDOWS\system32\cmd.exe                              –  □  ×

Microsoft Windows [Version 10.0.10061]
(c) 2015 Microsoft Corporation. All rights reserved.

C:\Users\Denise>ping 209.46.18.200

Pinging 209.46.18.200 with 32 bytes of data:
Reply from 209.46.18.200: bytes=32 time=342ms TTL=128
Reply from 209.46.18.200: bytes=32 time=50ms TTL=128
Reply from 209.46.18.200: bytes=32 time=53ms TTL=128
Reply from 209.46.18.200: bytes=32 time=50ms TTL=128

Ping statistics for 209.46.18.200:
    Packets: Sent = 4, Received = 4, Lost = 0 (0% loss),
Approximate round trip times in milli-seconds:
    Minimum = 50ms, Maximum = 342ms, Average = 123ms

C:\Users\Denise>
```

Figure 4.3
A command-line interface requires that you type commands from the keyboard at a prompt, such as C:\Users\ Denise> shown in the last line of text in this window.

Managing Application Programs and Memory, and Coordinating the Flow of Data

The OS manages the installed application programs and provides you with the ability to run a program, install a new program, and uninstall a program no longer desired. When working at a computer, many people will have more than one program running at the same time. The OS manages computer resources, allocating data and software to and from the CPU and memory as needed, and determines the order in which tasks are performed. The OS also manages the flow of data between the CPU, cache memory, RAM, and the input and output devices. If you exceed the capacity of RAM, the OS uses space on the hard disk to store overflow data. The hard disk space allocated to store RAM contents is called **virtual memory**. In Windows, the Task Manager displays information about how the OS manages and coordinates computer resources (Figure 4.4).

Figure 4.4

The Windows 10 Task Manager shows the many tasks the OS has to manage while you are working.

Task Manager		13%	62%	0%	0%
File Options View					
Processes	Performance	App history	Startup	Users	Details	Services				
Name	Status	CPU	Memory	Disk	Network
Apps (3)					
Food & Drink		0%	99.2 MB	0 MB/s	0 Mbps
Health & Fitness		0.6%	101.6 MB	0 MB/s	0 Mbps
Task Manager		2.3%	7.8 MB	0 MB/s	0 Mbps
Background processes (24)					
Adobe® Flash® Player Utility		0%	2.3 MB	0 MB/s	0 Mbps
Application Frame Host		0%	11.7 MB	0 MB/s	0 Mbps
COM Surrogate		0%	1.5 MB	0 MB/s	0 Mbps
Host Process for Windows Tasks		0%	2.7 MB	0 MB/s	0 Mbps
InstallAgent		0.6%	1.2 MB	0 MB/s	0 Mbps
Microsoft Distributed Transactio...		0%	0.7 MB	0 MB/s	0 Mbps
Microsoft OneDrive (32 bit)		0%	3.6 MB	0 MB/s	0 Mbps
Microsoft Windows Search Filte...		0%	0.8 MB	0 MB/s	0 Mbps
Microsoft Windows Search Inde...		0%	6.7 MB	0 MB/s	0 Mbps

Fewer details   End task

Configuring Hardware and Peripheral Devices

The OS configures all devices that are installed or connected to the computer. A small program called a **driver** contains the instructions the OS uses to communicate and route data to and from the device. When the computer is booted, the OS loads each device driver. If you plug in a new device after the computer is started, the OS searches the device for the driver, loads it automatically, and displays a message that the necessary files are being installed (Figure 4.5). This ability is called **plug and play**. If a device driver is not found, the OS will prompt you to install the driver from another source.

Figure 4.5

When new hardware has been plugged in, the OS displays a message indicating the files needed to run the device are being installed.

The OS is also used to manage other aspects of the hardware—for example, to adjust the screen's resolution, adjust the volume, and change the default settings for a device such as the window that opens when a music CD is played. The OS provides options for managing the power plan for the computer, including the time interval before the display is turned off or the computer is put into sleep mode when no activity is detected. The power plan options allow for different settings when the computer is running on battery power or plugged into a power outlet.

Providing a File System

The OS keeps track of the files stored on a computer's storage devices and provides tools you can use to find and then manage those files by moving, copying, deleting, or renaming. In addition, utility programs to search, back up, restore, clean up, and defragment storage devices are included in the OS package. Figure 4.6 shows a Windows 10 File Explorer window with a red box outlining the ribbon interface that has buttons to perform file management tasks.

Managing Software Updates and Security

Software often needs to be updated as program fixes, security enhancements, and new or modified device drivers become available. By default the OS is generally set up to download updates automatically, as shown in Figure 4.7, free of charge to registered users who have activated the software.

ribbon interface with buttons to manage files

Figure 4.6

In a Windows 10 File Explorer Window, buttons on the Home tab are used to manage files and folders.

Click the Check for updates button if you want to download and install updates before an automatic update is performed.

Figure 4.7

To access the *Windows Update* panel of the Settings app in Windows 10, click the *Settings* option in the left pane on the Start menu, and then click the Update & security icon.

By default, Windows is set to automatically download and install updates.

Explore Further | What Is UEFI?

UEFI was created to deal with the limitations of decades-old BIOS firmware used to boot up a computer. Many companies are replacing their old BIOS firmware with this newer interface.

1. Research to find a description of UEFI and to learn why computer companies are moving to replace BIOS with UEFI.

2. Create a document that describes, in general and in your own words, why UEFI is a more secure boot process and why BIOS is considered obsolete. Include the URLs for the websites you used to complete this activity.

3. Save the document as **UEFI-YourName** and submit it to your instructor in the manner she or he has requested.

4.2 Popular OSs for Computing Systems

Tutorial
What's New in
Windows 10?

When you purchase a new computing device, an OS is preinstalled so the device will work when you turn it on. The OS that is preinstalled may depend on the hardware, since some hardware is designed specifically for a particular OS. The term **computing platform** refers to the combination of hardware architecture and software design that allows applications to run. For example, buying an iMac computer means you will have the Mac OS installed because Apple computers are not designed to run Windows software. Four OSs typically installed on work, school, and home computers are Windows, Mac OS, UNIX, and Linux. You may also encounter a network OS on a PC.

Windows

Good to Know

Microsoft stopped providing support for Windows XP in April 2014. While the OS is still in use on some PCs today, home and business users are advised to upgrade to a version of Windows that is Windows 7 or higher to avoid problems that occur when updates are no longer provided. Extended support for Windows 7 is slated to end January 2020.

Windows, created by Microsoft Corporation, is the most popular OS because a wide variety of hardware is designed to run Windows and because software applications designed for Windows are plentiful. Windows has evolved from Windows 1.0, released in 1985, to Windows 10, released in 2015. You will encounter a variety of Windows OSs since the Windows brand is so prevalent and not everyone upgrades to the most current release.

Windows is updated as Microsoft develops new versions to keep up with hardware innovations, adds new functionality and/or redesigns existing functions, and overall strives to make the OS faster and more user-friendly. A new release is usually assigned a version number, such as 10, to differentiate the OS; however, with the release of Windows 10 in 2015, Microsoft adopted a new strategy: instead of releasing a new version of Windows every few years, it will use periodic updates to introduce new features and technologies in the Windows as a Service model.

Each Windows version generally comes in a variety of editions for various home and business environments. For example, Windows Server 2016 is used by businesses that need advanced security and management for networks.

The UI for Windows 8.1, released in 2013, is vastly different from the UI for Windows 10, released in 2015 (see Figure 4.8). The Start screen with live tile interface for Windows 8.1 was a game changer for PC users comfortable with the

Figure 4.8

Windows 8.1 Start Screen (left) and Windows 10 Desktop with Start button menu (right)

desktop in Windows 7 and earlier releases. With Windows 10, Microsoft responded to customer feedback about Windows 8.1 and brought back the familiar desktop interface with a redesigned Start button. The redesigned Start menu offers Windows 8.1-style tiles in the right pane, along with access to all installed applications and settings in the left pane. Windows 10 also includes **Cortana**, a personal digital assistant, which can search the web, locate files on your device, and remind you of meetings or events in your calendar. Cortana responds to voice commands or keyboard input. It also keeps track of your likes and responses to alerts, and uses that information to personalize your interactive experience.

Check This Out ✓

http://CC2.Paradigm
College.net/Windows
History

Go here to read the history of Windows developments from 1975 to today.

Mac OS

The **Mac OS** is the OS created by Apple, Inc., with the first release in 1984 for the Macintosh computer. The first Macintosh computer used a GUI interface and became the basis for the design of other GUI OSs down the road.

The Apple Mac OS X family is the most recent OS, with the El Capitan version, released in October 2015, shown in Figure 4.9. Apple uses a unique naming convention for Mac OS X, with a version sporting the name of an animal, such as Snow Leopard (2009) and Mountain Lion (2012), or a popular place, such as Mavericks (2013), Yosemite (2014), and El Capitan (2015). (El Capitan is also the name of a rock formation in Yosemite National Park.) Like Microsoft, Apple releases new versions to update functionality, responsiveness, and efficiencies to strive for faster, more user-friendly experiences. Server versions of Mac OS X are also available.

Historically, Macs were less prone to viruses since hackers went after Windows software because of its prevalence in the marketplace. However, with the rise in Mac sales in the past few years, virus attacks now hit the Mac world more frequently.

Mac computers have always been popular with graphic artists and those working in multimedia environments because the hardware is designed with high-end graphics processing capability. Consumer demand for mobile products from Apple, such as the iPhone and iPad, have increased brand presence of Macs in the marketplace.

Figure 4.9

Mac OS X El Capitan

UNIX

UNIX is an OS that has been around since the late 1960s and is designed for servers. Originally designed to be multi-user and multitasking, the OS is often used for web servers because of its robust ability to support many users. UNIX is available in several versions and is able to run on a variety of devices, including hardware built for Windows and Macs. In fact, the Mac OS from Apple is based on the UNIX OS. Although UNIX is a highly stable OS, the cost and higher level of skill required to install and maintain a UNIX computer make it less prevalent for typical computer users.

UNIX was designed as a server OS.

Linux

Linux was created by Linus Torvalds in 1991 and is based on UNIX. Linux can be used as a standalone OS or as a server OS. What makes Linux preferable to some users is that the OS is an **open source program**, meaning that the source code is available to the public and can be freely modified or customized. Linux, like UNIX, can run on a variety of devices and is available as a free download on the web, as well as by purchase from Linux vendors. Linux, because of its open source design, is available in many distributions (versions), such as Red Hat and Ubuntu. Figure 4.10 illustrates Linux Ubuntu. You can order some computers with Linux preinstalled upon request.

Figure 4.10

Ubuntu is one of the many distributions available for the open source Linux OS.

The open source software movement is increasing in large part owing to the lower costs associated with using free software. Linux can be found in use at companies such as IBM and HP, and a popular mobile OS is based on Linux.

Network OSs

A **network operating system (NOS)** incorporates enhanced functions and security features for configuring and managing computers and peripherals connected in a networked environment. Some PC OSs, such as Windows and Mac OS X, have basic networking features built in that let you connect and share files and devices within a home network. An NOS is used in the business world, where more advanced security and management features for connecting, sharing, and providing access to multiple resources are essential for maintaining large networks. Windows Server 2016 is the network OS produced by Microsoft.

Tutorial
What Types of Tasks Does Network Operating Software Handle?

Blog Topic To Upgrade Your OS or Not to Upgrade—What Will You Do?

When a newer version of an OS is released, some people immediately upgrade, relishing the opportunity to be on the leading edge and experience what's new. Others prefer to delay the upgrade and stick with the tried and true, assuming that it is more prudent to wait for the manufacturer to work out all the bugs.

1. Assuming that cost is not a factor in the decision to upgrade, write and post a blog entry that supports immediately upgrading or taking the wait-and-see approach. Give reasons for your position.

2. Read at least two of your classmates' blogs and post a comment to each.

3. Submit your blog URL and the URLs of the two classmates' blogs to your instructor in the manner she or he has requested.

Explore Further   Conduct a Survey and Look Up Statistics on OS Usage

Microsoft Windows and Apple Mac OS X are the most commonly used operating systems. Each of these OSs comes in several versions. Which OS and version is the most popular?

1. Survey a minimum of 10 friends, family, or classmates outside your class to find out which OS, including the version number or name, they use on their primary computing devices.

2. Next, using your favorite search engine, look up current statistics on OS market share on the web.

3. Create a document or presentation that shows the compiled results of your personal survey and the results you found on the web.

4. Add a short paragraph that describes the comparisons you found. Include the URL of the site you used for your web research.

5. Save the document or presentation as **OSStats-YourName** and submit it to your instructor in the manner she or he has requested.

4.3 Popular OSs for Mobile Devices

Tutorial
What Is 4G?

A variety of mobile devices, such as smartphones and tablets, use a **mobile operating system**, an OS designed specifically for a mobile device. The OS is stored on a ROM chip. This type of OS is designed to manage hardware and applications with less memory than a personal computer OS yet run fast and efficiently. The mobile OS often manages input from a touchscreen and/or voice commands, and routes data to and from wireless connections including cellular and Wi-Fi networks. Mobile devices also have cameras that are used for video calling and taking pictures. Mobile OSs manage small application programs, called *apps*, with support for multitasking among contacts, messages, calendars, music, video, social media updates, web browsing, and numerous other mobile tools. Several hardware manufacturers produce mobile devices, and some have developed their own OSs for use on their hardware. The most common mobile OSs include Android, iOS, and Windows 10 Mobile.

The mobile market changes rapidly as wireless technologies and software develop to take full advantage of faster speeds and capabilities. Competition in the industry is fierce, and companies that lag in new development quickly run into trouble. For example, the market share for Symbian, a mobile OS once used on most Nokia phones and popular in Europe, declined to less than 1 percent after Nokia announced a partnership with Microsoft. Consider also the struggle by BlackBerry to remain viable. A market leader in the early smartphone days, BlackBerry saw its share of the market decline to less than 2 percent in 2015 as a result of its delay in releasing a device with touch-enabled multimedia, web browsing, and apps similar to Apple and Android offerings.

> **Security Alert** | **Password Protect Your Mobile Device**
>
> Imagine your lost smartphone or tablet resulting in someone posting embarrassing updates or photos on your Facebook account. Secure your device by locking it in case it falls into the wrong hands. Some devices provide for a touch or swipe motion to unlock; others require a typed passcode.

Android

Android is the leading mobile OS, used on many smartphones and tablets (Figure 4.11). The OS is based on Linux, making it an open source OS. In 2007, Android was released by the **Open Handset Alliance**, which is a consortium of 84 technology and mobile companies. A sampling of members includes Google, Samsung, LG, T-Mobile, and Sprint. The goal of the alliance is to develop open standards for mobile devices. Android is now maintained and developed by the **Android Open Source Project (AOSP)**, which is led by Google.

Each Android release is named after a dessert. The version in use at the time of writing is Android 6.0 Marshmallow. Android currently enjoys the highest market share for mobile devices, and Google Play, the website for Android apps, listed more than 1.7 million apps in October 2015.

Figure 4.11

Android is the OS of choice for mobile devices, including LG smartphones.

iOS

Apple developed **iOS** as the mobile OS for its iPhone, iPod, and iPad (Figure 4.12). The OS is based on Mac OS X. Users can download apps for their Apple devices only from the App store on their iPhone or iPad, or from iTunes on a Mac. Development of new apps for Apple devices is tightly controlled by Apple, meaning that new apps are generally virus-free, stable, and reliable. In the summer of 2015, over 1.5 million apps and games were available in the App Store and iTunes for Apple devices.

Windows 10 Mobile

Microsoft Windows 10 Mobile (Figure 4.13) is the edition that replaced the earlier mobile OS from Microsoft, Windows Phone. Windows Phone introduced the tile interface, which became the basis for Windows 8.1 for standalone (desktop) computers. In all three versions of Windows (Phone, 8.1, and 10), live tiles stream updates to the user's mail, calendar, and web apps.

Windows 10 Mobile for smartphones is considered to be just like the desktop edition of Windows 10 but optimized for the smaller screen—apps and settings operate similarly in both versions of Windows 10. The consistent design of Windows 10 across devices means that if you clear an alert on your smartphone, the alert also disappears on your laptop or tablet.

BlackBerry OS

BlackBerry (formerly Research in Motion) developed **BlackBerry OS** for BlackBerry devices (Figure 4.14). Although known for its superior messaging security and its BlackBerry Messenger tool, BlackBerry suffered a huge decline in market share before releasing four new smartphones in 2015 as part of a turnaround campaign. One of the new smartphones, called the Priv, incorporates the renowned BlackBerry security with the Android OS, which allows users to download apps from the Google Play store. Although no longer common as a consumer device, BlackBerry smartphones are still found in corporate and government offices.

Figure 4.12
The Apple iPad Air tablet uses the iOS interface.

Figure 4.13
Windows 10 Lumia 950 smartphone.

Figure 4.14
The BlackBerry Priv smartphone was released by BlackBerry in 2015 as part of a turnaround campaign to gain back customers.

Explore Further   **Which Smartphone Would You Choose?**

Assume you have just won a contest in which the prize is a free talk, text, and data plan for one year that more than meets your needs. All you need to do to claim your prize is to buy any smartphone you want.

1. Visit your preferred smartphone provider store or use the Internet to conduct your survey of smartphone providers and find your dream smartphone.

2. Once you have made your selection, create a document that explains your smartphone choice, the features of the smartphone, and your rationale. Include in your rationale a discussion of the mobile OS that resides on the smartphone and whether the mobile OS influenced your choice.

3. Include the URLs of any websites you used and/or the name and location of the store you visited.

4. Save the document as **Smartphone-YourName** and submit it to your instructor in the manner she or he has requested.

4.4 Embedded OSs and Cloud OSs

Computing consoles such as automated tellers, GPS navigation systems, video game controllers, medical equipment devices, point-of-sale cash registers, digital cameras, and a multitude of other consumer and commercial electronics need a specialized OS designed for the device's limited use. In these computing devices, an **embedded operating system** is installed. Embedded OSs are smaller and interact with fewer resources to perform specific tasks fast and reliably. Smart TVs use an embedded OS referred to as a *TV OS* to present a UI and manage the content options.

Cloud OSs, while not yet widely used, are a viable option for people with multiple devices who want seamless integration of software and documents.

Windows Embedded

Windows Embedded is a family of OSs in various releases, based on the familiar Windows OS, designed for use in task-specific devices that need to present a UI and manage input, output, and limited resources. For example, Windows Embedded and Windows Embedded Compact are variations recommended by Microsoft for an ATM or a digital picture frame.

Embedded Linux

Embedded Linux applications can be found running smart appliances, in-flight entertainment systems, personal navigation systems, and a variety of other consumer and commercial electronics. Similar to the standalone Linux OS, Embedded Linux has several distributions because it is an open source program.

TV OSs Embedded in Smart TVs

Televisions have evolved into entertainment hubs with a variety of choices for viewing content—traditional cable and satellite signal programming, streamed music, videos, movies, news, and more. Inside newer smart TVs an OS is embedded that is a **TV operating system**. The TV OS is the program that runs the set-top box, runs other connected devices, presents the interface for accessing content, and allows the viewer to navigate channels or streamed media. A TV OS uses apps to connect to resources, such as Netflix and YouTube, and accepts input from the remote control device or via wireless keyboard, smartphone, or tablet. A variety of TV OSs are in use, such as the LG webOS, Samsung Tizen, and Panasonic Firefox OS.

ATMs are just one of many kinds of electronic devices that require an embedded OS.

Car console and navigation systems use embedded OSs.

A TV OS presents a UI with access to apps that enable users to access content from a variety of resources in today's smart TVs.

Android Wear is the OS embedded in some smartwatches.

Android Embedded in Devices

Android, the Linux-based OS, is not just for smartphones and tablets. Some home automation systems that control lighting, heating, air conditioning, and interactions with a smart appliance, such as a washer or dryer, are using an embedded version of the Android OS. Android Auto may be the OS running the console and navigation system in your car, Android TV may be the OS on your game console, and you might be checking time on a smartwatch controlled by Android Wear.

Cloud OSs

Some companies, such as Google, are developing OSs that operate like a virtual desktop. The interface may look and feel like a traditional desktop, but your settings, documents, pictures, contacts, and other files are stored in the cloud. This means you can access the objects from any device anywhere you have an Internet connection. A **web-based operating system** is not a true OS like Windows, and you still need a standalone OS on the computer to start your computer and access the web browser. The appeal of these systems is that extra software for applications does not have to be installed, and the ability to synchronize documents among multiple devices seamlessly is worthwhile as more people use multiple computers.

Cloud OSs are like a virtual desktop, with all settings, applications, and documents stored on cloud servers.

> **Check This Out** ✓
>
> http://CC2.Paradigm College.net/CloudOS
>
> Go here to learn about eyeOS, a free cloud-based OS for those who register and create a user account.

Security Alert **Protect Your Documents in the Cloud**

Storing all your files in the cloud is not without risk of hackers or others making unwanted intrusions into your personal data. Make sure the service provider encrypts data, and choose a password that is difficult to hack. See Chapter 7 for information on encryption and creating strong passwords.

iCloud The Apple **iCloud** is built into every new iOS device. Once set up, iCloud automatically provides access to your email, contacts, calendar, notes, reminders, documents, pictures, movies, and more, on multiple Apple devices, as shown in Figure 4.15. You can work on documents in the cloud and access them from any connected device—including a Windows-based PC. If you download an app on one device, you have access to it on your other devices too. Apple typically includes 5 GB of free storage when you sign up for iCloud.

Chrome OS The Google **Chrome OS** is a Linux-based OS available on specific hardware called Chromebooks, manufactured by Acer, Asus, Toshiba, and HP. In 2014 Dell began shipping the first Chromeboxes, desktop PCs with the Chrome OS. Chromebooks boast fast startup with built-in virus protection, automatic updates that promise not to slow down your device over time, and cloud-based applications, such as Google Docs, Gmail, Google Drive, and Cloud Print. You can also sync your favorite websites, documents, and settings with other devices that use the Chrome browser.

Google is constantly updating Chrome OS as it receives feedback from users and reviewers. Figure 4.16 shows the desktop edition with version 19.

Good to Know

Chrome OS led to the establishment of the Chromium projects with the goal to develop a fast, simple, and secure open source OS for people who spend most of their time on the web.

Figure 4.15

After signing in with your Apple ID, the iCloud service connects you to Mail, Contacts, Calendar, and Find iPhone, and synchronizes documents, pictures, and movies from any other connected Apple device or PC

Figure 4.16

The desktop in Google Chrome OS version 19.

Career Connection

Careers in the Cloud

Cloud computing is growing, and businesses that use and supply cloud services are looking for IT professionals with the right cloud technology skill sets. According to Forbes.com, in 2015 there were 3.9 million jobs in the United States affiliated with cloud computing. The following skills were the top five most in demand: Structured Query Language (SQL), Java, overall software development expertise, Linux, and JavaScript. If you are interested in a career in cloud computing, look for certificate, diploma, or degree programs in that field. Cloud certification exams from companies such as Amazon, VMware, Cloud U, CompTIA, and Google are also available, although these exams are better suited to individuals with some work experience in an IT environment.

Blog Topic   Is the Future Bright for Web-Based OSs?

Within a team, discuss the following question: *Will cloud-based OSs eventually take over from traditional computing environments in which all the software and files are stored on a local hard drive?* Consider the advantages and disadvantages of using a system in which all settings and files are stored in the cloud. What, if any, barriers will prevent these working environments from becoming commonplace?

1. Write and post a blog entry for your team with a summary of your team's position.
2. Read at least two of your classmates' team blogs and post one comment from your team to each.
3. Submit your team's blog URL and the URLs of the two classmates' team blogs to your instructor in the manner she or he has requested.

Explore Further   Favorite Electronic Gadgets

Of all the many electronic gadgets available, which are the most popular? You can get some idea by working with a classmate to survey family and friends and analyzing your results.

1. Ask at least 10 family members or friends to name their favorite electronic gadget other than a smartphone or tablet. Examples can include MP3 player, GPS, gaming system, and digital camera.
2. Compare the results of your informal survey with a classmate's results and discuss the following questions: Which devices are named most often in both lists? Are there any devices that appear on only one list? Was there a response that surprised you?
3. Create a document that summarizes the two survey results and your discussion.
4. Save the document as **FavoriteDevices-YourName** and submit it to your instructor in the manner she or he has requested.

4.5 OS Utilities for Maintaining System Performance

Just as a car needs regular tune-ups to keep it running smoothly and efficiently, so does a computer. Files on the computer should be regularly maintained by removing unwanted files, and regularly backing up important files to prevent loss of data. Most OSs provide a utility to schedule regular maintenance. File maintenance utilities often include a file manager, a utility to clean up unwanted files, a disk defragmenter, and a backup and restore program.

Utilities that protect your computer from malware, such as viruses and spyware, are discussed in Chapter 7, Computer Security and Privacy.

File Manager

You open a **File Explorer** window to perform file management tasks, such as moving, copying, deleting, and renaming files. You can also set up your filing system by creating a new **folder**, which is where you store related files. A folder on a computer is similar to a paper file folder you would use in an office for paper documents you want to keep together. Open File Explorer in Windows 10 by clicking the File Explorer icon on the Windows taskbar.

In Mac OS X, the **Finder** utility is used to perform file management routines. Open a Finder window by clicking the Finder icon on the dock. See Figure 4.17 for a comparison of the Windows File Explorer and Mac Finder.

Figure 4.17

Perform file management tasks in a Finder window on a Mac (left), or in a File Explorer window (right) on a Windows PC.

Click here to access the menu of file management options.

folder

Use buttons on the Home tab to perform file management tasks.

Disk Cleanup Utility

The Windows **Disk Cleanup** utility (Figure 4.18) allows you to scan a particular storage device or drive to select various types of files to be deleted. Files the utility will flag for deletion include temporary Internet files, temporary application files, downloaded files, files moved to the Recycle Bin, and offline web pages. To open Disk Cleanup in Windows 10, click in the search box on the Windows taskbar, type *Disk Cleanup*, and then press Enter.

Disk Cleanup begins by calculating how much disk space can be freed up.

Next, the utility allows you to choose the types of files to be removed. Some options are selected by default.

Figure 4.18

In Windows, the Disk Cleanup utility is used to help remove unnecessary files that clutter a hard disk drive.

Disk Defragmenter

As time passes, a disk can become fragmented as a result of files being moved or deleted. Files are stored on a disk in groups called *clusters*, and several clusters are sometimes needed to store one document. Sometimes the clusters needed for a document are not stored adjacent to one another. This is called a **fragmentation**. When you reopen a document that has been fragmented, the OS has to gather back together all the fragmented clusters and arrange them in the correct order. As more fragmentation occurs, disk efficiency decreases. A **disk defragmenter** rearranges the fragmented files back together to improve file retrieval speed and efficiency. Figure 4.19 shows the Windows **Optimize Drives** window, which is used to perform a disk defragmentation manually.

The disk defragmenter utility is used primarily by someone with an older PC. Today's hard disk drives are much faster and larger than the HDDs in older computers. If your computer was bought recently and has a large hard disk drive with lots of free space available, or if the PC has a solid-state drive, you do not need to run the disk defragmenter utility.

The Mac OS X file system works differently than the file system used on a Windows PC. Mac users do not generally need to defragment a disk because a Mac automatically defragments files on its own. For those rare instances when Mac users need to defragment their hard disks, a third party utility program is needed.

An HDD is scheduled to be optimized weekly by default.

Figure 4.19

The Windows Optimize Drives window is used to analyze a drive for the percentage of fragmentation, optimize the drive, and change optimization settings.

Back Up and Restore Utility

All computer users should back up important files regularly to prevent loss of data from disk corruption, accidental deletion, or other damage that keeps the files from being usable. A **backup utility** is a program that allows you to back up selected files or an entire disk to another storage medium. To begin a backup in Windows, go to the System and Security category in the Control Panel and then click the link to **File History**.

Files backed up using a backup utility are not stored in a readable format because they are compressed to save space. To copy files back to a disk drive in their original state, the files need to be restored. During a restore, a file or group of files is decompressed. Open the File History window to restore a file or group of files from a backup in Windows.

In Mac OS X, the **Time Machine** is used to back up and restore files. Click the Time Machine icon on the dock to start a backup operation. Figure 4.20 shows the Mac Time Machine utility and the Windows File History utility.

Figure 4.20

Go to Time Machine (left) on a Mac or File History (right) on a Windows PC to back up or restore files.

Explore Further   A Computer Maintenance Checklist

This topic introduced a sampling of common utility programs that are provided with the OS and used to perform computer maintenance. A comprehensive computer maintenance plan includes other tasks, such as wiping clean the screen and other peripherals.

1. Search the web for articles on computer maintenance to learn about other tasks recommended by computer experts.

2. Individually or working with a classmate, develop a computer maintenance checklist that you could use at home or at work to maintain your computer. Group the tasks by frequency, such as daily, weekly, monthly, and yearly.

3. Create the checklist in a document and arrange it in a format that is easy to follow.

4. Save the document as **MaintenanceChecklist-YourName** and submit it to your instructor in the manner she or he has requested.

4.6 OS Troubleshooting Tools

In a perfect world, the printer would always print, the connection to the Internet would always work, and your computer would always operate at blazing fast speed! Causes of computer problems can be complex and not easily resolved. However, knowing how to use a few of the tools provided in the OS package can help you fix some problems and get back to work.

Windows Security and Maintenance Window

The Windows Security and Maintenance window opened from the Control Panel shown in Figure 4.21 is a good place to begin when something is not working. The window displays messages when the OS has detected potential issues that need your attention. If the problem you are experiencing is not listed in one of the messages, click the <u>Troubleshooting</u> link to open the Troubleshooting window, and then click the link that most closely describes the problem you are having to open tools to help you resolve the problem. The prompts that display in those tools will vary depending on the issue you are troubleshooting.

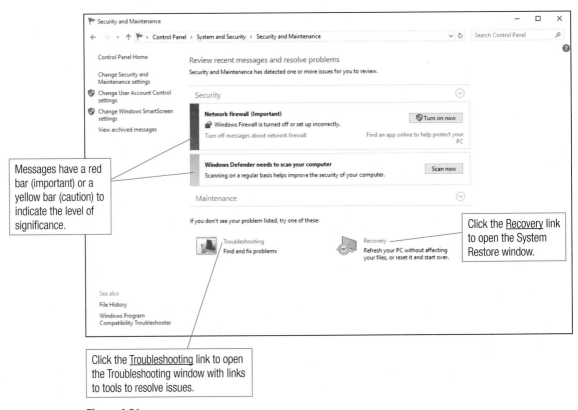

Messages have a red bar (important) or a yellow bar (caution) to indicate the level of significance.

Click the <u>Recovery</u> link to open the System Restore window.

Click the <u>Troubleshooting</u> link to open the Troubleshooting window with links to tools to resolve issues.

Figure 4.21

The Windows Security and Maintenance window displays messages about issues encountered on your computer and provides buttons and links to tools that can be used to resolve the issues.

Windows System Restore Feature

Sometimes a problem occurs after installing something new like a device driver, an application, or an update that inadvertently cause a problem with something else. Or you may accidentally delete or write over a system file and as a result cause a program or device to become unusable. In these cases, **System Restore** is a way for you to turn back the clock to when the computer was functioning normally. System Restore will undo a recent change while leaving all documents intact. You can access System Restore from the Security and Maintenance window. Click the <u>Recovery</u> link located at the bottom right of the window (see Figure 4.21 on page 106), and then click the <u>Open System Restore</u> link. At the first System Restore window (shown in Figure 4.22), click Next to begin a restore operation. At the next window, select an event from a list of changes that have been made to your system (Figure 4.23) and then follow the prompts that appear.

Good to Know

You can use a Windows utility named *Refresh* located in the *Update & security* panel of the Settings app to restore the OS without losing your personal files, personalization settings, or Windows Store apps. All software you installed from CDs, DVDs, or websites, is removed. Refresh is like reinstalling Windows but without losing your data files.

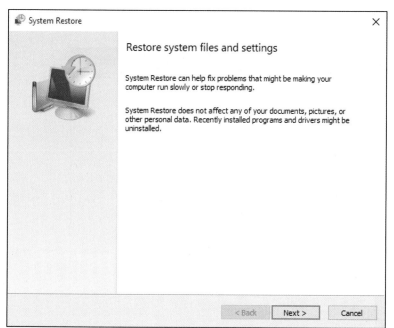

Figure 4.22

Click the Next button in the first System Restore window to start the process of undoing changes made to your Windows computer.

Figure 4.23

At the second System Restore window, select the restore point from the event list and then click Next to begin the restore process.

Help and Support

OSs offer extensive help and support that you can search to find answers to most questions and issues. In Windows you can access the Get Started app by typing *Help* in the search box on the Windows taskbar, and then clicking *Get Started* at the top of the search results list. In the Get Started app, click a category in the left panel to view available help topics displayed as icons in the right panel. Click an icon to read help information. Figure 4.24 shows the help topic icons for the Get connected category in the Get Started app.

In most cases, you can locate help more quickly by typing a short phrase that describes the feature or other issue in the search box on the Windows taskbar and then clicking a link in the search results list.

On a Mac device, access the Help utility from the menu bar along the top of the screen, type a search phrase in the search text box, and then select a topic in the results list that appears, or choose *Show All Help Topics* to browse help in a window. Figure 4.24 shows the results of a search using the phrase *fix sound* in Mac Help.

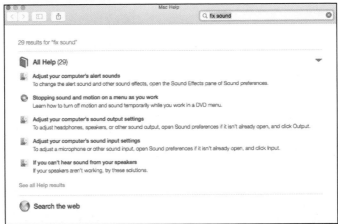

Figure 4.24

Windows Get Started app (top) and Mac Help (bottom) allow you to search for solutions to a computer issue in extensive online resources.

Career Connection

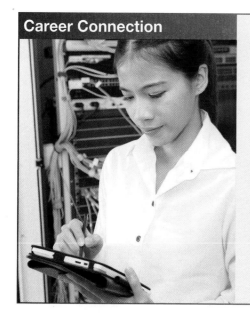

Careers in Technical Support

Help desk and technical support ranked sixth among the 10 most in-demand IT skills forecast for 2016 by *Computerworld*. IT executives reported a growing need for help desk and support technicians because of a growth in projects and bring-your-own-device programs that have added complexity and volume of work to the IT department. Certifications to demonstrate your ability to work well in this field include CompTIA A+ certification geared toward workers in desktop support, and MTA (Microsoft Technology Associate), MCSA (Microsoft Certified Solutions Associate), and MCSE (Microsoft Certified Solutions Expert), which validate your skills in troubleshooting Microsoft technology. Go to **http://CC2.ParadigmCollege.net/Certifications** to learn more about Microsoft certifications.

Blog Topic   How I Fixed My Computer

Almost everyone has had to troubleshoot a computer issue at some point. Think about the last time you had a problem with your computer and how you resolved the problem. If you do not have an experience that you can recall, ask a family member or friend to describe his or her experience to you.

1. Write and post a blog entry that relates the computer issue and the way it was resolved. Include tips or techniques learned from the experience to prevent the problem from reoccurring.

2. Read at least two of your classmates' blogs and post one comment to each.

3. Submit your blog URL and the URLs of the two classmates' blogs to your instructor in the manner she or he has requested.

Explore Further   Common Computer Problems

Everyone who uses a computer will eventually experience a problem. Some computer problems seem to crop up more commonly than others. Knowing about these common computer problems and their solutions will save you time when you encounter them.

1. Find articles that describe five common computer problems and how to fix them.

2. Create a presentation with one issue per slide and include recommendations for how to fix each problem.

3. At the end of your presentation, add a slide listing the URL(s) of websites that you used for research.

4. Save the presentation as **ComputerProblems-YourName** and submit it to your instructor in the manner she or he has requested.

Topics Review

Topic	Key Concepts	Key Terms
4.1 Introduction to the OS and OS Functions	System software consists of the OS plus a set of utility programs used to maintain a computer.	system software
	OS software provides a UI, manages the computer's hardware and software, and provides a system for managing files.	operating system (OS)
	Starting a computer is called *booting*; starting from a no-power state is a cold boot and restarting a powered-on computer is a warm boot.	booting
		cold boot
	At startup, the OS core called the kernel, which manages memory, devices, and programs, is loaded into RAM.	warm boot
		kernel
	Use the Shut Down command to turn off the power to a computer so that programs and files are properly closed.	Shut Down
	The UI is the method with which you interact with the computer. A GUI uses visual images, such as icons, that the user clicks. With a command-line interface, commands are typed at a prompt.	user interface (UI)
		graphical user interface (GUI)
		command-line interface
	The OS coordinates the flow of data and activities between hardware resources and application programs. For example, when RAM has reached capacity, the OS uses hard disk space, called *virtual memory*, to store RAM contents.	virtual memory
		driver
	The OS configures hardware and peripheral devices by using a driver. A driver is a small program with instructions that tell the OS how to communicate with a device. With plug and play capability, a driver is automatically installed by the OS when a new device is plugged in.	plug and play
	The OS keeps track of all files stored on a system and provides the tools with which to manage those files.	
	The OS performs automatic updates for program fixes, security enhancements, and new or modified drivers.	
4.2 Popular OSs for Computing Systems	A computing platform is a combination of hardware architecture and software design for a specific OS.	computing platform
	Windows is the most popular OS. A variety of hardware is designed to run Windows OS and Windows applications.	Windows
		Cortana
	Windows 10 restored the familiar desktop interface and introduced a redesigned Start button that combines the live tile interface from Windows 8.1 with a menu system.	Mac OS
		UNIX
	Cortana, in Windows 10, is a personal digital assistant that responds to voice commands or keyboard input to help you work.	Linux
		open source program
	Mac OS X is the OS used for Apple Mac computers. Mac OS was the originator of the GUI.	network operating system (NOS)
	UNIX was developed in the 1960s for servers and is a popular choice for web servers.	
	Linux, created in 1991, is an open source OS (meaning that it can be freely modified or customized) that runs on a variety of devices.	
	A NOS, such as Windows Server 2016, has enhanced functions and security features for managing networked environments.	

continued…

Topic	Key Concepts	Key Terms
4.3 Popular OSs for Mobile Devices	Mobile OSs, stored on a ROM chip, handle smaller hardware and apps with less memory. Mobile OSs include support for cameras, touchscreen and/or voice commands for input, and video calling. Android was released by the Open Handset Alliance, a collaboration of 84 technology and mobile companies that develops open standards for mobile devices. The AOSP is now tasked with maintaining and developing Android. iOS is the mobile OS developed by Apple for the iPhone, iPod, and iPad. Windows 10 Mobile is the mobile OS developed by Microsoft for Windows smartphones. BlackBerry developed the BlackBerry OS to support its family of BlackBerry devices.	mobile operating system Android Open Handset Alliance Android Open Source Project (AOSP) iOS BlackBerry OS
4.4 Embedded OSs and Cloud OSs	Consumer and commercial electronic devices use an embedded OS designed for their limited use. Windows Embedded is a family of embedded OSs used on a variety of task-specific devices. Embedded Linux is similar to standalone Linux and is used in a variety of consumer and commercial electronics. Smart TVs use an embedded OS called a TV OS to present a UI, manage content, and manage input from a remote control, wireless keyboard, smartphone, or tablet. Android is used as the embedded OS for many electronic devices and includes releases such as Android Auto and Android Wear. A web-based OS is a virtual desktop for accessing files and apps anywhere via the Internet. iCloud is built into every iOS device and syncs documents in the cloud to all devices, including PCs. Chrome OS is available on Chromebooks and supports cloud-based Google apps.	embedded operating system Windows Embedded Embedded Linux TV operating system web-based operating system iCloud Chrome OS
4.5 OS Utilities for Maintaining System Performance	File Explorer for Windows and Finder for Mac are utilities for file maintenance, such as moving or deleting files. A folder is a place for storing associated files. Disk Cleanup is a utility used to remove unwanted files. Fragmentation occurs when file clusters for the same file are not stored next to each other. A disk defragmenter utility, such as Windows Optimize Drives, increases disk speed and efficiency by putting file clusters back together. Newer computers with faster and very large hard disks or solid-state drives do not need to be defragmented. A backup utility, such as the Windows File History or Mac Time Machine, is used to back up files and restore backed-up files to their original state.	File Explorer folder Finder Disk Cleanup fragmentation disk defragmenter Optimize Drives backup utility File History Time Machine

continued…

Topic	Key Concepts	Key Terms
4.6 OS Troubleshooting Tools	The Windows Security and Maintenance window displays messages about issues and has tools to resolve problems. System Restore reverses a recent system change. The Windows Get Started app or Mac Help is used to find answers to questions or issues.	System Restore

 Recheck
Recheck your understanding of the topics covered in this chapter.

 Workbook
Chapter review and assessment resources are available in the *Workbook* ebook.

Chapter 5

Application Software

Whether you turn on a computing device for work, for school, for personal tasks, or for entertainment, it is application software that you are using. **Application software**, also called *applications*, is a category of programs used by an individual to carry out a task or project. For example, if you need to update your budget, you might open a financial program. If you have a photograph with red eyes, you might open a graphics editing application to edit the picture. An application exists for just about any purpose. Software is what makes our computers useful to us since it is the programs that provide us with the ability to create, write, calculate, draw, edit, manipulate, and otherwise work with text, graphics, audio, and video.

In Chapter 4, you learned about system software and the role of the operating system (OS) to route and manage data between the hardware and the other programs that are running. Once a computer is started and the OS is loaded, you are ready to start the application in which you want to work. In this chapter, you will learn about software applications commonly used in the workplace and by individuals. You will also learn how to manage the software on your computing device, and you will survey mobile apps for a smartphone, tablet, or wearable device.

Precheck

Check your understanding of the topics covered in this chapter.

Learning Objectives

5.1 Describe typical uses for a word processor, spreadsheet, presentation, and database management software application

5.2 Identify personal information management, accounting, project management, and document management software applications

5.3 Distinguish applications used for graphics, publications, multimedia, and web projects

5.4 List and explain types of applications intended for personal use

5.5 Describe the uses and benefits of web-based and open source applications

5.6 Explain how to acquire, install, uninstall, and upgrade software programs

5.7 Describe the functionality of a mobile application and give examples of mobile apps

 SNAP If you are a SNAP user, go to your SNAP Assignments page to complete the Precheck, Tutorials, and Recheck.

5.1 Productivity Applications for the Workplace

Software for the workplace generally includes programs for producing word processing documents (working with text), spreadsheets (calculating and managing numbers), presentations (slide shows), and database management systems (keeping track of data). These software programs are called **productivity software** because they are used in the workplace to perform a wide variety of business-related tasks.

A group of productivity software applications will typically be bundled together in what is called a **software suite** or **productivity suite**. While many variations of a software suite exist, a minimum bundle includes word processing, spreadsheet, presentation, and email applications. For example, the Microsoft Office Standard Suite includes Microsoft Word for word processing documents, Microsoft Excel for spreadsheets, Microsoft PowerPoint for presentations, and Microsoft Outlook for email. Microsoft offers its popular Office suite in several different bundles (called *editions*) to provide groups of programs to suit a variety of office environments.

Microsoft also publishes a version of Office designed for Mac computers. Alternatives to Microsoft Office and Apple productivity applications include OpenOffice, a free productivity suite made available by the open source community, and web-based productivity software offered by cloud providers, such as Google and Zoho. These applications are introduced in Topic 5.5.

Regardless of the suite you use, the productivity applications will have similar features. In this topic, you will learn the features and uses for four productivity applications: word processing, spreadsheet, presentation, and database management software.

Word Processing Applications

A **word processing application** is software used to create documents containing mostly text. Images and other multimedia are often included with text in a document to add visual appeal and assist with understanding content. Figure 5.1 presents a trip planner document for the Grand Canyon in Microsoft Word. Apple's word processor is called Pages. With a word processing program, individuals create a variety of documents, such as essays, reports, letters, memos, contracts, brochures, catalogs, menus, newsletters, mailings, labels, articles, blogs, and journals. Word processing programs generally include the following features:

- text formatting options to change the typestyle, color, size, and style of text, called *fonts* and *font attributes*
- bold, underline, italic, and other text effects, such as shadow and strikethrough
- spelling and grammar checking, as well as a thesaurus

Figure 5.1

A word processor is used to create any kind of document that is mostly text, such as this trip planner for the Grand Canyon created in Microsoft Word.

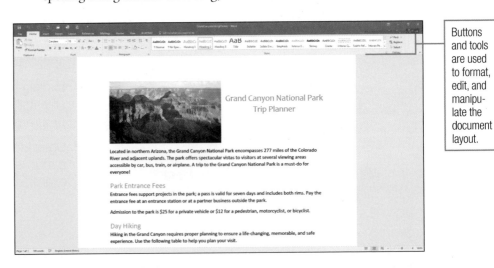

Buttons
and tools
are used
to format,
edit, and
manipu-
late the
document
layout.

- paragraph alignment options, spacing, tabs, indents, borders, and shading
- page numbering, margins, columns, and page breaks for formatting pages
- bulleted or numbered lists, tables, images, charts, and other graphics
- footnotes, endnotes, captions, and citations
- preformatted templates for cover pages, reports, letters, and other documents
- personalization of a standard document and labels for a mailing
- collaboration tools such as track changes, comments, share, and compare

Spreadsheet Programs

A software program in which you work primarily with numbers that you organize, calculate, and chart is called a **spreadsheet application**. Data is entered in a cell within a worksheet. A worksheet is a grid of columns and rows, with each column and row intersecting at a placeholder for data called a *cell*. You perform calculations on values stored in cells, and those calculations can be simple mathematical operations or complex formula statements.

Formulas in spreadsheets automatically recalculate whenever you change a number in a cell that is included in a formula. People like to perform "what-if" analysis with spreadsheets, which involves changing a value or formula to see what will happen to another value. For example, in a budget spreadsheet, you could increase your income in one cell and watch how that change affects the amount of money you have left after paying expenses in another cell. Spreadsheet programs also have charting capabilities so you can graph the values in a pie, column, or other type of chart. Figure 5.2 illustrates a school budget worksheet in Microsoft Excel. The Apple spreadsheet program is called Numbers.

Spreadsheets are used for any work that primarily tracks numbers such as budgets, revenue, expenses, asset tracking, inventory control, production control, gradebooks, research data, payroll, billing, costing, estimating, attendance recording, and scheduling. Spreadsheet programs generally include these features:

- preprogrammed formulas used in statistics, finance, math, date, and logic analysis
- formatting options to change typestyle, color, size, alignment, and numeric display
- sorting and filtering options to organize large blocks of data
- various chart styles and options to graph data and add other visual elements
- multiple worksheet tabs for grouping, consolidating, and managing data

> **Good to Know**
>
> You will encounter different versions of Microsoft Office in the workplace, because some business offices do not upgrade to the most recent version. You are most likely to see Microsoft Office 2010, Microsoft Office 2013, or Microsoft Office 2016 on Windows computers. Microsoft will stop providing support for Microsoft Office 2010 in October 2020.

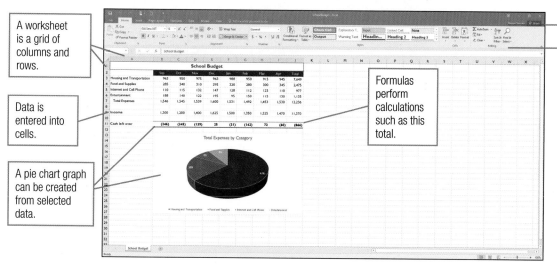

A worksheet is a grid of columns and rows.

Data is entered into cells.

A pie chart graph can be created from selected data.

Formulas perform calculations such as this total.

Buttons and tools are used to format and edit text and values, insert charts, and enter formulas.

Figure 5.2

Spreadsheet software is used to track, analyze, and graph numerical data such as this school budget worksheet in Microsoft Excel.

- page layout and format options for printing large worksheets
- tools to perform what-if analysis
- collaboration tools such as track changes, comments, and share

Presentation Software

Slides for an electronic slide show that may be projected on a screen during an oral presentation or on a video display at a self-running kiosk are created in a **presentation application**, such as Microsoft PowerPoint or Apple Keynote. Presentation software helps you organize, describe, and explain key points, facts, figures, messages, or ideas. Slides allow you to use text, images, audio, and video plus animation and transition effects to provide a dynamic presentation experience. Figure 5.3 shows a group of slides in a presentation created with Microsoft PowerPoint. Presentation programs generally include the following features:

- several slide layouts for arrangement of titles and content
- predesigned presentation designs and themes for backgrounds, colors, fonts, and effects
- formatting options to change typestyle, color, size, and alignment of content
- tools for inserting pictures, clipart, photos, shapes, charts, tables, and other graphics
- sound and video media options
- slide transition and animation schemes to make dynamic slide shows
- options for customizing a slide show
- collaboration tools such as track changes, comments, and share

The slide pane shows miniatures of all the slides in the presentation. Icons let you know if animation and/or transition effects have been applied.

Buttons and tools are used to insert slides, format text, apply transition and animation schemes, and insert graphics, audio, and video.

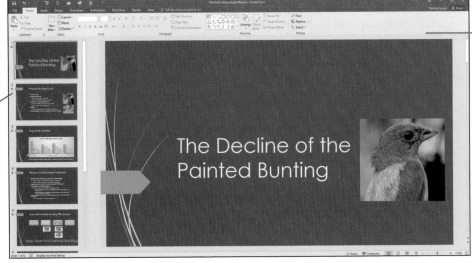

Figure 5.3

Presentation software, such as Microsoft PowerPoint, is used to create a series of slides that are presented in a slide show.

Database Management Software

Tutorial
How Can Databases Make a Difference in Our Lives?

A **database management application** is a software program that organizes and keeps track of large amounts of data. The data is stored in such a way that information can be extracted in useful lists and reports. For example, a manager could request a list of all customers residing in a certain zip code, or all employees with no absences.

With database software, you set up the structure for storing data, input and maintain the data, and produce lists and reports to serve a variety of purposes. Businesses use databases to keep track of customers, patients, clients, vendors, employees, products, inventory, assets, contacts, claims, equipment, service records, and more. Any data that needs to be organized and stored can be set up in a database. Figure 5.4 illustrates a database created in Microsoft Access to keep track of used textbooks for sale. Database applications generally include these features:

- tables for designing the structure of data in columns (called *fields*) and rows (called *records*)
- forms for entering and maintaining data in a user-friendly interface
- queries for extracting and displaying data by criteria
- reports for printing or displaying data with rich text formatting options
- the ability to join related tables for queries and reports that extract data from two or more tables

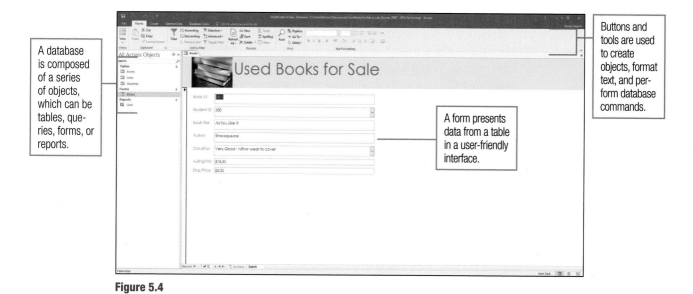

Figure 5.4

Database management software helps a business track and organize data such as this used textbook database shown in Microsoft Access.

Explore Further   Tips for Using Microsoft Word, Excel, or PowerPoint

Many people are self-taught Microsoft Office users who have learned how to get their work done by trial and error, by looking up a feature, or by being shown how to use a feature by someone else. Learning tips and tricks for one of the applications might save you some time or effort the next time you need to create a document, spreadsheet, or presentation.

1. Pick Microsoft Word, Microsoft Excel, or Microsoft PowerPoint—the application for which you most want to learn a few tips—and find and read one online article with tips for using the software.
2. From the article, choose the five tips you found most helpful and create a one-page handout that explains the tips in your own words. Include the URL for the article.
3. Save the document as **MSOfficeTips-Your Name**.
4. Submit the document to your instructor in the manner she or he has requested.

5.2 Other Workplace Productivity Applications

Tutorial
How Do You Identify
the Format That a File
Is Saved In?

Businesses use software to do more than deliver information through documents, spreadsheets, presentations, and databases. They also use applications to manage communications, calendars, contacts, financial information, projects, and documents. In some industries, specialized software is designed to complete tasks unique to the industry, and large companies use enterprise-wide software programs to manage large-scale operations. In this topic, you will be introduced to some of these other types of applications found in a workplace.

Personal Information Management Software

Managing messages, schedule, contacts, and tasks can be onerous with the volume of emails, appointments, contacts, and to-do lists a typical worker encounters. A **personal information management (PIM) application** helps you organize this type of information. Reminders and flags help you remember and follow up on important emails, appointments, events, or tasks.

Figure 5.5 displays the Calendar in Microsoft Outlook, which is part of the Microsoft Office suite. Outlook is used by individuals at home to manage personal information. When Outlook is used in a workplace, an Exchange server gives users additional features such as sending and tracking meeting requests and tasks to other employees. IBM Notes (formerly called Lotus Notes) is another PIM application. Apple devices include iCal, Contacts, and Mail programs. PIM apps are also included on smartphones. The ability to sync calendars, contacts, and email on multiple devices means you have the latest information wherever you may be. PIM software also allows you to share your calendar or contact information with other people inside or outside your workplace.

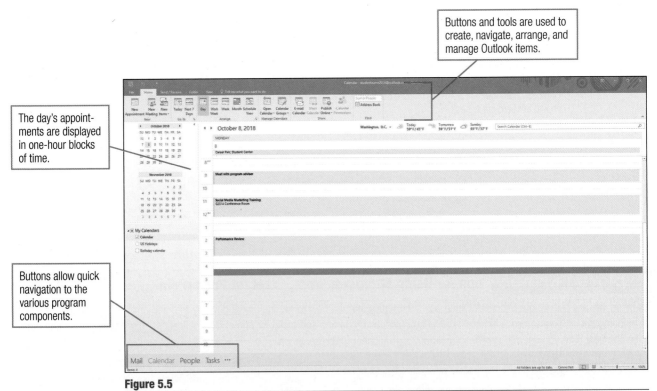

Buttons and tools are used to create, navigate, arrange, and manage Outlook items.

The day's appointments are displayed in one-hour blocks of time.

Buttons allow quick navigation to the various program components.

Figure 5.5

Microsoft Outlook is an application you can use to manage messages, schedules, contacts, and tasks.

Accounting Software

All businesses need an **accounting application** to record and report financial information related to assets, liabilities, equity, revenue, and expenses. These programs provide the basis for financial reporting and tax calculations. Accounting software is generally organized by accounting activity, such as invoicing, purchasing, inventory, payroll, banking, bill paying, payment receiving, and memo processing. Accounting programs also support costing and estimating features for customer- and vendor-related functions. Several accounting software programs are designed for small, medium, and large businesses. Figure 5.6 shows the payroll summary screen for QuickBooks, an accounting program used by many small businesses.

Good to Know 🎓

Sage software is another popular accounting program. Formerly called Simply Accounting, Sage is used by over 6 million small- and medium-sized businesses to keep track of transactions around the globe.

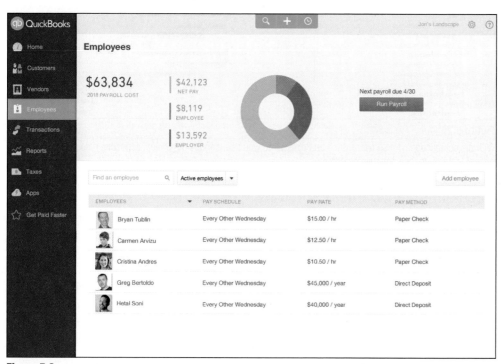

Figure 5.6

QuickBooks is a popular accounting software application for recording and reporting the financial activities for a small business. The payroll module shows a summary of payroll costs and employees.

Project Management Software

Large projects that need several resources and are to be completed on a schedule and within a budget are often managed using a **project management application**. Project management software is used to enter all the tasks needed to get a project done, establish time frames, assign resources, and allocate budget money to each task. Once the project is created, the program develops a project schedule and shows interdependencies between tasks for any tasks that cannot start until a previous task is completed. A typical way to display a schedule is in a Gantt chart, which plots tasks in time lines as shown in Figure 5.7 on page 120. Maintaining the data also allows you to view the impact on the schedule or budget if changes are made to tasks, resources, or time lines. Several project management software programs are available, including Microsoft Project, Clarizen, Wrike, Mavenlink, Basecamp, and ProjectLibre.

One advantage to using project management software is the collaborative tools included with the program. Each team member can be given access to the project file to update his or her task information and view other tasks or documents related to the project. This allows everyone to stay up-to-date and deal with issues that arise in a timely manner.

Check This Out ✓

http://CC2.Paradigm College.net/PMI

Go here to learn about the Project Management Institute, the leading nonprofit professional association for project managers. The PMI develops globally recognized project management standards, certifications, professional development tools, and other resources for individuals and businesses.

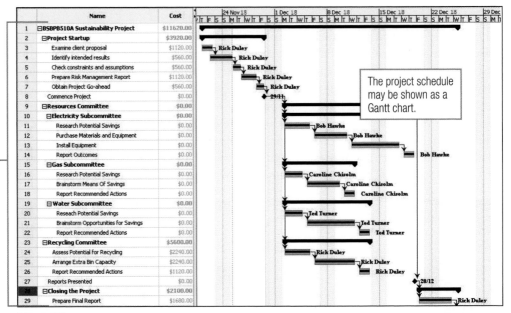

	Name	Cost
1	⊟BSBPB510A Sustainability Project	$11620.00
2	⊟Project Startup	$3920.00
3	Examine client proposal	$1120.00
4	Identify intended results	$560.00
5	Check constraints and assumptions	$560.00
6	Prepare Risk Management Report	$1120.00
7	Obtain Project Go-ahead	$560.00
8	Commence Project	$0.00
9	⊟Resources Committee	$0.00
10	⊟Electricity Subcommittee	$0.00
11	Research Potential Savings	$0.00
12	Purchase Materials and Equipment	$0.00
13	Install Equipment	$0.00
14	Report Outcomes	$0.00
15	⊟Gas Subcommittee	$0.00
16	Research Potential Savings	$0.00
17	Brainstorm Means Of Savings	$0.00
18	Report Recommended Actions	$0.00
19	⊟Water Subcommittee	$0.00
20	Reseach Potential Savings	$0.00
21	Brainstorm Opportunities for Savings	$0.00
22	Report Recommended Actions	$0.00
23	⊟Recycling Committee	$5600.00
24	Assess Potential for Recycling	$2240.00
25	Arrange Extra Bin Capacity	$2240.00
26	Report Recommended Actions	$1120.00
27	Reports Presented	$0.00
28	⊟Closing the Project	$2100.00
29	Prepare Final Report	$1680.00

The project tasks, estimated costs, durations, and dependencies are entered to create a project schedule.

The project schedule may be shown as a Gantt chart.

Figure 5.7

With project management software, such as ProjectLibre, you can manage the project schedule, resources, and budget to finish on time and within budget.

Document Management Software

A **document management system (DMS)** is a program that manages the creation, storage, retrieval, history, and eventual disposal of documents or other files stored in a central repository. Paper documents are scanned, coded or tagged, and stored electronically. DMS programs provide advanced search tools for retrieval as well as sharing of documents. A document's life cycle is managed through the DMS, and all documents are stored in a common file format, such as PDF. DMS programs use secure servers and controlled access to ensure privacy and security. Some industries, such as the legal industry, use DMS programs to manage the thousands of documents that are

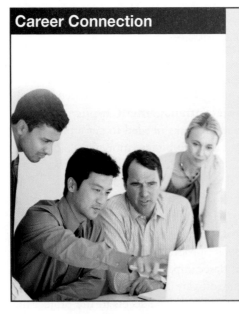

Career Connection

Project Manager—Among the Top 25 Jobs Posted Online

Any organization that launches a large project involving many resources and multiple teams needs to have a skilled project manager to keep the project on time and on budget. According to PayScale, a company that compiles salaries from over 40 million individuals, the average salary for a project manager in information technology was $86,378 in May 2015. WANTED Analytics, a company that collects and analyzes hiring trend data from over 150 countries, reported in May 2015 that project manager was among the top 25 most common jobs posted online. If you are well organized, like to lead groups of diverse teams, and have excellent communication skills, consider investigating what it takes to be a project manager.

exchanged between lawyers in litigation cases. A DMS is the cornerstone of a paperless office. The DMS program called LogicalDOC is shown in Figure 5.8.

Figure 5.8

Companies use a DMS program such as LogicalDOC to electronically manage all documents, including paper documents that are scanned, coded, and stored on central servers.

Other Specialized Software

Industries such as automotive, construction, manufacturing, and engineering use industry-specific software—for example, computer-aided design (CAD) or computer-aided manufacturing (CAM) programs—to create complex designs and drawings. Medical establishments use medical software programs to track patient records, billings, and insurance claims. Hotels and travel agencies use programs to manage bookings, guests, and resources. These are just a few examples of industry-specific software applications.

Large companies, referred to as *enterprises*, have higher-level needs to manage the multitude of activities and processes involved in transactions with customers, vendors, inventories, and human resources. These companies often use an **enterprise resource planning (ERP) application**, which is a software solution designed for large-scale organizations. Companies such as SAP and Oracle provide ERP software for these environments, often along with extensive customization, training, and support.

Explore Further | Which Industry-Specific Software Will You Use?

Chances are, industry-specific software is used in your field of study. For example, contractors use materials- and labor-estimating software, restaurants use meal service software, and airlines use reservation systems. What industry-specific software will you be required to use in your future career?

1. Research industry-specific software applications used in your field of study. If possible, interview someone who works in your field and ask that person to describe specialized software he or she uses in the workplace.

2. Create a document that describes the software applications used in your field and how the software is used to track, manage, and report information.

3. Save the document as **MyIndustrySoftware-YourName**.

4. Submit the document to your instructor in the manner she or he has requested.

5.3 Applications for Working with Graphics, Publications, Multimedia, and the Web

Graphics software is used for creating, editing, and manipulating drawings, photos, clip art, and scanned images. **Desktop publishing (DTP) software** incorporates text, graphics, and the use of colors for creating high-quality documents for marketing, communication, education, or other commercial purposes. **Multimedia software** includes programs that use text and images with video, audio, and animations to create interactive applications that market products or services, or educate or entertain people. **Web authoring software** is designed to create content provided over the Internet. In this topic, you will be introduced to applications used by businesses and individuals to work with graphics, publications, audio, video, and animations and for creating web pages.

Graphics Software

Graphic artists, illustrators, photographers, and other professionals use specialized software to create and edit images. Painting and drawing programs provide tools for artists to draw pictures, shapes, and other images to which they can add special effects. Adobe Illustrator is an example of a graphics program used to create, edit, and manipulate illustrations.

   Photo editing software is used by photographers and others to edit pictures and add special effects and text to pictures taken with a digital camera. Adobe Photoshop is a popular choice of both professionals and individuals. Tools are available in Photoshop to crop out unwanted portions of a picture, remove red eye, retouch areas, correct color brightness and contrast, add text, add special effects, and even add in a person or object copied from another photo. Figure 5.9 shows a photo edited using Adobe Photoshop to add a blue sky background and butterfly to baby's feet.

Figure 5.9

Adobe Photoshop is often used to touch up photos or add special effects.

Desktop Publishing Software

Word processing software provides tools to arrange text and graphics in a document; however, a word processor does not let you precisely position objects and control text flow around objects. For professional publications, desktop publishing software is used to produce a print-based document, such as a corporate newsletter, annual report, price list, restaurant menu, catalog, brochure, or book. Programs such as Adobe InDesign, Microsoft Publisher, and QuarkXPress are popular choices for desktop publishing. DTP programs use rulers, grids, and guides as well as other tools and features that allow DTP professionals to precisely place text and graphics on a page. In addition, the software provides more control over word spacing, space between and around objects and text, and a wider range of fonts, sizes, and colors for text formatting. Figure 5.10 illustrates an advertising circular in QuarkXPress for Mac.

Figure 5.10

QuarkXPress is a desktop publishing application used to do page layout for professional publications.

Multimedia Software

For content delivered via the web or distributed on CD, DVD, or Blu-ray disc, professionals use multimedia programs to create animations, add audio and video, and author interactive multimedia applications. **Animation software** is used to create images or objects that have movement or otherwise interact with users. Adobe Flash is an application often used to create interactive applications delivered over the web on Windows-based PCs and for desktop applications. In Flash, the designer works with a time line and a stage in which text, graphics, and other objects are placed in the sequence the movement or interaction is supposed to occur.

In 2015, YouTube changed its standard for delivery of video from Flash to HTML5, which is supported across all devices (Apple devices do not support Flash content). HTML5 also delivers video content over the Internet more efficiently than Flash. This change at YouTube is widely believed to signal the obsolescence of Flash within the technology community, although Adobe is still supporting Flash for the desktop environment. Web browsing via a smartphone or tablet is expected to grow, leading to the expectation that HTML5 will replace Flash as the new standard for developing multimedia content.

Video editing software, such as Final Cut Pro from Apple (Figure 5.11 on page 124) and Adobe Premiere Elements, provide tools to create videos referred to as *clips*. Video shot with a digital camera can be manipulated by cutting, adding, or moving scenes; creating split screens; or adding music, audio effects, or text for titles or credits. Some audio editing capability is also included, as well as tools to organize the

Figure 5.11
Final Cut Pro video editing
software from Apple is a
package used by many
professional multimedia
producers.

Figure 5.11
Final Cut Pro video editing
software from Apple is a
package used by many
professional multimedia
producers.

display of content on removable discs. For example, video editing programs also create the menus and burn the content to a DVD or Blu-ray disc.

Audio recording and editing software, such as free, open source Audacity and Adobe Audition, include tools for recording and editing music, sound clips, and podcasts (audio clips posted on the web). Other multimedia applications capture screen images and computer activity for creating training segments and demonstrations.

Web Authoring Software

Web authoring programs, such as Adobe Dreamweaver and Microsoft Expression Web, are used by businesses to create and maintain interactive websites. Alternative open source programs, such as openElement shown in Figure 5.12, are also available. Web pages are stored in programming code that is interpreted by browsers. Web authoring software provides tools for individuals to create and manage all the pages and external resources for a website by working in either design view or code view. Nonprogrammers can create a web page in design view and let the software automatically generate the programming code needed for browsers. Experienced web developers often work in code view and switch between views as pages are fine-tuned. Figure 5.12 is a web page shown in code view, with the software prompting the user that an unnecessary semicolon is present.

Figure 5.12
The web page source code in
Javascript is shown here using
the web authoring software
program called openElement,
an open source program. Web
browsers interpret this code to
display the text and multimedia
that you see when you view
the page.

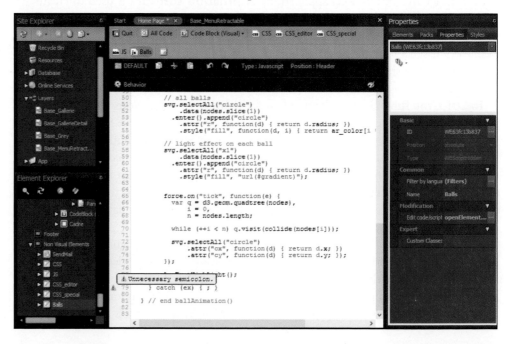

Multimedia for the Nonprofessional

A variety of graphics and multimedia programs are available to meet the needs of both professional and nonprofessional users. Most of the programs showcased in this topic are more expensive software programs geared toward professionals or hobby enthusiasts. Less expensive or free programs are used by nonprofessionals or individuals who want to work with multimedia at home. For example, Windows Live Essentials is a free suite offered to Windows users that includes a program to work with video (Movie Maker) and photos (Photo Gallery). The Windows OS also includes programs for drawing (Paint) and recording sound (Voice Recorder). Figure 5.13 shows how the exposure of a photograph can be adjusted using Photo Gallery. Apple devices are packaged with the iLife suite which includes iPhoto, iMovie, and GarageBand for working with photos, video, and audio.

> **Check This Out** ✓
>
> http://CC2.Paradigm College.net/Windows LiveEssentials
>
> Go here to download Windows Live Essentials for free.

> **Check This Out** ✓
>
> http://CC2.Paradigm College.net/Picasa
>
> Go here to download Picasa—a free image editing and organizing program from Google. Pictures are stored in web albums, which can be shared with others.

Figure 5.13

Photo exposure can be adjusted using Windows Live Photo Gallery, part of the free Windows Live Essentials suite from Microsoft.

Explore Further   Are You a Skilled Photo Editor?

Web-based photo editing software programs allow you to edit photos without downloading and installing software on your computer. Each program offers a basic set of tools for nonprofessionals.

1. Find a free online image editing program for which you want to experiment editing a photo.

2. Using a digital camera, take a photo of something related to your field of study. For example, take a picture of a park if you are going to be a landscape designer, a house if you are going to work in construction, or a hospital if you plan to work in the medical field. Upload the photo to the image editing website

and experiment with the software's editing tools to edit the image. For example, crop out a part of the picture, change the color, retouch the photo, add shapes, add special effects, add text, and so on.

3. Save the revised image as **PhotoEditing-YourName**.

4. Submit the original photo and the edited photo to your instructor in the manner she or he has requested.

5.4 Software Applications for Personal Use

Software programs for personal use include a wide range of applications that cover almost every hobby, interest, and need. For example, you can install software to help you manage personal notes, ideas, and thoughts at work, at school, or at home, manage your personal finances, prepare tax returns, play games, design a garden, and create a genealogy map. Programs help you organize recipes and plan trips, as well as educate and provide reference information. In this topic, you will survey a variety of applications for personal use.

If you have an interest or a hobby that is not mentioned in this topic, chances are that a related software program has already been created. Search the web for an application if you have not already found one.

Note Taking Software

While in meetings, classes, or at home, you often need a place to record notes, thoughts, or ideas. **Note taking software**, such as Microsoft OneNote (Figure 5.14), is used to store, organize, search, and share notes of any type. Notes can be entered by clicking anywhere on the screen and typing or writing by hand using a stylus. Documents, audio, video, images, emails, appointments, contacts, and web links can be attached or inserted into a note to collect everything related to a topic in one place. You can organize notes into notebooks and tabs and use search and share tools.

Figure 5.14

Microsoft OneNote, shown here in the Mac edition, is a useful tool to organize notes on any topic related to school, work, or home.

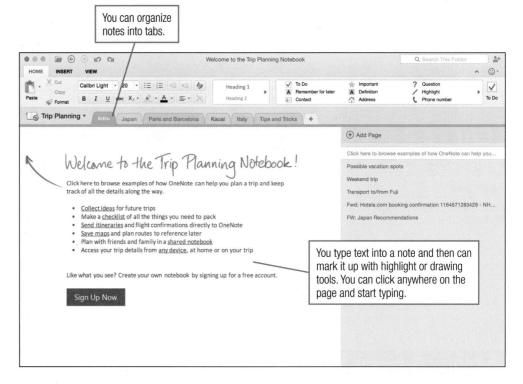

You can organize notes into tabs.

You type text into a note and then can mark it up with highlight or drawing tools. You can click anywhere on the page and start typing.

Software to Manage Personal Finances and Taxes

Keeping track of a checking or savings account and personal investments is accomplished with **personal finance software**. Most personal finance software programs allow you to download activity from your banking account directly into the personal finance program. You can balance your checking account, analyze home expenses, and track investments. Quicken (Figure 5.15) is a popular program used for managing finances.

Tax preparation software guides you through the completion of the complex forms required to file your income taxes with the government. These programs generally estimate your tax bill using an interview-style series of questions and input boxes. Programs generally alert you to missing information and/or deductions that can help minimize taxes. Tax forms can be printed and can also be filed with the government electronically.

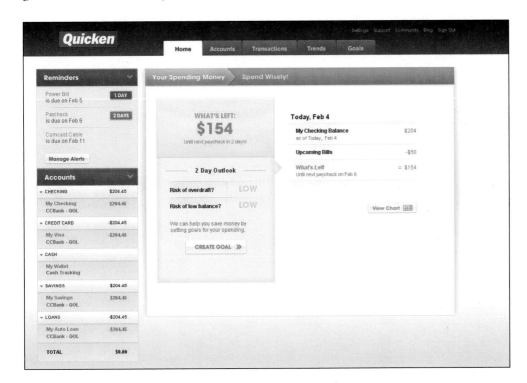

Figure 5.15
Quicken is a software program for managing personal finances such as cash and personal expenses.

Legal Software

Legal software, such as Quicken WillMaker, MyAttorney, and Family Lawyer, help you prepare legal documents such as wills, contracts, leases, loan agreements, and living trusts. These programs provide standard legal documents that you customize for your purposes by responding to a series of questions, forms, or dialog boxes that prompt you for input.

Legal software helps individuals create legal documents such as a last will and testament.

Hobby Software

Software applications for creating a family tree; scrapbooking; planning trips; managing recipes and planning meals; designing homes, decks, and gardens; and creating and printing custom greeting cards are just a few examples of **hobby software** you can use to pursue your favorite leisure activities.

Software is available to help individuals with just about any hobby imaginable.

Entertainment Software

Entertainment software includes programs for playing interactive games and videos. Some games are designed to be played individually. Others involve subscribing to online services where you can join hundreds of thousands of other game enthusiasts and play against others online. For example, with more than 7 million subscribers, World of Warcraft (WoW) is a highly successful online game involving role-playing and multiple players that boasts a 2014 Guinness World Record for the longest video game marathon at 29 hours and 31 minutes.

Games are often available in multiple versions such as an edition for a PC, a version that can be played online through a browser, and a smaller app for downloading to a smartphone. Tetris (Figure 5.16) is one example of a game that is available in all these flavors.

Figure 5.16

Tetris, shown here in the four-player ultimate edition, celebrated 30 years of gaming in 2014. The fan favorite puzzle game had over 425 million paid downloads, and more than one billion games played online per year at its 30th birthday!

Blog Topic   What Is Your Favorite Game?

Do you play video games? If yes, which game is your favorite? Which game do you find most challenging, or the most relaxing? How much time per week do you spend playing games?

1. Write and post a blog entry with your answers to the questions. If you do not play computer games, ask someone you know who does to describe a favorite game for you.

2. Read at least two of your classmates' blog entries and post one comment to each.

3. Submit the URLs of your blog and the two classmates' blogs to your instructor in the manner she or he has requested.

Education and Reference Software

Educational software is designed to teach children and adults about subjects such as math, spelling, grammar, geography, science, and history through an interactive reference or game format. Figure 5.17 shows the ScienceFlix program created by Scholastic for teaching children in grades four through nine about science. You can also find software to help you learn a foreign language and to teach you how to type. **Reference software** uses multimedia tools to provide rich content information in encyclopedias, dictionaries, translation guides, atlases, and other reference resources.

Tutorial

How Can Software Help You Learn?

Figure 5.17

Scholastic educational materials are found in schools all over the world. The interactive ScienceFlix program contains over 4,000 objects for students to explore about science topics.

Security Alert | **Be Cautious with Free Software**

The lure of free software can be enticing. Be cautious with web ads that offer free software of any type, but especially those that offer to manage personal finances. Read the details, including the fine print, before downloading the software or submitting your email address or any other personal information. Often these programs are used to collect personal information for resale, or they may contain malicious code such as a virus.

Explore Further | **Survey Note Taking Software**

The ability to organize, store, sort, and search notes electronically can save you time finding information, and help you study for tests and exams. Several free note taking applications are available for PC, Mac, Android, iOS, and Linux. Which note taking software would you like to use?

1. Search for online reviews on free note taking software and read at least two articles.

2. Decide on one program that you think would work best for you, given the program's features and ease of use.

3. Create a document that describes the note taking application you selected and give your reasons for choosing it. Include the URLs of the articles you read for this topic.

4. Save the document as **NoteTakingSoftware-YourName**.

5. Submit the document to your instructor in the manner she or he has requested.

5.5 Cloud and Open Source Applications

Check This Out ✓

http://CC2.Paradigm College.net/Prezi

Go here to learn about Prezi—a cloud-based presentation program that uses a virtual canvas for presenting ideas. By signing up for a free account, you agree that your prezis will be searchable, accessible, and reusable by anyone.

In Chapter 1, you were introduced to Cloud Computing and the SaaS delivery model for software applications. Recall that SaaS stands for *software as a service* and means that the software you are using is not installed on your computing device. SaaS applications are hosted by a third party and made available to you from a web browser. Open source programs are often provided for free, meaning that you can download and install the software on a computer without paying a license fee. In this topic, you will survey three web-based and two open source software alternatives for productivity applications. If you need new software, consider using one of the programs described in this topic, or search for another cloud or open source alternative application.

Web-Based Productivity Applications

The main advantage to using a web-based application is that you have access to the software and your files from any location at which you have an Internet connection. Table 5.1 provides a summary of three popular web-based productivity application alternatives. If you decide to use a cloud application, consider spending time working with a few different suites until you find the one with the features and interface that works best for you. In Figure 5.18 on page 131, the same text is shown in the word processing application from each of the three providers summarized in Table 5.1.

Table 5.1

Summary of Three Popular Web-Based Productivity Applications

Criterion	Google Drive	Office Online	Zoho
Amount of free storage offered at time of writing	15 GB	15 GB	5 GB
Applications	Documents Spreadsheets Presentations Forms Drawings	Word Online Excel Online PowerPoint Online OneNote Online	Sheet (Spreadsheet) Show (Presentation) Writer (Word Processor) Plus several apps for collaboration and business processes
URL	https://www.google.com	https://office.live.com	http://www.zoho.com
Sign-in process	Sign in with a Gmail account and then click Google Apps, Drive, New, and the desired application.	Sign in with a Microsoft account and then click the desired application.	Sign in with a Zoho account and then click the desired application.

Figure 5.18

Web-based programs from different developers vary slightly. For example, compare the text formatting options in the Google, Microsoft, and Zoho online word processing applications.

Tutorial

How Did the Open
Source Movement
Evolve?

Open Source Applications

Apache OpenOffice is a free productivity suite that includes word processor, spreadsheet, presentation, graphics, and database programs. OpenOffice is a project of The Apache Software Foundation that provides support for open source software initiatives. In Figure 5.19, you see the opening menu of OpenOffice, which lists the available applications, and the window for OpenOffice.org Writer. The interface for OpenOffice is intuitive for people who have experience with Microsoft Word 2003 and earlier versions (before the ribbon interface). As of February 2016, the OpenOffice software suite had been downloaded over 160 million times. OpenOffice is updated and maintained by volunteers.

Figure 5.19

OpenOffice is a free, open source productivity suite that includes a word processor (shown here) as well as spreadsheet, presentation, drawing, database, and formulas applications.

Another free open source productivity suite is LibreOffice (Figure 5.20). LibreOffice runs on Windows, Macintosh, and Linux computers and includes the applications Writer, Calc, Impress, Draw, Base, and Math. LibreOffice is a project of the not-for-profit organization The Document Foundation. Similar to OpenOffice, LibreOffice is created and maintained by volunteers, and was actually born when a team of OpenOffice developers decided to create LibreOffice as a separate suite.

A few writers in the technical community have speculated that LibreOffice will overtake OpenOffice as the preferred open source productivity suite, and some are predicting that the two projects will merge, creating one open source desktop suite. Given the similarities in the two programs, a merge of the two programs into one would be a likely scenario.

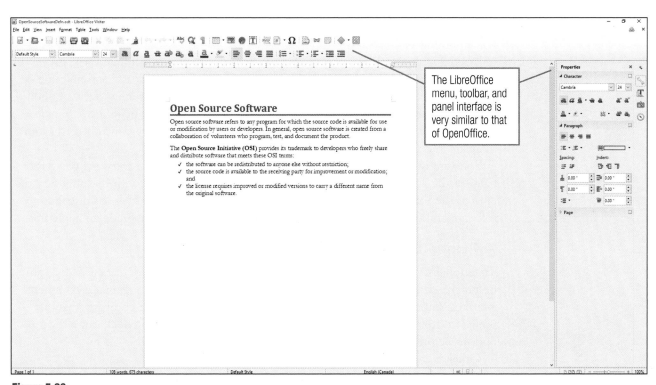

The LibreOffice menu, toolbar, and panel interface is very similar to that of OpenOffice.

Figure 5.20

LibreOffice is another free open source productivity suite with the same applications as OpenOffice. The word processor shown here is very similar to the one in OpenOffice—a result of LibreOffice being created by OpenOffice developers.

Explore Further   **Discover Zoho**

Zoho is a web-based applications provider with 15 million users in 2015. Try out Zoho and compare it with what you are using now for productivity applications. *Note: If you are already a Zoho user, complete this activity using another web-based productivity application.*

1. Go to **http://CC2.ParadigmCollege.net/Zoho**, sign up, and activate a free account.

2. Launch Writer, Sheet, or Show—the application you want to use for your comparison—and experiment with the program to learn the available features. For example, enter some sample text and try formatting options and spell check features.

3. Create a document that compares the Zoho application with the same type of application you normally use. Consider doing the

comparison in a table or chart to compare the two programs feature by feature.

4. Save the document or spreadsheet as **ZohoComparison-YourName**.

5. Submit the document or spreadsheet to your instructor in the manner she or he has requested.

5.6 Acquiring, Installing, Uninstalling, and Upgrading Software

Tutorial

How Does a Software as a Service (SaaS) License Differ from a Traditional Software License?

Software applications can be acquired in various ways such as purchasing from a retailer either in the store or online, buying directly from the software publisher, or downloading from a website such as Tucows downloads (http://www.tucows .com/downloads). At software download websites, people often look for software that is low cost or free. You should exercise caution when using software download websites. Many times, free software is bundled with other programs you do not want, and the installation screens can be confusing to navigate as you try to avoid getting the extra unwanted software. Many download websites advertise that all software has been tested to be virus and spyware free; however, this does not prevent the bundling of extra software and the placement of many ads that entice you to buy software you do not need. You may also find your browser home page is redirected after installing software from a download website. Despite these issues, if you are careful, and you need a software program for a limited use or timeframe, a download website can be a good resource. On Mac computers, new software should be acquired and installed within the Mac App Store whenever possible, to avoid these issues. The Apple software distribution platform is strictly controlled to avoid malware and unwanted additional software.

Software is a licensed product, meaning that when you install software, you have paid for the right to use the product, while ownership remains with the publisher that created the software. In this topic, you will learn the various models for distributing software and the general steps you take to install, uninstall, or upgrade an application.

Software Distribution Models

Traditional software suites, such as Microsoft Office and Adobe Creative Cloud, can be purchased as **packaged software** at a retailer's store or from several e-commerce websites. You can also buy the software online directly from the company that published it. Pricing for software suites can vary, so it is wise to check out a few options before making a purchase.

Other ways to acquire software include the following:

- **Shareware** is available to download for a free trial period. Once the trial period expires, you need to pay a fee to the software publisher to unlock the application. Other forms of shareware continue to work beyond the trial period but generally have features made inaccessible until the fee is paid.
- **Freeware** can be downloaded and installed at no cost and without restrictions. An example of a popular freeware program is Apple iTunes.
- Open source software is generally available for free and downloaded from a website.
- **Subscription software** is purchased from providers that generally charge a monthly or annual fee for access to the software and storage services. Fees vary based on the number of users and the amount of storage space.

Installing Software

When you buy packaged software at a retail store, you usually receive a DVD inside the package. Insert the DVD into the appropriate drive on your computing device, and the software will automatically begin the installation process. Follow the prompts to complete the installation routine.

Good to Know

Software packages that have been opened are generally not returnable. Check the system requirements before paying for packaged software to make sure the software will work with your PC hardware and with your OS.

In some cases, you may purchase a license card, which has instructions to go to a website, download the software, and install the software with the license key printed on the card. If you have downloaded software from a website, you generally have two methods for installing the software on a Windows-based computer:

- You can opt to run the installation program directly from the website. After clicking the download link, you will have the option to run or save the installation file. Choose run to install the program directly from the source website and then follow the prompts that appear. In the Windows OS, you will be prompted with a security warning message and will have to allow the installation to proceed.
- Alternatively, you can save the downloaded file to your hard drive and run the installation later. After clicking the download link, select the save option to download the file to the default downloads folder, or choose Save as to either navigate to another drive and folder or create a new folder in which to store the file. When the download is complete, open the window to view the file and then double-click the file name to start the installation routine. Follow the prompts that appear in the installer window (Figure 5.21). In the Windows OS, you need to click the option to allow the installation to proceed at the security warning message. Choose the method that saves the downloaded file if you want to have a copy of the software program installation file in case you need to reinstall it again at a later date.
- On a Mac computer, downloaded software is saved automatically to the Downloads folder located next to the Trash icon on the dock. Open the folder and double-click the installer program to start the installation. Some installer programs open a pop-up window instructing you to drag the installer program to the Applications folder, while other installer programs automatically copy the file to the Applications folder and begin the software installation. Follow the prompts that appear once the installer program is running.

Packaged software purchased at a retailer generally includes a DVD that you use to install the software.

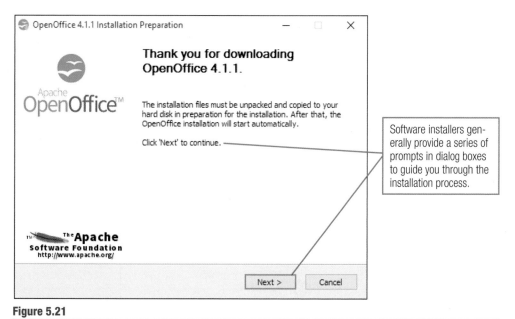

Software installers generally provide a series of prompts in dialog boxes to guide you through the installation process.

Figure 5.21

Installing software you have downloaded generally involves proceeding through an installer wizard that prompts you along the way.

When you install software, you are required to accept a license agreement (unless the software product is open source) similar to the one shown in Figure 5.22. The license agreement, called a **software license agreement (SLA)** or **end-user license agreement (EULA)**, varies by software publisher. Although the terms and conditions are generally long and filled with legal terminology, you should read the agreement and not just blindly click I Accept or I Agree or Yes to move on. The SLA or EULA specifies the number of computers you can legally install the software on. For example, some publishers will allow installation on up to three computers, while others may restrict it to one.

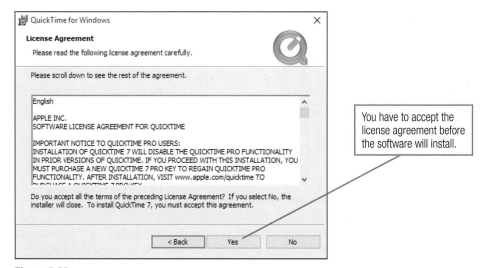

You have to accept the license agreement before the software will install.

Figure 5.22

Software such as Apple QuickTime requires that you agree to a license agreement for the software installation to proceed.

Uninstalling Software

If you have installed a software application that you no longer use, uninstall the program from the hard drive to free up resources. To do this on a Windows-compatible computer, open the Control Panel and click the link Uninstall a program in the *Programs* category (Figure 5.23). At the Programs and Features window, click to select the program you want to remove in the list of software applications and then click the Uninstall button. An uninstall routine will automatically run. Close the Control Panel when finished. In some cases, programs are not completely removed until you restart your computer.

Figure 5.23

Open the Control Panel on a Windows-compatible computer and then click Uninstall a program to open the Programs and Features window and remove software you no longer want.

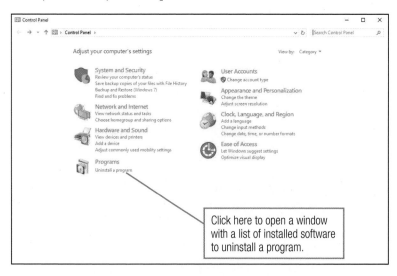

Click here to open a window with a list of installed software to uninstall a program.

On a Mac computer, you uninstall an application by finding the application icon (in the Finder window) and dragging the icon to the Trash. The icon is a shortcut to the program's installation bundle, which includes all related program files. To remove a program's shortcut icon from the dock, simply drag the icon off the dock.

Upgrading Software

Upgrading software means installing a newer version of a program you are already licensed to use (not to be confused with updating, which installs fixes or patches to the existing version). Usually, when you install an upgrade, the older version is replaced; however, in some applications, you can opt to keep the older version and the newer version on the same computer. Some software applications prompt you when an upgrade is available, and clicking the prompt will take you to the website where you can download the newer version. Some upgrades are free, while others require payment for the upgrade at a price lower than the original purchase. Registering software when you buy it is a good idea because it helps ensure you are notified of upgrades and qualify for reduced pricing.

Blog Topic   **Why Pay for Software?**

As you have learned in this chapter, there are several alternatives to paying for a software license for a traditional packaged suite such as Microsoft Office. Despite these free alternatives, software suites like Microsoft Office have loyal supporters who consistently buy upgrades. Why do you think people pay for software? What benefits do paying customers receive that users of freeware do not?

1. Write and post a blog entry with your thoughts on why people prefer to pay for software such as Microsoft Office, instead of using OpenOffice, LibreOffice, or other free, web-based applications.

2. Read at least two of your classmates' blog entries and post one comment to each.

3. Submit the URLs for your blog and your two classmates' blogs to your instructor in the manner she or he has requested.

Security Alert   **Downloader Beware**

Exercise caution at software review websites that provide links to download free software. Many of these sites have ads with links that look deceptively similar to the actual download links you are supposed to click. These links lead to software the advertiser wants you to download, not the software you are looking for. Clicking one of these links by mistake often means you end up with unwanted software on your PC that can be difficult to remove completely. To be safe, download a program from the actual company's website, and be careful to click the download link in the main body of the web page (not around the outside edge where ads are typically run). These precautions can help ensure you get the software you want.

Explore Further   **SLA Terms for Microsoft Office**

Do you know the usage rights in the Microsoft Office SLA? For example, can you legally install the software on more than one computer?

1. Find and read the software license agreement for Microsoft Office desktop application software at **http://CC2.Paradigm College.net/MicrosoftSLA**. Specifically, find out how Internet activation works, whether the software can be transferred to another user, and the number of computers the software can be installed on.

2. Create a document with the answers to the questions in your own words.

3. Save the document as **MSOffice-SLA-YourName**.

4. Submit the document to your instructor in the manner she or he has requested.

5.7 Mobile Apps

Mobile devices, such as smartphones, tablets, and smartwatches, have a different software edition designed specifically for mobile use. A program for a smartphone or tablet is called a **mobile application** or *app*. An app is designed usually for one purpose, to work on a smaller screen, and to accept touch input from finger gestures. Functionality for on-screen keyboards, handwriting recognition, and speech recognition capabilities are also part of app design. Other important features include compatibility and synchronization with PC software and information sharing with other programs or users. In this topic, you will survey apps for mobile devices.

Downloading Apps for a Smartphone or Tablet

Apps by the thousands are available for Android, Apple, Windows, and BlackBerry devices to accomplish just about any type of task you can imagine. For example, apps are available for working with emails, schedules, contacts, maps, GPS data, weather information, news, travel details, games, banking, calculating, currency conversion, messaging, and social media such as Facebook, Twitter, and Instagram. These are just a few of the categories of apps you will find at the Android, Apple, Windows, and BlackBerry stores. Smartphones and tablets have an icon or tile that you tap to launch the store where you find and download apps. Figure 5.24 displays the Google Play store website, where Android apps are bought and downloaded.

Good to Know

As of January 2016, Microsoft revealed that the free Microsoft Office Mobile apps for Android and Apple devices had been downloaded more than 340 million times, surpassing the downloads tally for Windows 10.

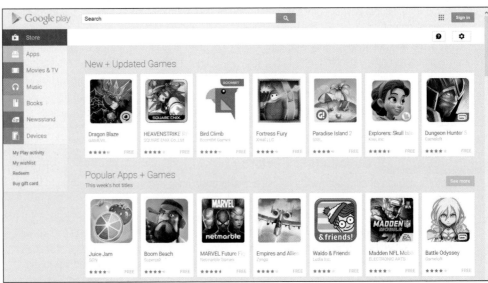

Figure 5.24

Android apps are found at Google Play. New apps are added frequently, with many offered for free or at a low cost.

Blog Topic **What Is Your Favorite Mobile App?**

What is your favorite smartphone or tablet app? Why? How often do you use the app in a typical day?

1. Write and post a blog entry that describes your favorite app, why it is your favorite, and how often you use it in a typical day.

2. Read at least two of your classmates' blog entries and post one comment to each.

3. Submit your blog URL and the URLs of the two classmates' blogs to your instructor in the manner she or he has requested.

Built-in Apps

Android, Apple, Windows, and BlackBerry smartphones and tablets come equipped with several built-in apps, such as the ones shown on the iPhone in Figure 5.25. Typically, PIM apps for keeping track of appointments, contacts, to-do lists, reminders, and notes are standard, as are apps for email, messaging, maps, music, games, and social networks.

Figure 5.25

Smartphones and tablets come equipped with built-in apps, such as the ones shown on this iPhone. Apple includes a mobile edition of productivity applications such as Numbers, Pages, and Keynote.

Mobile Productivity Apps

Microsoft has Word, Excel, PowerPoint, and OneNote editions designed for a smartphone or tablet. You can review, edit, and sync documents to and from email, OneDrive, Sharepoint, or other web-based services. Microsoft has released Office Mobile apps for Android in the Google Play store and for iPhone and iPad in the iTunes store as free downloads. Apple has mobile editions of Pages, Keynote, and Numbers for the iOS devices iPhone and iPad (Figure 5.25). Google Mobile is a suite of productivity apps for Android devices. Figure 5.26 shows the Office mobile app screen for Microsoft Excel and Microsoft Word.

Figure 5.26

Microsoft Excel Mobile (left) and Microsoft Word Mobile (right) are used to view, edit, and create spreadsheets and documents on your smartphone or tablet.

Wearable Technology Apps

The growth of wearable technology devices is also driving growth in the development of wearable technology apps. The challenges for wearable app developers are the constraints of battery life, small screen, and less computing power. These are the same challenges encountered for smartphone app developers, but they are magnified for developers of wearable devices. Developers also have to consider the usage for a wearable app. In most cases, the wearer will want a quick interaction with a display that provides information at a glance, while withstanding constant movement. Fitness apps are abundant for bands and smartwatches—everything from apps that measure heart rate to apps that monitor glucose levels and issue fatigue alerts. Alarms, billable hours trackers, maps, weather forecasts, schedule and note reminders, email alerts, shopping lists, recipe card displays, boarding passes, and conversion tools are just a few of the other wearable tech apps now available.

Mobile apps for wearable technology are a growing trend, with IDG predicting that 111.9 million wearable devices will be sold in 2018.

Productivity apps for wearable devices will see growth as the devices become prevalent in the workplace. To coincide with the release of the Apple Watch in 2015, Microsoft released a smartwatch PowerPoint app that lets the wearer navigate slides in a presentation, view the time elapsed, and see the number of slides in the deck. Watch for innovative wearable apps to come soon!

Explore Further   Popular Apps for Android, Apple, and Windows Mobile Devices

With thousands of apps available for mobile devices, finding the most useful apps for a smartphone or tablet might not be easy.

1. Find and read at least two online articles that rate the top free apps for an Apple, Android, or Windows mobile device. Pick five apps that you think are noteworthy.

2. Create a presentation that contains five slides describing the five apps—one app on each slide. Include a sixth slide with the URLs

of the articles you used.

3. Save the presentation as **MyTop5Apps-YourName**.

4. Submit the presentation to your instructor in the manner she or he has requested.

Topics Review

Topic	Key Concepts	Key Terms
5.1 Productivity Applications for the Workplace	Application software, or apps, are programs used by individuals to carry out tasks, or otherwise get things done. A productivity suite, also known as a *software suite*, is a group of bundled programs that includes a word processing, spreadsheet, presentation, and database management program. The Microsoft Office suite is offered in several editions, some of which include Microsoft Word, Microsoft Excel, Microsoft PowerPoint, Microsoft Outlook, and Microsoft Access. A word processing application is used to create, edit, and format documents that are mostly text, but may also include multimedia to improve the appearance or comprehension of content. A spreadsheet application is used to organize, calculate, edit, format, and chart numbers that are entered in cells within a grid of columns and rows called a worksheet. Spreadsheets are often used to perform what-if analysis, where a value is changed to view the impact on other values. A presentation application is used to create slides for an electronic slide show that communicates key points, facts, figures, messages, or other ideas. Large amounts of data are organized, stored, and maintained in a program called a database management application. In database management software, you set up the structure to store data, input data, maintain data, and then produce lists and reports for various purposes.	application software productivity software software suite productivity suite word processing application spreadsheet application presentation application database management application
5.2 Other Workplace Productivity Applications	Personal information management (PIM) software is used to organize emails, appointments, contacts, and to-do lists. Accounting software applications are used to record and report the financial activities of a business related to assets, liabilities, equity, revenue, and expenses. A business will use project management software to create and maintain a project schedule and project budget. Document management software is used for managing the storage, retrieval, history, and eventual disposal of documents stored in a central repository. Industry-specific software applications are programs used to perform tasks unique to a specific business environment, such as computer-aided design or travel bookings. Enterprise resource planning (ERP) software is designed to support large-scale operations with higher level needs.	personal information management (PIM) software accounting application project management application document management system (DMS) enterprise resource planning (ERP) application

continued...

Topic	Key Concepts	Key Terms
5.3 Applications for Working with Graphics, Multimedia, and the Web	Graphics software refers to painting and drawing programs with tools to create, edit, and apply special effects to pictures, shapes, or other images.	graphics software
	Desktop publishing software is used to place text and graphics on a page with more control over spacing and a wider range of fonts, sizes, and colors for professional, print-based publications.	desktop publishing (DTP) software
	A multimedia software program uses text with images, video, audio, and animations to create interactive applications.	multimedia software
	A website and its associated web pages are created and maintained using a web authoring program.	web authoring software
	Photo editing software is used to edit pictures and add special effects and text.	photo editing software
	Animation software applications are used by a multimedia professional to create images with movement or otherwise interact with viewers.	animation software
	Video editing software is used to manipulate video recorded with a camcorder and add music, audio effects, and text to create videos called clips.	video editing software
	Recording and editing music clips, sound clips, or podcasts is done using an audio recording and editing software program.	audio recording and editing software
	Low-cost or free multimedia programs are available for nonprofessionals to work with graphics, pictures, video, and sound.	
5.4 Software Applications for Personal Use	Note taking software provides a way to store, organize into notebooks and tabs, search, and share notes of any type.	note taking software
	Personal finance software allows you to balance your bank accounts and manage personal investments.	personal finance software
	Prepare and file your tax return using a tax preparation software program.	tax preparation software
	Legal documents, such as wills and contracts, can be prepared using legal software, which contains forms for completing legal documents.	legal software
	Hobby software applications are available to help you with just about any type of leisure activity, such as scrapbooking, meal planning, or genealogy.	hobby software
	A program for playing a game or video is referred to as *entertainment software*.	entertainment software
	Learning about subjects such as math and geography is made easier using an educational software program that uses multimedia to add interactivity and games to improve comprehension and retention of content.	educational software
	A reference software program uses multimedia tools to provide rich content in an encyclopedia, translation guide, and other references.	reference software

continued…

Topic	Key Concepts	Key Terms
5.5 Cloud and Open Source Applications	The main advantage to using a web-based application is that you have access to the software and your documents from any location with an Internet connection.	
	Google Drive, Office Online, and Zoho are all cloud providers that offer free storage space and a suite of productivity applications for free.	
	Apache OpenOffice, a free, open source productivity suite updated and maintained by volunteers, includes a word processor, spreadsheet, presentation, graphics, and database program.	
	LibreOffice, a project of The Document Foundation, is another open source productivity suite with applications called Writer, Calc, Impress, Draw, Base, and Math.	
5.6 Acquiring, Installing, Uninstalling, and Upgrading Software	Software is a licensed product, meaning that you pay for the right to use the software but you do not own the program code.	packaged software
	Packaged software is a program or suite that can be purchased in a retail store, at e-commerce websites, or directly from the software publisher.	shareware
	Shareware is a downloadable software program for which you pay a small fee if you decide to keep the program after a trial period.	freeware
	Freeware is a software program provided for your use without purchase, such as Apple iTunes.	subscription software
	Subscription software is a program generally purchased from cloud computing providers where you pay a monthly or annual charge.	software license agreement (SLA)
	Packaged software contains a DVD or license card inside the package with which you install the application.	end-user license agreement (EULA)
	Download and install software directly from a website by running the install program at the source website or by saving the install program on your hard disk drive to install at a later time.	
	All software programs except open source applications require that you agree to or accept a software license agreement (SLA) or end-user license agreement (EULA) which contains the terms and conditions for using the program. For example, the agreement specifies the number of computers you can legally install the software on.	
	Uninstall software from the computer when you are no longer using it to free up computer resources by opening the Control Panel on a Windows PC or by dragging the program icon and dock shortcut to the trash on a Mac.	
	Installing a newer version of a software program is called *upgrading*; upgrades are generally made available for free or at a price lower than purchasing the software new.	

continued...

Topic	Key Concepts	Key Terms
5.7 Mobile Apps	A mobile application, or app, is a program designed for use on a mobile device such as a smartphone, tablet, or smartwatch that is designed to work on a smaller screen. The app accepts input from touch, handwriting, and voice, and includes compatibility with PC software. All smartphones and tablets come equipped with several built-in apps that typically include personal information management, communication, messaging, maps, music, and game apps. Microsoft, Google, and Apple all have separate mobile productivity apps that run on their smartphones and tablets. Wearable technology apps are designed for use on devices, such as fitness bands and smartwatches. These apps accommodate smaller hardware resources that provide for a quick interaction, display information at a glance, and withstand constant movement.	mobile application

Recheck

Recheck your understanding of the topics covered in this chapter.

Workbook

Chapter review and assessment resources are available in the *Workbook* ebook.

Chapter 6

Using Social Media to Connect and Communicate

Precheck

Check your understanding of the topics covered in this chapter.

In Chapter 2, you learned that Web 2.0 refers to second-generation websites that provide for two-way communication, where individuals interact with organizations and with one another by sharing ideas, feedback, content, and multimedia. A large component of Web 2.0 involves social networking sites, such as Facebook, Twitter, and Instagram, that are used daily by millions of people of all ages around the world. Businesses and other organizations also use social media technologies to connect and interact with customers or clients. Media sharing services, blogs, and wikis are other components of Web 2.0 that focus on user-generated content.

In this chapter, you will learn about social networking, social bookmarking, media sharing, blogging, and wikis. You will also be introduced to ways organizations have incorporated social media technologies into their strategies to increase brand loyalty or attract new business.

***NOTE:** The nature of social media websites is such that they constantly evolve in response to innovation or new trends. The screens shown and instructions provided in this chapter are subject to change. Often, updates or changes to software mean that changes occur to the layout, design, or procedures. You can use the Help function at a website if the figures or steps provided in this chapter do not match what you are seeing on your screen.*

 SNAP If you are a SNAP user, go to your SNAP Assignments page to complete the Precheck, Tutorials, and Recheck.

Learning Objectives

6.1 Describe social networking and list popular social networking websites

6.2 Explain how social bookmarking is used to track and share information, and give examples of social bookmarking websites

6.3 List key features of popular websites used for sharing music, videos, photos, and presentations

6.4 Identify websites used for blogging and explain how to create a blog and a blog post

6.5 Describe how wikis generate content from users and describe two well-known wiki websites

6.6 Relate examples of social media strategies used by businesses to connect and communicate with customers

6.1 Social Networking

Tutorial
How Can HootSuite Help You Organize Your Communications?

Social media is a term used to describe any online tool in which users generate content and interact with others. A website that provides a platform for people to connect with groups of people and interact is called a **social networking website**. Generally, social networking sites provide a means to build a list of friends, with whom you share information, and publish a profile that contains information about yourself. In this topic, you will be introduced to the social networking sites Facebook, LinkedIn, and Google+ (which help you connect with friends, family, and business contacts) and reddit (an open source community for sharing stories).

Facebook

Facebook is the most popular social networking site used by people who want to connect with friends and family. The social network ranked first in a 2015 worldwide survey of social networking websites by Statista (an Internet statistical portal) and by GlobalWebIndex (a digital consumer market research company).

New Facebook users start by creating an account, setting up their profile, and adding friends to their Friends list. To add friends, you search by a person's name and look at his or her profile page. If the person is someone you want to add to your Friends list, click the Add Friend button. A friend request is sent to the individual, who can then accept or ignore it. Once an individual accepts your friend request, the two of you can see each other's Facebook activity.

People post updates to Facebook about what they're doing and share links, photos, videos, music, games, news items, quotes, and just about anything else that appears to be of interest. People comment on a person's Facebook posts, generally with brief notes. Users can chat with friends who are online or use the Facebook Messenger tool to send private messages.

Users can create or join Facebook groups to gather with people who share a similar interest or goal. Businesses and other organizations create Facebook pages to share information and interact with customers, clients, or other interested visitors. For example, Figure 6.1 shows the Facebook page for the US Department of Education.

Good to Know

Facebook was founded in February 2004 as a network for college students only. In 2006, Facebook opened up to everyone, and quickly exploded to become the most used social network worldwide. In December 2015, Facebook reported more than 1.59 billion active monthly users, with mobile users representing 1.44 billion.

Figure 6.1

Education news is shared and discussed in comments with the general public on the Facebook page for the US Department of Education.

Check This Out ✓

http://CC2.Paradigm College.net/FBSeguin Concepts

Go here to see the Facebook page for this textbook.

LinkedIn

LinkedIn, the most visited business-related social networking site, launched in May 2003 and reports that new members join the network at a rate of more than two per second. The social network ranked seventh in the March 2015 worldwide survey by Statista. LinkedIn reports over 414 million members, with students and recent college graduates the fastest growing demographic. It is a professional network where users connect with business contacts.

Tutorial

How Can Social Media Help You Land a Job?

Creating an account with LinkedIn allows you to create a professional profile with your current and past employment positions, education credentials, and links to websites (such as your current company's website). Your profile can be expanded to represent in resume-like fashion a summary of your qualifications and prior work experiences. Once your profile is established, you begin connecting through LinkedIn with people in your workplace and with other professionals in your field and related fields. The Search tool in LinkedIn can be used to find people by name, job title, company name, or location. You can also join professional association groups to keep up with news in your field.

Good to Know

LinkedIn mobile users viewed 1.45 million jobs per day in 2014.

A Jobs board shows current job listings and includes a search tool to find job listings by job title, keywords, or company name. Figure 6.2 shows the LinkedIn Careers page for Adobe.

Figure 6.2

The LinkedIn Careers page for Adobe has information about working at Adobe and current job postings.

Google+

In 2011, Google launched a social networking site called **Google+**. The social network ranked ninth in a March 2015 survey by Statista, with 300 million active monthly users. Sign in at Google+ with your Gmail account or create a new account, add content to your profile, and then start adding people to your network.

In Google+, people or websites that you connect with are organized into categories called *circles*. The default circles are Family, Friends, Acquaintances, and Following. By maintaining your social network in separate circles, you can share activity with only the people for whom the content is of interest. For example, you can post information about a family reunion and share it only with your Family circle. Add websites with which you want to keep up-to-date to your Following circle. Type a note, upload a photo or video, or enter a link at the *Share what's new* box at the top of your page, and then share the item by adding names, names of circles, or email addresses.

Businesses and other organizations have Google+ pages. Figure 6.3 shows a page of photos posted by the US Navy on its Google+ page.

Figure 6.3

At the US Navy Google+ page, you can scroll through photos that show live action of navy activities.

reddit

The reddit mascot is named *Snoo*.

reddit is a social networking website where registered users submit content with text, links, or photos. Other registered users, called *redditors*, vote to move the content up or down the list. Each page updates stories constantly as new submissions are posted and voting occurs. The position of an entry on the page shifts depending on its submission score, which is the number of upvotes minus the number of downvotes. Content is organized by categories, such as gaming, videos, news, movies, and sports, called *subreddits*, to which you can subscribe. Each subreddit is independent, with a set of guidelines and rules to follow, moderated by volunteers. Users comment on stories and can add friends. In January 2016, reddit had over 231 million unique visitors.

Mobile Apps for Social Networking

Popular social networking websites have free mobile apps that are preinstalled on a smartphone so that you can post messages, upload photos, or otherwise stay connected from your mobile device. If your mobile device is missing an app for a social network, download the app from Google Play, iTunes, or the Windows store.

Anonymous social networking apps became a rising trend in 2014. An **anonymous social network** allows users to post content viewable by everyone on the network without using their real names. One popular anonymous social network is Yik Yak, a free mobile app for Android or iOS devices. Yik Yak uses GPS technology to pinpoint the location of mobile devices and then allows users to create and view posts, called *yaks*, within a small radius—anyone within 1.5 miles of a message can read and respond to yaks. Yik Yak began as a popular app among college and university students to communicate about class cancellations and campus life. The app soon spread to high school and middle school students. The app's developers had to build geofencing technology into their system to block the app from being used on high school or middle school grounds after complaints that the app became a vehicle for misuse and cyberbullying by the younger student population.

Another anonymous social network, Secret, shut down its network in April 2015 after just 16 months of operation. Although the future of anonymous social networking is unclear, many of these apps have a large number of active users.

Table 6.1 lists three mobile social networking apps that ranked in the top 15 worldwide for active accounts in March 2015, according to Statista.

Social networking apps are free for a mobile device.

Table 6.1

Three Top 15 Ranked Social Networking Apps

Social Network	Number of Active Users in March 2015	Rank in Top 15
WhatsApp	700 million	Third
WeChat	468 million	Sixth
Skype	300 million	Eighth

Security Alert Know Your Privacy Settings

Make sure you check the privacy settings at the social networks you use when you set up your account. Recheck the settings periodically to be sure you are not sharing more personal information than you intended. Always recheck your settings when a network updates or changes its privacy options or policies. Ask your friends not to tag you in photos they post if you don't want friends of friends to see what you've been up to.

Blog Topic Is It Fair That Social Media Posts Can Be Used Against You?

You have probably seen news stories about athletes who lost scholarships, college applicants whose admission offers were rescinded, and employees who were fired—all because they posted on a social network something considered inappropriate or offensive. Do you think your social network posts should affect your ability to attend school or to work? Should a social network post be treated the same as a notice on a public bulletin board? Is it fair that an employer or potential employer can judge you based on your social media activity?

1. Write and post a blog entry that answers the above questions and gives your reasons.

2. Read at least two of your classmates' blogs and post one comment to each.

3. Submit your blog URL and the URLs of the two classmates' blogs to your instructor in the manner she or he has requested.

Explore Further Find a New Social Network

This topic surveyed only four social networks; many more exist. The popularity of mobile social networking is leading to the development of new social networks every year. What new social network would you like to explore?

1. Find a social networking app or website that you have not used before. Learn the purpose of the social network and read reviews and user ratings. Think about whether you would use the network or stick with your existing social networks.

2. Create a document or presentation that describes the app, whether you would use it, and give your reasons. Include the URLs for the websites you used.

3. Save the document or presentation as **NewSocialNetwork-YourName**.

4. Submit the document or presentation to your instructor in the manner she or he has requested.

6.2 Social Bookmarking

Tutorial

How Are People Using
Social Bookmarks?

A category of social networking that provides tools to organize, store, and share content with others is known as **social bookmarking**. You have probably saved or bookmarked a link that you visit frequently within your browser. Bookmarked links are stored in folders on your local hard drive. Social bookmarking is similar to browser bookmarking except that a saved link, called a **bookmark**, is saved in a social network that is accessible from any device with Internet connectivity. At social bookmarking sites, you can search bookmarks that others have created.

Bookmarks can be organized by tagging a website. A **tag** is a keyword you assign to describe or categorize a selected photo, article, or item on a web page. Tags help users at the social bookmarking site find content. For example, if you find a recipe for Greek souvlaki you want to share, you can tag the recipe at the source website, while creating the bookmark with keywords such as *recipe*, *greek souvlaki*, *greek*, and *entrée*.

Each social bookmarking website has a **bookmarklet**. A bookmarklet is an icon that allows you to perform an action on the current web page with one click. For a social bookmarking website, the bookmarklet captures the current web page's URL and saves the page reference for you in your bookmarks account. The bookmarklet performs actions in the social bookmarking website similar to what happens when you add a web page to the Favorites list or bookmarks bar in your browser. When you create an account at a social bookmarking website, look for instructions on copying the bookmarklet to your browser's toolbar.

Many web pages display bookmarklets for popular websites near content you might want to bookmark. Depending on the bookmarklet, you may need to select the desired content and sign in to your account before the bookmark is created. Web pages also display bookmarklets you can use to share content via a social media account. For example, a Facebook or Twitter bookmarklet may be used to post content on your Facebook page or Twitter account. Figure 6.4 shows three bookmarklets that can be clicked to bookmark or share the content shown.

In this topic, you will explore three social bookmarking sites: Pinterest, StumbleUpon, and Delicious.

Figure 6.4

Bookmarklets on the Chrome toolbar and NASA web page can be used to bookmark or share content.

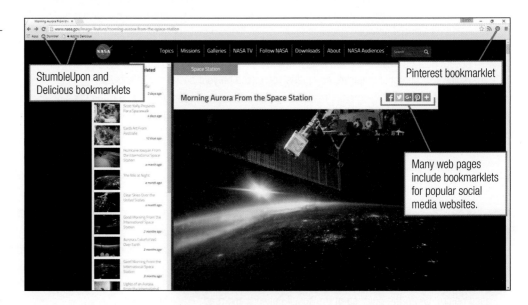

StumbleUpon and Delicious bookmarklets

Pinterest bookmarklet

Many web pages include bookmarklets for popular social media websites.

Pinterest

Pinterest is a virtual pinboard, or visual bookmarking tool to find and save ideas or other content of personal interest. The website launched in March 2010 and quickly joined the ranks of Facebook and Twitter in the top 10 social networking websites. Users click the Pin It button (bookmarklet) to pin pictures of things they have seen on the Internet that they like and want to share. Pinterest users can add a Pin It button to their browser's toolbar, or many websites include the Pin It button next to an image or other content that can be copied to Pinterest. Click the Pin It button, select the image to pin, and then choose the board to pin it to. You can also upload your own pictures to share on a board.

A board is a collection of related pictures and users can assign boards unique names. For example, you can create a board for technology and collect pictures of cool gadgets. You can browse and follow boards created by other Pinterest users to get ideas for yourself. If you like something you find on someone else's board, you can repin the item to your own. In August 2014, Pinterest launched a messaging feature that allows users to discuss a shared pin without leaving the social bookmarking website.

Figure 6.5 displays items in the Travel category that could be pinned to an individual board or shared via the messaging feature.

Good to Know

According to Pinterest, 75 percent of its daily traffic initiates from a smartphone or tablet. Pinterest also says one-third of all new Pinterest accounts come from men, despite the widely held belief that Pinterest is a female-dominated social network.

Click here to choose a category of pins to browse.

Click here to view your own boards and pinned images.

The Pin It bookmarklet can be added to the Chrome toolbar.

Figure 6.5

Pinterest is a visual social bookmarking site where users pin pictures to boards that link to items of interest.

StumbleUpon

StumbleUpon allows you to browse recommended web pages and save the pages you like to a personal profile. When you join StumbleUpon, you choose which content categories you want to see. Once your interests are established, you navigate through various web pages StumbleUpon finds for you by clicking the Stumble button in the black StumbleBar at the top of the screen (Figure 6.6). Use the Like (thumbs-up) button and the Dislike (thumbs-down) button on the StumbleBar as you view pages so that StumbleUpon can tailor the recommendations to your preferences. Each time you click the Stumble button, another web page appears. You can share a page you find with others, and you can follow another StumbleUpon user (called a Stumbler) if you like the same web pages.

View web pages you have liked, add more categories to your interests, and browse lists, channels, or other Stumbler pages once you have created a profile and used StumbleUpon to like pages. Click your avatar and explore pages using the options that appear.

Figure 6.6

StumbleUpon shows recommended web pages for you based on your likes and dislikes.

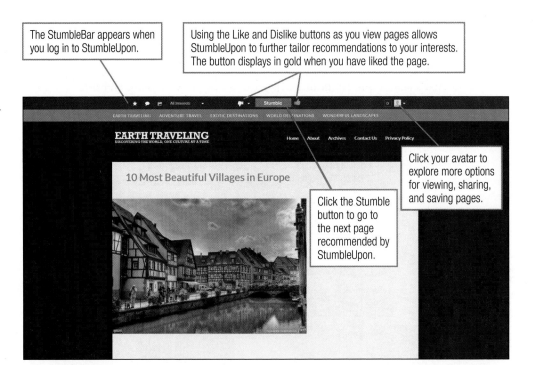

The StumbleBar appears when you log in to StumbleUpon.

Using the Like and Dislike buttons as you view pages allows StumbleUpon to further tailor recommendations to your interests. The button displays in gold when you have liked the page.

Click your avatar to explore more options for viewing, sharing, and saving pages.

Click the Stumble button to go to the next page recommended by StumbleUpon.

+ Add to Delicious

Click the Delicious bookmarklet to save a link to your account.

Delicious

Create an account at **Delicious** to save and share links to web pages that have articles, pictures, videos, blogs, or some other content that you want to bookmark. Use the Delicious bookmarklet to save links in your Delicious account. You will have to add the Delicious bookmarklet to your browser's Favorites or Bookmarks bar. As an alternative, use the *Add Link* option in the Delicious sidebar menu to type a link that you want to save. Delicious has an import utility found on the Manage tab of its Settings page that will import bookmarks you have saved in a browser.

When viewing a web page that you decide to save, click the Delicious bookmarklet, sign in to your account if you are not already logged in, enter tags or accept the default tags, type a comment if desired, and then click the Save link button. You can mark links as private or public, and you can follow other Delicious users.

Once you have a collection of links, you can sort and search your personal collection or the collections of people you are following. Figure 6.7 on page 153 displays a Delicious page with saved bookmarks.

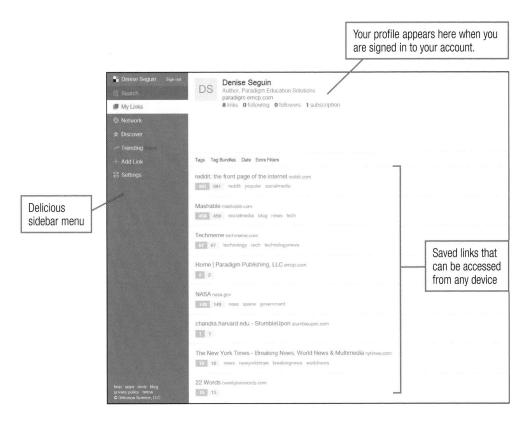

Figure 6.7

Use Delicious to collect links to websites, pictures, videos, blog entries, articles, or any other web content you want to save and/or share.

Some social bookmarking websites have connectors to Facebook and Twitter, allowing users to register using an existing Facebook or Twitter account instead of an email address.

Table 6.2 provides names and URLs to six social bookmarking sites, including the three discussed in this topic.

Table 6.2

Social Bookmarking Websites

Social Bookmark	URL
Delicious	https://delicious.com/
Digg	http://digg.com/
Diigo	https://www.diigo.com/
Newsvine	http://www.newsvine.com/
Pinterest	https://www.pinterest.com/
StumbleUpon	http://www.stumbleupon.com/

Explore Further   Start Social Bookmarking

Explore a social bookmarking website to learn what it offers.

1. From the list in Table 6.2, choose a social bookmarking website you have not used before and create an account at the website.

2. Experiment with the tools available at the site by adding at least 10 bookmarks to content that you like on the web. Bookmark different types of content, such as a blog, news article, picture, and video. Consider also customizing your profile and sharing some links with others.

3. Capture an image of your page at the social bookmarking website, showing your saved links. Use a screen capture program, such as Windows Snipping Tool or PrintScreen. Depending on the method used, save the image as a JPEG file or paste the image into a document. Save the image or document as **SocialBookmarks-YourName**.

4. Submit the image or document to your instructor in the manner she or he has requested.

6.3 Media Sharing

Good to Know

A video sharing app named Vine, owned by Twitter and released in 2013, quickly gained popularity. The app lets users record and edit a video clip up to six seconds long, called a *vine*. The video is published on the Vine social network or shared on Facebook or Twitter as a looping video. According to Twitter, five vines are tweeted every second.

Photos, videos, music, and presentations are shared, viewed, and downloaded using **media sharing** websites. Popular media sharing websites are YouTube for videos, Flickr and Instagram for photos, Spotify for music, and Slideshare for presentations. Sharing media using social sharing sites allows you to publish content, work with content collaboratively, and distribute content to several people more easily than sending files or links as message attachments.

Some websites have applications for **peer-to-peer (P2P) file sharing**, in which users access each other's hard drives and exchange files directly over the Internet. BitTorrent is a P2P application often used for file sharing. People use P2P applications to share software, games, movies, music, and other content. Some P2P applications have been used to share copyrighted material without permission from the copyright owner, such as exchanging movies or music tracks between users, and are often the target for litigation from copyright holders.

Digital audio and video files are sometimes shared on the Internet as podcasts. A **podcast** is an audio or video post that is usually part of a series to which people subscribe. A software program called a **podcatcher** automatically downloads new podcast episodes to your computer or mobile device for you to listen to or watch whenever you like. Other podcasts are streamed from a website. In this topic, you will survey the media sharing services YouTube, Flickr, Spotify, and Instagram.

YouTube

YouTube, which is owned by Google, is the most popular video sharing website in the world. A YouTube video becomes a **viral video** when it spreads quickly via forwarded or shared links or word-of-mouth. With a YouTube account, you can search, browse, and watch videos; upload a video you have created; subscribe to someone's YouTube channel; and share videos with friends. Figure 6.8 shows a page from YouTube EDU, which hosts educational videos, some of which are lessons from teachers or full courses from leading universities. According to YouTube, over 1 billion users watch YouTube videos, with more than 50 percent watching from a mobile device. New content is uploaded at the rate of 300 hours of video every minute! Many people also go to YouTube to stream music or watch music videos.

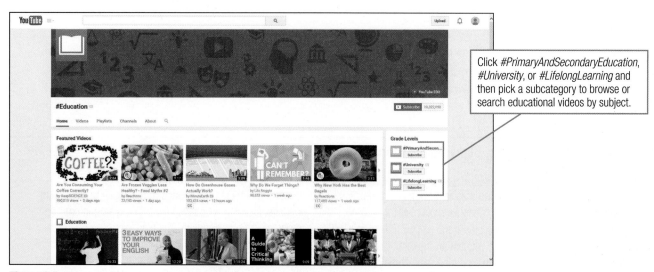

Click #PrimaryAndSecondaryEducation, #University, or #LifelongLearning and then pick a subcategory to browse or search educational videos by subject.

Figure 6.8

Go to YouTube EDU (http://CC2.ParadigmCollege.net/YouTubeEDU) to watch free lectures, courses, or other educational videos.

Flickr

Sharing photos is a popular media sharing activity because most people have digital photos they want family and friends to see. Uploading photos to a sharing site lets you easily send a link to share your photo album with other people. Although social networking sites such as Facebook and Twitter let you upload and share photos, these sites generally have lower photo storage limits than do dedicated photo sharing websites.

Many dedicated photo sharing websites are available. **Flickr** was among the original services, started in Vancouver, Canada, in 2004. In 2005, Flickr was bought by Yahoo. See Table 6.3 to review other photo sharing websites.

Generally, photo sharing websites let you upload pictures organized into albums, sets, or folders; tag and comment on pictures; and share the photos with others. You can share with other users of the site, or you can link to the photos through Facebook, Twitter, or blog posts, or through emails and other messaging tools. You can search for pictures uploaded by others, and some sites include a feature (such as the Commons at Flickr) that lets you search public photography archives. Figure 6.9 shows the Explore page for photos uploaded to Flickr.

Some photo sharing websites, such as Google Photos, include photo editing tools. In May 2015, Google announced the launch of Google Photos. Previously part of Google+, the Photos app was converted to a new standalone product that allows for free, unlimited storage of photos and videos from Apple or Android devices, or via the web. The free, unlimited storage applies for pictures with a maximum resolution of 16 megapixels and video with a maximum resolution of 1080p (also called *Full HD*).

> **Good to Know** 🎓
>
> A mobile app for photo and video sharing called Snapchat had over 200 million monthly users in 2016. The app, for Apple and Android devices, lets users take photos, record videos, add text and drawings, and then send the media, called *snaps*, to a list of recipients. Users set a time limit for which a recipient can see the snap, which ranges from 1 to 10 seconds. When the time period expires, the snap is deleted from Snapchat servers.

Table 6.3

Sampling of Photo Sharing Websites

Photo Sharing Website	Restrictions for Free Accounts	URL
Flickr	1 TB for photos and videos up to 3 minutes each	https://www.flickr.com/
Google Photos	Unlimited photos and videos for images up to 16 megapixels and video up to 1080p	https://photos.google.com/
Photobucket	2 GB for photos and videos up to 10 minutes each	http://photobucket.com/
Shutterfly	Unlimited photos	https://www.shutterfly.com/
Snapfish	Unlimited photos	http://www.snapfish.com/photo-gift/welcome

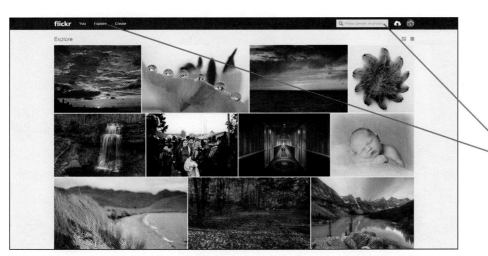

By default, Flickr searches everyone's uploads. Click Explore to browse recently uploaded photos or videos, or type a keyword or phrase to find photos using the search text box.

Figure 6.9

The recent photos on the Explore page at Flickr change constantly as new photos are added. As of May 2015, Flickr had approximately 11 billion photos stored on its servers.

Spotify

Spotify is a music and video streaming service launched from Sweden in 2008 that quickly became popular by allowing users to listen to music on most devices connected to the Internet. Spotify was one of the first to offer streaming of music via the web instead of requiring individuals to download tracks to a device. Spotify is also popular because of its vast collection of music, which includes over 30 million tracks and 2 billion playlists. The service was available in 58 countries and reported over 75 million active users in 2016. Spotify offers both a free account and a paid subscription account. A free account has ads between tracks and delivers music at a lower quality. The paid account, called Spotify Premium, is ad free and streams high-definition music. In addition, Premium users can listen to music offline.

Spotify users can share playlists and tracks that are currently playing with friends on the service. A feature called Discover Weekly delivers a personalized playlist of two hours of tracks every Monday to your phone or other device. The weekly playlist is compiled based on the previous tracks you have played and similar tracks listened to by other users. In 2015, Spotify announced it was adding video to its streaming service.

To use Spotify, sign up for an account at the Spotify website (see Table 6.4), and then download the app to your PC or mobile device and install it. Figure 6.10 displays the Spotify app for a PC. You can browse for tracks by genre or use the search text box to find a song by artist, title, playlist, or record label. You can easily save favorite tracks to your music library using the Save icon next to a track.

Table 6.4

Music Streaming Services

Music Service	URL
Apple Music	http://www.apple.com/music
Deezer	https://www.deezer.com
Google Music	https://play.google.com/music/listen#/sww
Rdio	http://www.rdio.com/home/en-us/
Spotify	https://www.spotify.com/us/
YouTube	https://www.youtube.com/

Figure 6.10

Spotify has a library of more than 30 million tracks available on iOS, Android, and Windows Phone devices, as well as streaming from the web on your desktop, laptop, and some smart televisions and gaming consoles.

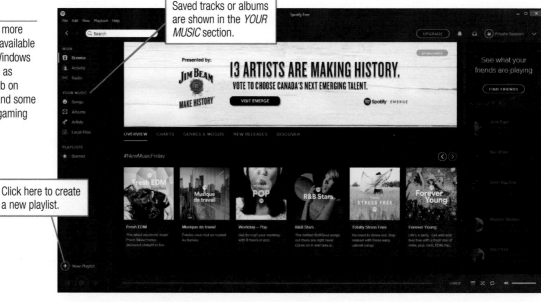

Saved tracks or albums are shown in the *YOUR MUSIC* section.

Click here to create a new playlist.

Music sharing sites are often the target of litigation by major music recording labels for copyright violations. For example, Grooveshark, a music sharing website started in 2007, became embroiled in lawsuits in 2010 for copyright infringements from four major music labels: EMI Music Publishing, Universal Music Group, Sony Music, and Warner Music Group. In April 2015, the company ceased operations as part of a settlement with the record labels. At the time Grooveshark shut down, the site streamed over 1 billion songs per month, stored over 15 million songs on servers, and had 20 million active users.

Instagram

Instagram is a free app used by over 400 million users for sharing photos from an Apple or Android phone or tablet. After taking a photo with a mobile device, you can use Instagram to add a special effects filter to the picture, and then share the photo to your Instagram page or your favorite social networking site. In March 2015, Instagram added a new feature called Layout that lets you combine multiple pictures into one, and then flip and rotate images to create interesting visuals. Figure 6.11 shows the Layout feature being used to flip an image. You can download the Instagram app from the App Store or Google Play.

Instagram was started in October 2010 and grew to one million users in just over two months. In April 2012, Facebook purchased Instagram. According to Instagram, on average, approximately 80 million photos are posted each day.

Check This Out ✓

http://CC2.Paradigm College.net/Music Resource

Go here to find a music resource authorized by the Recording Industry Association of America and the Music Business Association.

Check This Out ✓

http://CC2.Paradigm College.net/Mashable

Go here for up-to-date news on digital culture, social media, and technology.

Figure 6.11

The Layout feature in Instagram (left) is used to flip an image, creating the result shown at the right.

Explore Further   Share a Presentation

Slideshare is a website at which you upload and share presentations created in PowerPoint, PDFs, Keynote, or OpenOffice. The slide hosting website also allows you to upload and share documents and videos. In this activity, you will experiment with sharing a presentation.

1. Create a presentation with at least three slides that describes the methods or websites that you use to share media, such as photos, videos, or music. If you do not share media, create one slide for each of the websites mentioned in this topic that summarizes what you learned.

2. Save the presentation as **MediaSharing-YourName**.

3. Go to **http://CC2.ParadigmCollege.net/SlideShare** and sign up for a new account or log in if you already have an account.

4. Upload the MediaSharing-YourName presentation. Add appropriate tags and a description and select the Education category.

5. Email the presentation to your instructor from SlideShare, or submit the presentation and a screen capture of the presentation in SlideShare to your instructor in the manner she or he has requested.

Tutorial

When Do Blogs Go Beyond Words?

6.4 Blogging

A **blog** is basically a journal posted on a website, with the most recent entry at the top of the page. Older blog entries are usually archived by month and can be displayed by clicking the month to expand the blog entry list. The word *blog* is derived from *web log*. The collection of all of the blogs on the web is referred to as the **blogosphere**. Writing and maintaining a blog is called **blogging**. An entry in a blog is called a **blog post**, *post*, or *entry*. The individual who writes the blog content is referred to as a **blogger**. Blogs exist on just about any topic one can think of and are mostly text and pictures; however, posts also contain links to other web pages and sometimes video and audio. The popularity of YouTube led to a form of blogging that uses videos—called **vlogging**. A **vlog** is a blog that uses video as the primary content. A **vlogger** is the person who creates a video blog.

Blog websites include tools that allow individuals to create, update, and maintain blogs without a programming background. Blogs are interactive, meaning that people post comments on blog posts, and the authors and their audiences can have conversations about the posts. In this topic, you will learn about two widely used blog hosting websites, WordPress and Blogger, as well as one microblogging website, Twitter.

WordPress

WordPress (https://wordpress.com) is a blog hosting website that uses the WordPress open source blogging software. Sign up for a free blog by providing a blog address, user name, password, and email address. A blog address begins with the domain you want to name your blog and ends with *.wordpress.com*. For example, if you type your name as the blog address, the URL you would give to people to find your blog will be *yourname.wordpress.com*. After registering for a new blog, go to your email and activate the blog from the confirmation email message. In the message, a link is provided to start your first post. Figure 6.12 shows the window for creating a new post. Type a title and the body of the blog entry in a word processor–style window. Buttons are available to add a photo, video, quote, or link. Click the Publish button to add the entry to the blog.

Figure 6.12

New blog posts are created at WordPress by typing inside a window similar to that of a word processor.

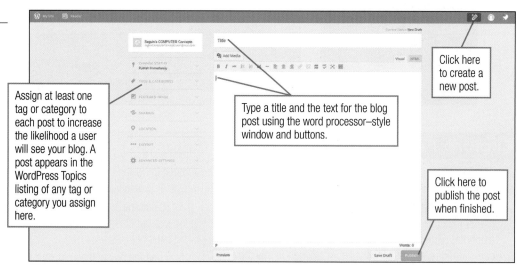

Assign at least one tag or category to each post to increase the likelihood a user will see your blog. A post appears in the WordPress Topics listing of any tag or category you assign here.

Type a title and the text for the blog post using the word processor–style window and buttons.

Click here to create a new post.

Click here to publish the post when finished.

Blogger

Blogger (https://www.blogger.com) is another popular choice for creating a blog. Sign up for the blog using your Gmail account. After you customize your profile, you are ready to create your first blog. At the Blogger page, click the New Blog button, type a title for the blog, enter a valid blog address, choose the template with the colors and style you want to use, and then click the Create blog! button. Blog addresses in Blogger end with *.blogspot.com* (*.blogspot.ca* if you reside in Canada), so the URL for a new blog would be *yourblogaddress.blogspot.com* (*yourblogaddress.blogspot.ca* in Canada). Once the blog is created, you can start publishing blog posts. At the screen shown in Figure 6.13, type the post title and text in the word processor–style window. Add links, pictures, video, or quotes as needed, and then click the Publish button when finished.

Once the first post has been added to the blog, additional posts are created by clicking the New post button. You can change the template at any time using the Design page, and you can preview the template in both PC and mobile environments (Figure 6.14).

WordPress and Blogger are two of many blog hosting websites. See Table 6.5 on page 160 for more blogging services.

Type title and text for blog post. Use toolbar to format or insert items.

Click here to publish the post when finished.

Figure 6.13

Blogger is a popular blog hosting service because the tools are easy to use and navigate for beginner bloggers.

Manage and customize Blogger blogs using the Design page. Click Design while viewing the blog to see this page.

Choose a template that looks good in both PC and mobile environments.

Figure 6.14

The Blogger template design can be changed at any time, and you can preview how the blog will look on both a PC and a mobile device.

Table 6.5

Blog Hosting Services

Blog Hosting Service	URL
Blogger	https://www.blogger.com/
LiveJournal	http://www.livejournal.com/
Medium	https://medium.com/
Quora	https://www.quora.com/
Squarespace	http://www.squarespace.com/
Tumblr	https://www.tumblr.com/
Twitter	https://twitter.com/
WordPress	https://wordpress.com/

Microblogs

A few blog services such as Twitter and Tumblr are microblogging hosting services. A **microblog** is a blog that restricts posts to a smaller amount of text than a traditional blog. A **microblogger** is someone who typically posts about what he or she is doing, what he or she is thinking about at the moment, or links to interesting content (stories, pictures, videos). Tumblr is a popular microblog that includes social networking and social bookmarking features. A post in Tumblr is called a *tumblelog*. Many Tumblr users use their blogs to bookmark videos or pictures they have found on the web and share them with their followers. Tumblr users also frequently reblog items seen on someone else's page at their own pages.

Twitter is by far the most popular microblog, with posts limited to 140 characters or less. A post in Twitter is called a **tweet** and contains information about a breaking news story, opinion, status update, or other topic the author finds interesting. Because of the short nature of a tweet, many users post to Twitter from their mobile devices. Clicking the Tweet button opens a small window in which the user types a new post. Twitter users type the **hashtag symbol (#)** preceding a keyword or topic (with no space) in a tweet to categorize messages. Clicking a hashtagged word in any post will show you all the other tweets categorized with the same keyword.

Many people like to follow other Twitter users to see their tweets, including business accounts to find out about new products, sales, or other specials (Figure 6.15, page 161). Twitter followers for some accounts reach millions. In February 2016, Katy Perry recorded the most Twitter followers at 82.8 million. Twitter is also a resource to learn about breaking news or other topics that are trending in social media. According to Twitter, after the announcement from Kensington Palace on May 2, 2015, of the birth of Her Royal Highness Princess Charlotte of Cambridge, over 1.1 million tweets circulated that day in conversation about the tweet.

Good to Know

Twitter was launched in July 2006 and by 2015 had 320 million monthly active users that collectively sent 500 million tweets per day!

Security Alert   **Be Careful What You Post Online**

What you write in a blog or in comments at social media websites reflects your ethics and your personality. Poor spelling and grammar portray sloppiness. Be mindful of your digital persona at all times. Do not engage in conversations or blogs that a potential employer might read and use to decide that you are not a good fit for the organization.

Figure 6.15

Businesses use Twitter to post tweets with daily deals, news about products, or exclusive deals on Twitter, called *twixclusives*.

Blog Topic   What Is in *Your* Digital Footprint?

Your *digital footprint* is the accumulation or trail of your online activities. For example, your social media activity, online shopping habits, online subscriptions, photos and videos you have uploaded, and any other activity on the Internet for which your name is associated is part of your digital footprint. Individuals who have grown up with the Internet as part of their life rarely think twice about the things they do online. What kinds of activities make up your own digital footprint? Do you consider your digital footprint when you blog, tweet, comment, or otherwise post content online? Should everyone monitor his or her digital footprint and be mindful of it when doing things online? Would *not* having a digital footprint be a drawback for a person?

1. Write and post a blog entry that answers the above questions and gives your reasons.

2. Read at least two of your classmates' blogs and post one comment to each.

3. Submit your blog URL and the URLs of the two classmates' blogs to your instructor in the manner she or he has requested.

Explore Further   Tweet a Social Media Fact

If you completed the blog topic exercises in previous chapters of this textbook, you are an experienced blogger. But do you tweet? In this activity, you have a chance to post a tweet with an interesting fact about social media.

1. Search the web for a fact about how Twitter has been used for social good.

2. Go to **http://CC2.ParadigmCollege.net/Twitter** and sign in. (You will need to sign up for a new account if you do not already have one.)

3. Compose a tweet to share the Twitter fact you found at Step 1. Precede your tweet with *#courseidentifier* so that your instructor

can locate your tweet. Your instructor will provide you with the hashtag keyword to use for *courseidentifier*. For example, the hashtag keyword might be *#comp100f2018*.

4. In addition, or as an alternative, your instructor may request that you make a screen capture of your tweet and submit the screen capture saved as **TweetForSocialGood-YourName**. In that case, submit the tweet in the manner she or he has requested.

6.5 Wikis for User-Generated Content

Tutorial
What Are the Differences between Wikis, Blogs, and Microblogs?

Good to Know

At the time of writing, over 5 million articles were available on *Wikipedia*.

A **wiki** is a website with **wiki software** that allows anyone (except those under a ban restriction) to create and edit content at the website. Clicking the edit tab, edit button, or edit link in a wiki opens the text in a word processor–style window, where you can add, delete, or edit content. This type of open content is used for collaboration and knowledge sharing. The postings on wikis that provide encyclopedic or other reference content are monitored by people to make sure entries are well written and accurate. In this topic, you will explore two well-known wiki websites: *Wikipedia* and wikiHow.

Wikipedia

The most used online encyclopedia is **Wikipedia**, supported by the not-for-profit Wikimedia Foundation. Individuals looking for new information about a subject often start at *Wikipedia*. Content at *Wikipedia* can be created by anyone; however, thousands of editors regularly review and update pages.

People who want to edit at *Wikipedia* are encouraged to create an account so that their postings will be identified with their name or alias. If you edit a page without being logged in to an account, the IP address for your PC is attributed to your content in the page history. New contributors to *Wikipedia* are encouraged to first post in the **Wikipedia Sandbox** (Figure 6.16), where they can learn how to edit content.

Figure 6.16

The *Wikipedia* Sandbox contains instructions on how to edit content, and new contributors are encouraged to post a test edit here before modifying a real article.

wikiHow

When people need a how-to instruction manual, **wikiHow** is often where they look. The website contains more than 187,000 how-to articles. According to wikiHow, the mission of the website is that "by creating the world's most helpful

Career Connection

Leading-Edge Social Media Careers

Businesses need to stay on top of social media trends and ensure that social media websites are used for positive brand messaging. Careers in social media require above-average research, analytical, and communication skills. Candidates must be able to design online social campaigns and manage multiple projects simultaneously. To find out more about this field, conduct a search online for job titles such as *social media strategist*, *social media specialist*, *online community manager*, *blogger*, *social media coordinator*, *digital marketing specialist*, and *search marketing specialist*. Read ads for these positions to see the qualifications employers are seeking and the responsibilities for each job.

instructions, we will empower every person on the planet to learn how to do anything." You can search for the instructions you need using keywords or browse articles by category at the home page. Figure 6.17 shows the beginnings of the how-to article "How to Grow Orchids." wikiHow is a for-profit wiki that shows ads to users who are not registered to finance the operation of the website.

Other wikis that you might want to investigate are listed in Table 6.6.

Figure 6.17

User-generated content at wikiHow consists of how-to articles such as this one that describes two methods for growing orchids.

Table 6.6

Popular Wiki Websites

Wiki	URL	Purpose
Wikibooks	https://www.wikibooks.org/	Free textbooks and manuals
Wikimedia Commons	https://commons.wikimedia.org/wiki/Main_Page	Freely usable images, photographs, or videos
wikiHow	http://www.wikihow.com/Main-Page	How-to instructions
Wikipedia	https://www.wikipedia.org/	Encyclopedia
Wikiquote	https://www.wikiquote.org/	Collection of quotations from notable people
Wiktionary	https://www.wiktionary.org/	Dictionary for words in all languages
Wikitravel	http://wikitravel.org/en/Main_Page	Worldwide travel guide

Explore Further   Explore a New Wiki

You have likely looked up information in *Wikipedia*, but have you used any other wiki? In this activity, you will explore another wiki of your choice.

1. Choose from Table 6.6 a wiki (other than *Wikipedia*) that you have not used before and look up information on a topic or subject of interest to you. For example, you might use Wikitravel to find an article on a destination that you want to visit.
2. Read the article at the wiki website.
3. Create a document that provides a brief summary of the wiki you used, the information you researched, and your perception

of the content's usefulness to you. Include the URL of the article at the end of the document.
4. Save the document as **WikiArticle-YourName**.
5. Submit the document to your instructor in the manner she or he has requested.

6.6 Social Media Strategies in Business

Tutorial

How Are Businesses Using Social Networking?

Business strategies for using social media incorporate a wide variety of techniques, such as using Facebook pages to provide customer support, invite feedback, offer a forum for new ideas, and allow users to exchange tips, post reviews, or otherwise interact with interested people. Businesses also offer coupons or information on specials using social media. Social media has also been employed to enhance a brand using hashtag campaigns with video or photo sharing invitations or contests to engage customers.

A category of e-commerce called **social commerce (s-commerce)** refers to the use of social networks to support the buying and selling of products or services. Social commerce employs techniques that encourage user-generated assistance in online selling, such as user ratings, referrals, reviews, and participation in online communities. Social networks offer assistance to businesses with social commerce activities. For example, Facebook maintains the "Facebook for Business" page with marketing information and success stories, and Twitter hosts a business blog that gives tips for using Twitter in s-commerce activities (Figure 6.18). Facebook, Twitter, and Pinterest have implemented Buy buttons that let customers complete a purchase without leaving the social network page.

This topic describes s-commerce strategies employed by Forever 21, Honda, and Lowe's.

Forever 21

In 2015, clothing retailer Forever 21 invited customers to post photos of their favorite summer outfits to Instagram, Facebook, or Twitter (Figure 6.19) using the hashtag *#F21xMe* or *#F21SummerCool* and include the tag *@Forever21*. The retailer featured the posts on Forever 21 social networks with shoppable links to the merchandise. The user-generated campaign was an effort by Forever 21 to promote sales using a strategy of shopper-to-shopper conversations. The person posting the photo experiences a celebrity-like atmosphere, and the shoppers viewing the photo get to see an outfit on someone with whom they can relate.

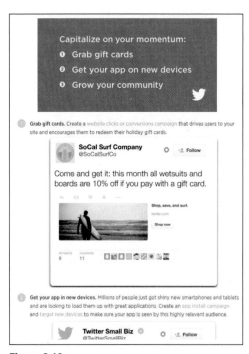

Figure 6.18

Twitter maintains a blog for businesses, with tips for using Twitter to connect with customers.

Figure 6.19

The *#F21xMe* campaign by Forever 21 engaged shopper-to-shopper interactions.

Honda

In August 2014, car company Honda launched the *#Cheerance* campaign (Figure 6.20). The five-day campaign was designed to spread cheer to people through amusing videos, GIFs, and visual jokes spread via social media. The campaign coincided with traditional media advertising to support Honda's annual summer sales clearance activities. The "Dancing with People" YouTube video at the campaign launch was viewed over 790,000 times. Honda also added close to 9,000 fans on Facebook and 4,600 new followers on Twitter during the week. As part of the campaign, Honda donated $100,000 to the Pediatric Brain Tumor Foundation.

Lowe's

The Lowe's Pinterest page is more than just a visual catalogue of the company's products. The page has inspiration boards with do-it-yourself ideas (Figure 6.21). Lowe's also runs a *#FixinSix* campaign on Vine, where it showcases home improvement tips in 6-second videos. The company actively engages with commenters on its Facebook page, where most comments receive a reply from a Lowe's employee. The company also runs multiple YouTube channels, with a channel for professional contractors called LowesForPros and a channel highlighting the company's community involvement called Lowe's in the Community.

Figure 6.20

Honda promoted its Cheerance event through Facebook posts.

Figure 6.21

Lowe's Weekend DIY Alert! board has more than 100 pins.

Career Connection

Social Media Managers

Businesses need to monitor and manage all the social media feeds that can affect their business strategies. A social media manager coordinates all the s-commerce activities of the business. Typically, the social media manager is someone who enjoys spending a lot of time online, has excellent writing skills, and enjoys communicating and connecting with all types of people. Jobs in social media management or strategy typically ask for individuals with degrees or diplomas in communications, public relations, or marketing.

Explore Further   Find a Business in Social Media

A business needs to engage in s-commerce to attract new customers and retain existing customers. Exploring a specific use of s-commerce will help you understand how companies are connecting with people.

1. Choose a familiar business that was not profiled in this topic and find its presence in a social media venue, such as Facebook, Twitter, Instagram, or Pinterest.
2. Examine the way the business is using social commerce. Do you think the strategy is successful? Would you engage with the business on its social media site? Why or why not?
3. Create a document or presentation that describes the results

of your research and answers the questions posed in Step 2. Include a screen capture or URL of the page(s) you reviewed.

4. Save the document or presentation as **SocialMediaBusiness -YourName**.
5. Submit the document or presentation to your instructor in the manner she or he has requested.

Topics Review

Topic	Key Concepts	Key Terms
6.1 Social Networking	Social media includes any online tool used by individuals to generate content and interact with others. A social networking website provides a platform for people to connect and interact with one another, individually or within a group. Facebook is the most popular social networking site used by people who want to connect with friends and family. LinkedIn is a social network used to connect with business contacts. Google+ uses circles to group people you want to connect with by categories such as Family, Friends, Acquaintances, and Following. reddit is a website where users submit content, and other registered users vote a story up or down the list. All the popular social networking websites provide free apps that are preinstalled on devices so that people can stay connected from their mobile devices. An anonymous social network allows users to post content without using their real names.	social media social networking website Facebook LinkedIn Google+ reddit anonymous social network
6.2 Social Bookmarking	Social bookmarking websites let you save and share links to content on the web, such as articles, pictures, videos, blogs, music, and other web pages. A saved link is called a *bookmark*. Bookmarks are created by tagging a website with one or more keywords called a *tag*. A bookmarklet is an icon that is installed on a toolbar in the browser and then used to link a web page to a social bookmarking website. Pinterest is used to pin images that you want to save and share to a board at your Pinterest account. StumbleUpon is a social bookmarking website that shows you pages that it determines might be of interest to you based on content categories in your profile and pages you liked in the past. Delicious is a social bookmarking site for saving and sharing links, and can import links you have saved to Favorites in your browser.	social bookmarking bookmark tag bookmarklet Pinterest StumbleUpon Delicious
6.3 Media Sharing	Media sharing websites let registered users upload and share photos, videos, music, or presentations. YouTube is owned by Google and is the most popular video sharing website in the world. A viral video is a video that spreads quickly via forwarded links, shared links, or word-of-mouth. Flickr is a photo sharing website that provides tools for users to upload, organize, and share photos. Spotify is a streaming music and video service with a library of over 30 million songs. The service can be used for free or with a paid subscription. Playlists and tracks can be saved and shared with friends. Instagram is a photo sharing app for use with a smartphone.	media sharing peer-to-peer (P2P) file sharing podcast podcatcher YouTube viral video Flickr Spotify Instagram

continued…

Topic	Key Concepts	Key Terms
6.4 Blogging	A blog is an online journal created at a blog hosting website, with the most recent post at the top of the page. All the blogs on the web collectively are referred to as the *blogosphere*. Writing and maintaining a blog is called *blogging*, and each entry on a blog is called a *blog post*, *post*, or *entry*. The person who writes a blog is called a *blogger*. A form of blogging that uses videos is called *vlogging*. A vlog is a blog with video as the primary content. A vlogger is someone who creates a video blog. WordPress is a blog website that uses the open source WordPress blogging software, in which a blog is typed inside a word processor–style window. Blogger, owned by Google, is a popular blogging tool that uses templates and a user-friendly interface. A microblog is a blog in which posts are restricted to a very small amount of text. A microblogger creates a microblog, which usually has posts about what is happening at the moment, with links to interesting content, pictures, or videos. Twitter is the most popular microblog. A post in Twitter, called a *tweet*, is limited to 140 characters or less, with the hashtag symbol (#) preceding a keyword that the author uses to categorize the tweet.	blog blogosphere blogging blog post blogger vlogging vlog vlogger WordPress Blogger microblog microblogger Twitter tweet hashtag symbol (#)
6.5 Wikis for User-Generated Content	A wiki website uses wiki software that allows any user not under a ban restriction to add or edit content. Wikis that provide encyclopedic information have thousands of editors who review and update content to ensure postings are well written and accurate. *Wikipedia* is the most used online encyclopedia. New contributors are encouraged to do a test edit in the *Wikipedia* Sandbox before editing a real *Wikipedia* article. wikiHow is a wiki website with thousands of how-to articles on a wide range of topics.	wiki wiki software *Wikipedia* *Wikipedia* Sandbox wikiHow
6.6 Social Media Strategies in Business	A category of e-commerce called *social commerce (s-commerce)*, refers to the use of social networks to support the buying and selling of products and services. Forever 21 used a hashtag campaign that invited customers to post photos of their favorite summer outfits, encouraging shopper-to-shopper interactions. Honda ran the five-day *#Cheerance* campaign, which coincided with the company's annual summer sales clearance events. During the week, amusing videos, GIFs, and visual jokes were circulated on social networks to spread cheer to people. Lowe's has a presence on popular social networks, using inspiration boards on Pinterest, *#FixinSix* home improvement videos on Vine, a company page on Facebook, and videos on multiple YouTube channels.	social commerce (s-commerce)

Recheck
Recheck your understanding of the topics covered in this chapter.

Workbook
Chapter review and assessment resources are available in the *Workbook* ebook.

Chapter 7

Computer Security and Privacy

 Precheck

Check your understanding of the topics covered in this chapter.

C hances are you spend most of your time online browsing the web, social networking, messaging, shopping, or doing research. A network intrusion can occur anytime you are online, leaving you vulnerable to security and privacy breaches. According to Interpol, **cybercrime** (illegal acts involving a computing device that occur on the Internet) is one of the fastest-growing crime areas, with organized crime groups increasingly controlling these illegal activities. Given the prevalence of cybercrime and other malicious computer threats, every person needs to understand and protect his or her computing equipment, data, and personal information from theft or misuse. In fact, some people believe each person has a responsibility to make sure his or her computer or mobile device is protected, because the security practices you follow affect others. If you allow your computer or mobile device to become infected with malware, your device could possibly infect others. Another possibility is that your infected device may be used to facilitate a network attack on another system without your knowledge.

Computer security, also known as *information security*, includes all activities related to protecting hardware, software, and data from loss due to unauthorized access or use, theft, natural disaster, and human error. In this chapter, you will learn about the various security and privacy concerns associated with using a computer connected to a network or the Internet, and strategies you can employ to secure your devices and data. You will also examine computer security issues related to mobile devices and ways you can secure a smartphone or tablet.

Learning Objectives

7.1 Explain various types of network risks that occur when computers are connected to a network or the Internet, and list preventive security strategies

7.2 Describe a botnet and a denial of service attack and the techniques used to protect against these types of intrusions

7.3 Distinguish various types of malware and discuss methods to prevent malware infections

7.4 Differentiate phishing, pharming, and clickjacking threats and identify best practices for thwarting these attacks

7.5 Recognize privacy concerns when using the Internet and strategies for safeguarding personal information

7.6 Identify mobile device security risks and techniques for minimizing risk

 SNAP If you are a SNAP user, go to your SNAP Assignments page to complete the Precheck, Tutorials, and Recheck.

7.1 Unauthorized Access and Unauthorized Use of Computer Resources

Connecting to a network at home, at work, or at school has many advantages that include sharing access to the Internet and the network's resources, storage, and software. However, these advantages come with risks. Network attacks occur often at business and government organizations. In this topic, you will learn about the types of risks associated with using a network, which include unauthorized access and unauthorized use, and ways in which a network can be protected from these threats.

No network is immune from the threat of intrusion by cybercriminals.

Unauthorized Access

Using a computer, network, or other resource without permission is referred to as **unauthorized access**. Unauthorized access happens when someone using programming or other technical skills gains entry without permission into a computer or other resource through the network. The term **hacker** refers to an individual who accesses a network without permission, and **hacking** describes activities involved in gaining unauthorized entry into a network's resources. Table 7.1 describes some recent network intrusions that made news headlines.

Some hackers have good intentions; they attempt to pinpoint weaknesses in network security and may even be hired by an organization to hack into the organization's own network. This type of hacker is called a **white hat**. A hacker who gains unauthorized access with malicious intent to steal data or for other personal gain is called a **black hat**.

Unauthorized access is often the result of network intrusions from hackers.

Wireless networks are used often in homes and workplaces. These networks become a target for hackers because they are relatively easy to infiltrate through methods such as war driving and piggybacking. Driving around with a portable computing device and trying to connect to

Table 7.1

Network Hacks That Have Made the Headlines

When the Hack Was Reported	Organization That Was Hacked	Data That Was Affected
December 2013	Target Corporation	Personal information for 70 million customers
July 2014	JPMorgan Chase	Personal information for 76 million bank account holders and 7 million small businesses
September 2014	Home Depot	Payment card data for 56 million customers
January 2015	Premera Blue Cross	Personal information and medical claims of 11 million patients
June 2015	US Office of Personnel Management	Personal information of 21.5 million federal government employees, contractors, and others

someone else's unsecured wireless network is **war driving**. Connecting to someone else's wireless network without the network owner's knowledge or consent to provide access is called **piggybacking** or *Wi-Fi piggybacking*. This often occurs when a neighbor is within range of another neighbor's or businesses' unsecured wireless network.

War driving is driving around a neighborhood looking for unsecured wireless networks.

Unauthorized Use

Using a computer, network, or other resource for purposes other than those intended is referred to as **unauthorized use**. Unauthorized use can occur when an employee uses the employer's computer for activities such as personal email, personal printing, or personal online shopping without the employer's permission. Another unauthorized use could occur when a student uses a computer on a school campus to send inappropriate messages or participate in other unacceptable conduct.

Strategies to Prevent Unauthorized Access

At home and in the workplace, unauthorized access is prevented by making sure that each authorized user is assigned a unique user name and password. Family members and employees are advised to choose a password that is not easy to guess and never to reveal it to anyone else or write it down in a visible location. Some workplaces require passwords to be changed every month, and the reuse of a password may be prohibited. When a device is not in use, the screen should be locked so that the password is required to sign back into the computer. Every computer user should choose a **strong password**, which is a password that is difficult to hack by humans or password detection software programs. A strong password meets the following criteria:

All networked computers and mobile devices should have user accounts with strong passwords.

- is a minimum of eight characters
- uses a combination of uppercase letters, lowercase letters, numbers, and symbols
- does not contain any dictionary words or words spelled backward
- does not contain consecutive or repeated numbers or letters
- has no personal information, such as a birthdate

In the workplace, entry to rooms with computing equipment is often secured with physical locks. Entry to these rooms may also require additional authentication before the door is unlocked. For example, the use of biometric devices is becoming more common. A biometric device authenticates a person's identity using physical characteristics, such as a fingerprint, iris scan, facial recognition, or voice recognition (Figure 7.1).

Good to Know

Many websites and financial institutions are now offering two-step authentication for signing into an account—a more secure authentication process. With two-step authentication, you are sent a randomly generated code via email message, text message, or an app on your smartphone. You then type in this code after entering your user name and password.

Figure 7.1

Access to computing equipment may be controlled using a biometric device, such as an iris or fingerprint scanner.

Figure 7.2

All computers and mobile devices connected to a network should have data pass through a firewall that blocks unwanted intrusions to the network.

Tutorial

What Is the Difference between a Hardware and Software Firewall?

All networked computing devices should also have a **firewall**, which is hardware, software, or a combination thereof that blocks unwanted access to the network (Figure 7.2). Operating systems (OSs), such as Windows, install with the firewall feature turned on by default (Figure 7.3). Incoming and outgoing network traffic is routed through firewalls that examine each message and block any communication that does not meet security criteria. Some routers that are used to share network or Internet access have a built-in firewall, which adds an extra layer of protection. Organizations with large networks install a piece of networking equipment that is a dedicated firewall.

Figure 7.3

In Windows, the firewall is turned on by default. You can view the firewall status or change the firewall settings in the Control Panel.

Check This Out ✓

http://CC2.Paradigm
College.net/Protect
Network

Go here to watch a video on steps to take to protect a home wireless network.

Securing a Wireless Network At home and at work, wireless routers and access points need to be secured from war drivers and piggybackers. The router or access point should require a network security key to gain access. Devices sold with a preset password should have the password changed to a strong password immediately. Wireless routers and access points should also use the highest security and encryption standard available for the device. **Encryption** scrambles communications between devices so that the data is not readable. **Wi-Fi Protected Access (WPA)** and **WPA2** are recent security standards that authenticate users and employ sophisticated encryption

A wireless access point is secured with a network security key and the highest level of encryption standard possible for the device.

techniques. Enable the WPA2 security standard if possible. Organizations may also install **intrusion detection software** that analyzes network traffic for suspicious data and alerts network administrators to possible system threats.

Strategies to Prevent Unauthorized Use

An **acceptable use policy (AUP)** describes for employees, students, or other network users the permitted uses and inappropriate uses for computing equipment and networks. Some organizations allow employees to use a workplace computer for personal use while the employee is on break; other organizations prohibit personal use of any kind.

Some organizations use monitoring software that provides reports on activities at each computer. For example, some software monitors websites visited and web searches conducted, and other software may even record social networking activity. Email monitoring is also conducted by some organizations.

Video surveillance, although usually part of a broader safety and security strategy, is another method organizations can use to monitor authorized access and authorized use of computers and networks.

AUPs spell out authorized and unauthorized activities on a network.

Blog Topic | **Should Employers Monitor Personal Use of a Business Smartphone?**

Many employers provide mobile employees with company-paid smartphones for business use. Does the employer have the right to monitor employees' Internet and messaging use of a business smartphone after business hours?

1. Write and post a blog entry that provides your response to the question.
2. Read at least two of your classmates' blogs and post one comment to each.
3. Submit your blog URL and the URLs of your classmates' blogs to your instructor in the manner she or he has requested.

Explore Further | How to Create a Strong Password That Is Easy to Remember

Passwords that meet all the criteria for a strong password can be difficult to remember. However, there are strategies that can help you create passwords that are both strong and easy to remember.

1. Find and read a minimum of two articles that describe techniques for creating a strong password.
2. Create a presentation that could be used as a self-guided tutorial for a new network user who needs to create a strong

password. Include the URLs of the articles that you read.
3. Save the presentation as **StrongPasswords-YourName**.
4. Submit the presentation to your instructor in the manner she or he has requested.

7.2 Botnets and Denial of Service Attacks

Tutorial
How Are Botnets Used
on the Internet?

Good to Know 🎓

According to
Kaspersky Lab (a
security company),
in the first quarter of
2015, cybercriminals
conducted over 23,000
botnet-assisted denial
of service attacks in 76
countries, with servers
in the United States,
Canada, and China as
the prime targets. In
the second quarter of
2015, Kaspersky Labs
noted that South Korea
became the third-place
target, displacing
Canada.

Two types of attacks on a computer network that cause disruption to network service are botnets and denial of service attacks. These malicious activities cause widespread network slowdowns and sometimes block authorized activity from taking place. In this topic, you will learn how a botnet spreads and how to prevent your computer from becoming compromised. You will also learn how a denial of service attack disrupts a network.

Botnets

A computer that is connected to the Internet and is controlled by a hacker or other cybercriminal without the owner's knowledge is called a **zombie** computer. A collection of zombie computers that work together to conduct an attack on another network is a **botnet**. Botnets are used by hackers or cybercriminals to send spam emails, spread viruses, or steal personal data. In some cases, the botnet may be used to conduct a denial of service attack.

A computer becomes a zombie when it is infected with software (usually a virus) that is hidden from the user. The computer can then be controlled remotely by the hacker or cybercriminal. Generally, the infection happens from one of the following events:

- The user clicks a link in an email or opens an email attachment that contains the malicious program code, which is then installed on the computer.
- The user downloads a video, image, or program from a website without realizing the file is a cover for the malicious program code; this method is often used at media sharing or peer-to-peer sharing websites.
- The user simply visits a website without realizing that the malicious code is being downloaded in the background.

Figure 7.4 illustrates a botnet spreading malicious code to a target computer. Once the target computer is infected, it joins the botnet. Table 7.2 (page 175) lists signs that may indicate your computer has become a zombie. Keep in mind that some of the symptoms listed in Table 7.2 could indicate other issues, such as lack of memory. Have the suspected PC checked by a professional to determine the cause of any symptoms.

To prevent your computer from becoming a zombie, make sure you have antivirus software automatically scheduled to scan and update, update the OS regularly, and have a firewall active at all times. If you think your computer is a zombie, immediately update your antivirus software and perform a full scan. In some cases, you may need to hire professional help to erase your hard disk drive and start from scratch by reinstalling only legitimate programs and data.

Figure 7.4

Zombie computers are
used, without their owners'
knowledge, as part of a botnet
to attack other computers.

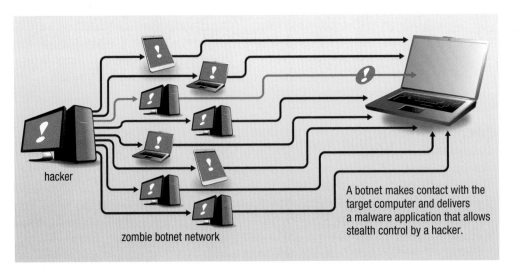

hacker

zombie botnet network

A botnet makes contact with the
target computer and delivers
a malware application that allows
stealth control by a hacker.

Table 7.2

Signs That Your Computer May Be a Zombie

Your Internet connectivity slows down consistently and dramatically and/or your browser closes frequently for no reason.
Hard disk activity occurs when you are not running any programs (including automatic antivirus or software updates).
Your computer or device becomes unresponsive, crashes frequently, or gives you unexplained error messages.
Hard disk space is filling up unexpectedly.
A different website (not the one you have set as your default) appears when you open the browser window.
New desktop icons or toolbars appear that you did not install.
Your email inbox contains undeliverable messages for people you did not email.

Denial of Service (DoS) Attacks

A **denial of service (DoS) attack** occurs when a network or web server is overwhelmed with network traffic in the form of a constant stream of bogus emails or other messages to the point that the server response time becomes slow or shuts down completely. Legitimate users are denied access, usually receiving a message that the server is busy. Popular or well-known companies and government websites are often the target of DoS attacks conducted by botnets. Figure 7.5 displays how a DoS attack is orchestrated.

Hackers or other cybercriminals perform DoS attacks for a variety of reasons, such as to draw attention to a social or political cause, to embarrass a company or government, to gain notoriety, or to make demands on a company. Organizations attempt to prevent DoS attacks by employing firewalls, intrusion detection software, and antivirus software tools.

> **Good to Know**
>
> In April 2015, Rutgers University's network was the target of a DoS attack that shut down Internet service across the campus. Some classes were canceled, and students were unable to complete assignments or tests in some classes. The university brought in the FBI to help find the attacker.

Figure 7.5
DoS attacks often target large corporate or government networks.

Explore Further   Best Practices for Preventing Botnets

Technology experts suggest that all computer users have a responsibility to ensure their PC or mobile device does not become part of a botnet. Learn how to protect your network and prevent your PC or mobile device from becoming a zombie.

1. Find and read at least two online articles that give strategies for how to protect a computer from becoming a zombie computer.

2. Create a document or presentation with a list of five best practices every computer user should adopt to help prevent the spread of botnets. Include the URLs of the articles you read.

3. Save the document as **PreventBotnets-YourName**.

4. Submit the document or presentation to your instructor in the manner she or he has requested.

7.3 Malware Infections

Any type of malicious software program that is designed to damage, disable, or steal data is called **malware**. Malware installs on your computer without your knowledge, usually from email or online activities. Malware programs can delete files, damage files, steal personal data, track your activities, display pop-up windows or messages, or turn your computer into a zombie. In this topic, you will learn about common malware that exists in the form of viruses, worms, Trojan horses, rootkits, and ransomware, as well as strategies to prevent malware from infecting your computer.

Viruses

A **virus** is a form of malware that, once installed on a host computer without the owner's knowledge, can replicate itself and spread to other media on the infected computer and to other computers on the network. A virus can infect a computer through a variety of means:

- downloading and installing infected software
- opening an infected file attachment in an email message (Figure 7.6)
- visiting an infected website
- plugging in an infected USB or other peripheral device
- clicking links in messages (including instant messages) or at untrustworthy websites

A **macro virus** is embedded in a document, which then infects the computer when the user opens the document and enables a macro. Microsoft Office documents were once a favorite target for macro viruses because of the popularity of the software suite. Microsoft improved security in its Office programs so that macros are automatically disabled when a document is opened. Always exercise caution enabling a macro in a document that was received via email.

In a **drive-by download**, the user's device is infected simply by visiting a compromised web page. The malware installs in the background when it encounters a browser, app, or OS that is out of date and has a security flaw. Always keep your OS and browser up-to-date, and use browser add-ons that block Flash or disable scripts.

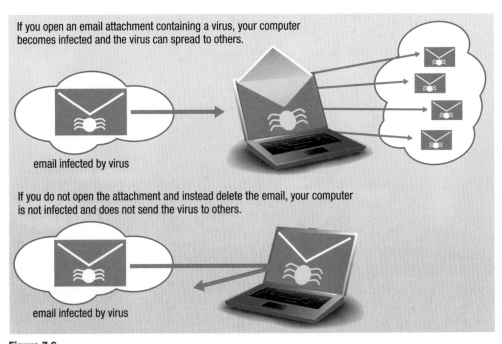

If you open an email attachment containing a virus, your computer becomes infected and the virus can spread to others.

email infected by virus

If you do not open the attachment and instead delete the email, your computer is not infected and does not send the virus to others.

email infected by virus

Figure 7.6

Opening an email attachment with a virus infects your computer and starts spreading the virus to others.

Worms

A self-replicating program that requires no action on the part of the user to copy itself to another computer on a network is called a **worm**. Your computer can become infected with a worm simply by being connected to an infected network (Figure 7.7). Worms typically exist to backlog network traffic or performance, or they may even shut down a network. In some cases, a worm is spread via a social network. For example, in March 2015, a worm was identified that propagated via Facebook. A user who posted an infected video spread the worm to all the user's friends and groups—effectively becoming a bot.

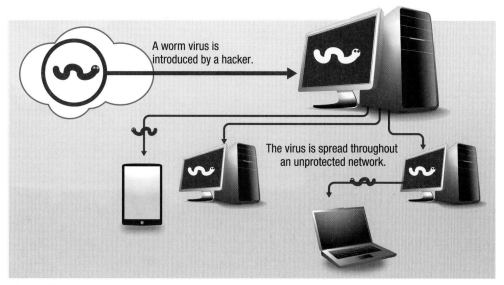

Figure 7.7

A worm automatically sends copies of itself to other computers on the network.

> ### Good to Know
> Macs, once considered safe from viruses, have been the focus of new malware, as hackers have turned their attention to popular Apple devices, such as the iPad and iPhone.

Trojan Horses

A program that disguises itself as a useful program but then infects your computer with malware when you run the application is called a **Trojan horse**. This type of malware is named after the legend in which Greeks concealed themselves inside a hollow wooden horse to invade the city of Troy. Residents of Troy thought the horse was a victory trophy and brought it inside the gates of the city, thereby allowing the city to be overtaken. Similarly, Trojan horse malware often appears as a useful program, such as antivirus software or an OS update, to entice you to run the application that installs the malware. Trojans do not replicate themselves, but the damage done by them can be disastrous. Some Trojans, for example, are designed to send personal information back to a cybercriminal.

A Trojan horse is disguised as a useful program, tricking you into running a program that installs the malware.

> ### Good to Know
> A program that is not classified as malware but is considered nuisance software, or within a "gray zone" of malware, is a potentially unwanted program (PUP). A PUP is usually not malicious but uses system resources, slowing down PC performance. PUPs can also covertly track your activities and modify system settings. A PUP is installed when you download some other software. Avoid PUPs by paying attention during installation of software. Deselect check boxes for additional software or add-ons, or say no when asked if you want to install these items.

Rootkits

A **rootkit** program hides on the infected computer and provides a **back door** (way to bypass computer security) for a hacker or other cybercriminal to remotely monitor or take over control of the PC. Using the remote access, the hacker or cybercriminal can run damaging programs or steal personal information. Unlike viruses and worms, the objective of a rootkit is intended not to spread to other computers but to control the target PC. Rootkits may end up on your computer by piggybacking on the installation of some other software or via a virus.

A rootkit is very hard to detect because the program is designed to be invisible by masquerading as an essential OS file. Antivirus software may overlook the file, and even the OS may think the file is a system file and prevent its removal. Companies that sell antivirus and security software usually offer a standalone utility program designed to detect and remove rootkits.

A hidden program called a *rootkit* can allow a hacker to monitor your activity or steal personal data.

Ransomware

A type of malware that locks a computer or restricts access to the computer, demanding that the user pay the malware creator to unlock the device or provide an unlock code, is called **ransomware**. In some cases, the contents of the hard drive are encrypted by the malware. Initially, ransomware installed when a user opened an email attachment that contained the malware. However, early in 2015, the FBI warned the public that it was seeing more incidents of users infecting their computers simply by clicking on a compromised website, often after being lured to the website via an email message or pop-up ad. In the first quarter of 2015, McAfee Labs (an Internet security company) reported a 165 percent increase in ransomware over 2014.

Malware Protection

All computer users need to have an up-to-date **antivirus program** running on their computers at all times. This type of program is set up to run automatic scans on a regular basis during a time when the computer is not likely to be in use. Most antivirus programs also scan all incoming emails automatically. You will need to check the settings in a particular program to ensure real-time protection is turned on.

New computers are sold with an antivirus program already installed for a trial period. Some OSs also include malware protection. However, you may want to use a different program or upgrade to a comprehensive suite of online threat

Some antivirus companies, such as Bitdefender, offer a free online scanning tool.

protection. Check reviews and look for information from trusted sources about the antivirus program that detects and removes malware the best. For example, you can buy a program or subscription for Bitdefender, Kaspersky, Webroot, or McAfee—these are just four of several companies that offer antivirus programs. Most antivirus software companies offer programs packaged in a suite of Internet security utilities or separate, standalone security programs. If you have one or more mobile devices, look for a suite that includes protection for smartphones and tablets. You will also find free antivirus software available from companies such as Microsoft or AVG. Microsoft provides Windows Security Essentials free for computers using Windows 7, and Windows Defender free for computers using Windows 8.1 and later (Figure 7.8).

Be wary of downloading free antivirus software from an ad or pop-up window that appears when you are on a website. Go directly to the website of a company that you know is trusted, and download free software from there. Regardless of the malware protection program you choose, make sure it runs automatically and scans regularly, and that a firewall is always active.

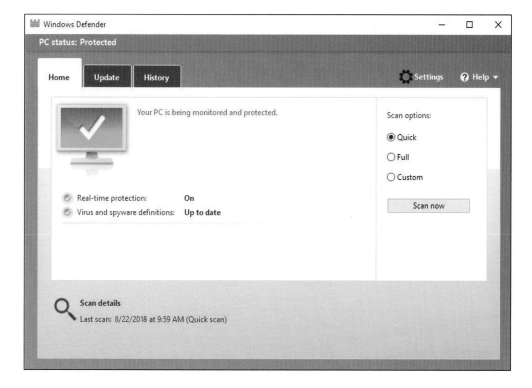

Figure 7.8
Windows Defender is included with Windows 10 and runs automatically to provide protection against malware and other unwanted software.

Security Alert   **Do Regular Backups**

Making regular backups of your data will provide the best protection of all. Create a routine to back up data regularly. Should malware strike your system, you will have another copy of important information safely stored somewhere else.

Explore Further   **What Is a Logic Bomb?**

Another type of malware that can cause damage to your computer is a logic bomb virus. What are the characteristics of this type of malware? What is the most common type of activity that activates the virus? Are there uses for a logic bomb that are not malicious?

1. Search online for information on logic bombs and read at least two articles to find answers to the above questions.

2. Create a document or presentation that summarizes in your own words what you learned about logic bombs. Include the URLs of the websites you used.

3. Save the document or presentation as **LogicBombs-YourName**.

4. Submit the document or presentation to your instructor in the manner she or he has requested.

7.4 Phishing, Pharming, and Clickjacking Threats

A growing area of cybercrime involves online fraud or scams designed to trick unsuspecting users into revealing personal information so the criminal can steal money from the individual or engage in identity theft. **Identity theft** occurs when an individual's personal information is obtained by a criminal, who then uses the information to buy products or services under the victim's name or to pose as the victim for financial gain. In this topic, you will learn about three scams used to obtain personal information: phishing, pharming, and clickjacking.

Phishing

Phishing (pronounced *fishing*) is the term that describes activities that appear to be initiated by a legitimate organization (such as a bank) in an attempt to obtain personal information that can be used in fraud, theft, or identity theft. A popular email phishing technique involves receiving a message that appears to be from a bank or credit card company and directs the user to click a link (Figure 7.9). The link goes to a bogus website that appears to be valid and may even include a real bank's logo and color scheme. At the phishing website, the user is prompted to enter personal information, such as a user name, password, bank account number, or credit card number. If the individual complies, a criminal now has critical personal information and will use it to transfer money from the individual's bank accounts or to charge purchases to a credit card.

Phishing is growing on social networking sites, owing to the high volume of activity on these sites. For instance, in 2015, coinciding with the excitement of the launch of the Apple Watch, Facebook and Twitter were used to lure people into entering personal information in a fake giveaway. Those who succumbed to the scam entered their full names and Facebook handle and were then asked to invite 100 friends to do the same—with 100 invites earning the user an Apple Watch. Twitter users who mentioned the smartwatch in a tweet were also directed to the scam at fake accounts named Apple Giveaways.

Tutorial

What Are Current Trends in Phishing Attacks?

Good to Know

According to the 2015 *Anti-Phishing Working Group* report, over 1 million unique phishing email reports were filed by consumers from January to September, which was double the number of reports received in 2014.

Check This Out ✔

http://CC2.Paradigm College.net/Report Phishing

Go here to submit a report about a phishing message you have received.

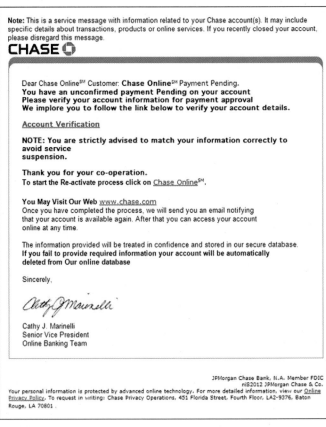

Figure 7.9

This message received by Chase customers was a phishing attempt to trick users into clicking the links and revealing account information.

Pharming

Pharming is similar to phishing except that the individual is tricked into typing in personal information at a phony website that appears to be the real website. One type of pharming attack generates an email that installs code on the user's computer without the user's knowledge, and the code then modifies files on the computer. In other pharming cases, the attack compromises the IP address for a Domain Name System (DNS) server. When an individual enters the correct web address for a website, such as his or her bank, the malicious code redirects the URL, sending the victim to a fake web page. The web page at the pharming website looks legitimate, so the individual proceeds to enter personal information.

Phishing and pharming scams employ **spoofing** techniques, in which a sender's email address is altered to a phony address that appears legitimate to the email recipient, or an IP address is altered to appear to be a trusted source.

Pharming scams redirect you to a phony website where you are prompted to enter personal information.

Clickjacking

Clickjacking occurs when a button, graphic, or link on a web page appears to be real but, when clicked, causes malicious software to run. The malicious software code is hidden so that users have no idea that they are not clicking a real link. The bogus button, graphic, or link directs users to another website, where personal information is requested or malware is installed.

In some Facebook clickjacking schemes, a bogus Like button redirects users to advertising pages where the scammers receive money for each wayward clicker. Techniques used in clickjacking scams often involve a breaking news story, exclusive content or contest lure, or a trending news item. Be cautious of clicking links or buttons for something that appears too good to be true or seems unlikely, such as a celebrity death hoax.

Clickjacking scams use buttons, graphics, or links to redirect users from legitimate websites or run malicious software.

Identity theft scams often initiate in email. Delete messages you receive that ask you to click a link to update information. Never click links in unsolicited email messages. Before typing personal information on any web page, examine the URL and other text on the page. Phony websites usually have spelling or grammar errors, or the URL for a false website will have a slightly different domain name or character substitution in the name, such as the number *1* instead of the letter *i*.

Explore Further   What Is Social Engineering?

Security experts know that the weakest link in computer security is human. Unfortunately, cybercriminals also know this and employ social engineering tactics to gain unauthorized access to a network or trick individuals into revealing personal information. How will you know a social engineer is trying to trick you?

1. Search online for articles on social engineering. Find and read at least two articles that describe social engineering tactics, including tactics used at social networking websites.

2. Create a document or presentation that summarizes in your own words what you learned about social engineering. Include the URLs of the websites you used.

3. Save the document or presentation as **SocialEngineering-YourName**.

4. Submit the document or presentation to your instructor in the manner she or he has requested.

7.5 Information Privacy

With so much information collected and stored online, individuals and companies are increasingly concerned with information privacy. **Information privacy** is the right of individuals or organizations to control the information collected about them. Consider all the websites at which you have set up accounts and the personal information you provided at each site. Consider also that some websites track the pages you visit and store information about you. Software may be installed on your computer that is tracking everything you do. In this topic, you will learn about privacy concerns related to online activities.

Cookies

A web server may send a small text file to be stored on your computer hard disk that contains data about you, such as your user name and the pages you visited. This text file is called a **cookie** and is used to identify you when you return to the website. In many cases, the use of cookies is welcomed; they are helpful when used to prefill a login screen or customize your viewing preferences at an e-commerce site. However, cookies might also be used for unwanted purposes, such as tracking your activities or gathering information about you without your permission.

All Internet browsers provide the ability for you to control how cookies are handled. Figure 7.10 shows the Cookies section in the Advanced settings panel for Microsoft Edge, where you can choose how to manage cookies. The default setting is *Don't block cookies*. This setting can be changed to *Block all cookies* or *Block only third-party cookies*. Blocking all cookies is not recommended because signing in to websites that you use frequently becomes difficult without the website cookie installed on your hard drive. A third-party cookie is a cookie placed on your hard drive by a domain that is different from the domain of the web page you are visiting. For example, if you are viewing a web page from the domain shoppingsite.com and a cookie is placed on your system from adtracker.com while viewing that page, the adtracker.com cookie is considered a third-party cookie. Third-party cookies are often designed to track your surfing habits. Many people choose to block third-party cookies as a precaution against behind-the-scenes tracking by websites.

Figure 7.10

Internet browser software such as Microsoft Edge provides options to help you manage cookies.

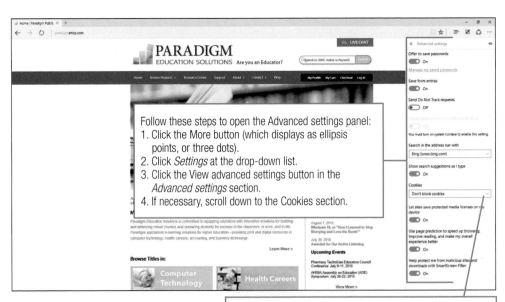

Follow these steps to open the Advanced settings panel:
1. Click the More button (which displays as ellipsis points, or three dots).
2. Click *Settings* at the drop-down list.
3. Click the View advanced settings button in the *Advanced settings* section.
4. If necessary, scroll down to the Cookies section.

The default option is *Don't block cookies*. Click here to choose either *Block all cookies* or *Block only third-party cookies*. Click in the browser window away from the panel to close the panel.

Spyware

Software programs that exist on your computer without your knowledge and track your activities are referred to as **spyware**. Some spyware may be on your workplace computer so that your employer can monitor your online activities. Other spyware may be used by websites to target ads to your preferences. Antivirus programs typically include spyware detection and removal.

A version of spyware called **keystroke logger**, or *keylogger*, may be activated as part of a rootkit or Trojan horse that records every keystroke you type and sends it back to a cybercriminal. Keystroke loggers may be used to obtain your bank account number and password or other personal information that leads to identity theft. Some keystroke logger software is promoted on the Internet to businesses as a computer security tool and to parents who want to monitor their children's online activity.

Programs responsible for pop-up ads that appear on your desktop or while viewing web pages are the result of software referred to as **adware**. These unwelcome ads often piggyback spyware onto your computer. Early in 2015, technology company Lenovo made headlines when an adware program called Superfish, preinstalled on new Lenovo PCs, was found to have a flawed design that left users vulnerable to a **man-in-the-middle (MITM) attack**. An MITM attack occurs when a hacker intercepts communications between a user and a website, usually for purposes of capturing personal information. In the Lenovo case, Superfish adware left a hole in the security on the user's PC that meant a hacker could install malware on the device. In May 2015, Lenovo was served with a class action lawsuit over the adware debacle.

Spam

Spam is electronic junk mail—unsolicited email sent to a large group of people at the same time. Spam messages entice readers to buy something, are phishing messages, or are vehicles used to distribute Trojan viruses in attachments or via a link the user clicks in the message, or are vehicles used to distribute Trojan viruses in attachments or via a link the user clicks in the message. Spam messaging has infiltrated social networks and text messages. According to Kaspersky Lab (an Internet security company), on average, between 53 and 62 percent of email was spam in the first half of 2015. A Kaspersky Lab analyst wrote that an increase in the use of real-life tragic events in spam was noticed in 2015. For example, the April 2015 Nepalese earthquake was used by spammers in emails asking the recipient to make a donation to help earthquake victims. Never click a link in an unsolicited email to make a donation. A **Twitter bot** is software programmed to follow people based on popular keywords. When a user clicks a link in the comment that appears as a response to a tweet, they receive spam or malware. Beware of followers with strange handles.

Obtaining a store loyalty card or registering for free accounts often requires you to provide your email address. These databases of names and email addresses are sold for marketing purposes, which is how you end up with spam. Many people use a free web-based email account at hosts such as Outlook.com or Gmail for online activities only. This helps to reduce the amount of spam invading the email inbox you use for personal or work messaging. Sign up for a new account when spam at the free account becomes onerous.

Spyware tracks your online activities.

Good to Know

The United States Secret Service issued an advisory in July 2014 about keystroke logger malware used on computers in business centers at major hotels in the Dallas/Fort Worth area to obtain large amounts of sensitive personal information from guests.

Spyware called a *keystroke logger* records every keystroke you type.

Spam is estimated to account for more than 53 percent of all email traffic!

Ways to Protect Personal Information

When shopping online or conducting other business that requires a financial transaction, make sure the URL at the website begins with *https* and that you see a small closed padlock next to the Address bar or in the Status bar of the browser window. These signs indicate a secure website using a protocol that protects data sent to the site with **Transport Layer Security (TLS)**, which encrypts transmitted data so that the data is unreadable if intercepted.

Table 7.3 provides strategies you can use to protect personal information while pursuing online activities. Ultimately, you are responsible for keeping sensitive information private and being diligent at websites where you provide personal data. Check privacy policies and do not reveal information that you do not feel is necessary for the purpose of the visit.

Table 7.3

Ways to Minimize Tracking of Your Personal Information

Fill in only the fields marked with asterisks at websites that ask you for personal information when registering for an account; these are the minimum fields required to obtain an account.
Consider changing the privacy option in the browser that you use to block third-party cookies.
At websites that require a birthdate, such as Facebook, make sure you hide the date in your profile.
Have different user names and use strong passwords for online shopping, social networks, and banking. Make sure the answers to security questions you have set up to recover your password from websites are not easily gleaned from other information about you that is online.
Do not allow apps or websites to tag your location. Geo-location apps on your smartphone may sound cool, but consider that a third party could be tracking your every movement.
Use a free web-based email account for online shopping and social networks and keep your regular email address for other purposes.
If your ISP does not use a spam filter on your email account, find and install anti-spam software on your own.
Delete spam messages right away without opening them.
Unsubscribe to mailing lists that you think are selling your email address for marketing purposes.
Regularly clear the history in your browser.
Make sure the antivirus program you use includes antispyware and that the program is set to automatically update and scan your computer regularly.
Make sure a firewall is active at all times you are online.
Do not reveal personal details in status updates or other posts that may allow someone to determine where you live.
Shred documents with personal information before discarding them.

Data Privacy in the Cloud

When storing pictures, documents, or other data at a cloud provider website, such as Flickr or Dropbox, find out the privacy and security policies that affect your data. Typically, you control the data privacy by restricting who can see a file. However, unanticipated issues could arise, such as an employee of the cloud provider being able to view the contents of your files. To be safe, never post at a cloud provider files containing sensitive information, such as your birthdate and social security number, that could make you vulnerable to identity theft.

At social networks, such as Facebook and Twitter, make sure you review and change privacy settings so that only the information you want public is viewable by anyone. In Facebook, check the information about you that is public. To do this, go to your Profile page in your Facebook account, click the button next to View Activity Log with the ellipsis (three dots), and then click *View As*. The next page shows you what your profile looks like to anyone who searches for your name in Facebook.

Change your profile if you see personal information that should not be shared with the general public. When posting information at social networks, also consider that friends who see the information could inadvertently share something personal about you with someone else.

Cybercriminals are trolling social networks for personal data they can mine for financial gain. Three popular methods cybercriminals use on social networks is to place offers for free gifts (such as a smartphone), post scandalous news or a death hoax about a celebrity, or post news about a tragic world event. Generally, once you click one of these items in your news feed, you are asked to fill out a survey, invited to download software that is really malware, or redirected to a website with a drive-by download. Often, you are encouraged to share the post on your timeline to entice your friends to do the same activity. Don't answer surveys in social networks, and do practice the advice *Think before you click!*

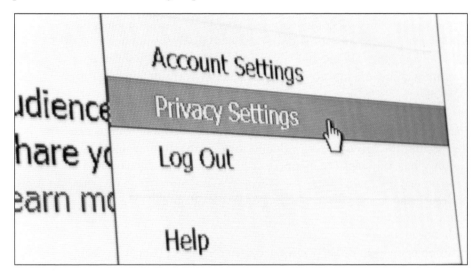

Change privacy settings at social networks, such as Facebook, and at cloud provider websites to control information about you that is available for others to view.

Good to Know

In Facebook, run the Privacy Checkup tool to go through a three-step process to review your current privacy settings. To start Privacy Checkup, click the Privacy Shortcuts button (to the right of the Notifications button) at the top of the your account window, then click *Privacy Checkup*. The utility shows you the audience for your posts, the apps you have logged in to using Facebook, and information in your profile that is visible to others.

Blog Topic   **Is Employer Monitoring an Invasion of Privacy?**

Video cameras, email monitoring, website monitoring, and keystroke loggers are some of the ways employers can keep tabs on what their employees are up to at the workplace. Generally, employees should not have an expectation of privacy when using employer-owned computing equipment. Still, is all this monitoring of activities an invasion of privacy? What about using the employer's computer during lunch hours and breaks? Shouldn't that be considered the employee's personal time?

1. Write and post a blog entry that provides your opinion about the questions.

2. Read at least two of your classmates' blogs and post one comment to each.

3. Submit your blog URL and the URLs of your classmates' blogs to your instructor in the manner she or he has requested.

Explore Further   **Learning about Privacy Notices**

Websites that collect personal information also have a privacy notice that spells out how the organization will use the personal data you provide. Have you ever read a privacy notice? What should a typical privacy notice include?

1. Go to the website of an e-tailer that you have used in the past, and find and read the privacy policy or privacy notice link. If you have not made an online purchase, visit the website of a well-known e-tailer, such as Amazon.

2. Create a document or presentation with a summary in your own words of how personal information will be used, stored, and safeguarded by the e-tailer. Include the URL to the policy you used.

3. Save the document or presentation as **PrivacyPolicy-YourName**.

4. Submit the document or presentation to your instructor in the manner she or he has requested.

7.6 Mobile Device Security

Mobile devices such as notebooks, ultrabooks, tablets, and smartphones have untethered people from their homes and offices; however, the portable nature of these devices makes them vulnerable to security risks. In this topic, you will examine the various security risks for mobile users and methods used to protect hardware and data from loss due to cybercrime, theft, or other circumstances.

Mobile Malware

According to Internet security company McAfee Labs, **mobile malware** (viruses designed for mobile devices) increased 49 percent from the last quarter of 2014 to the first quarter in 2015. Android devices are a popular target for malware because of the open source nature of their OS; however, no mobile OS is without risk. A smartphone or tablet may get a virus via an infected app downloaded from an app store or the web, an infected computer connected to the device, an attachment sent via email or text message, or a Bluetooth connection in close proximity.

Make sure your smartphones and tablets have mobile security software to shield the devices from malware. All app stores offer free mobile security apps.

Mobile malware is increasing each year. Each smartphone and tablet should be protected with mobile security software.

Lost or Stolen Mobile Devices

Securing a mobile device with locks, biometrics, and/or remote tools is necessary to protect against the loss of a device due to theft or absentmindedness. While the hardware may be easily replaced, the personal information and data stored on the device usually has the higher value for individuals and employers. The following tools assist with securing mobile devices and data (see also Figure 7.11):

- Many devices are equipped with fingerprint readers that restrict access to the authenticated user only.
- A strong password or passcode for access to the device should be enabled; should the device be stolen or lost, the password/passcode may provide enough time to employ remote wiping utilities.
- Physical locks with cables that attach a notebook to a table or desk in a public place are a deterrent to thieves looking for an easy target.
- Technology for remote wiping, locking, and tracking of a lost or stolen mobile device lets the owner wipe the device clean of data and track its location.
- Regular backups of data stored on mobile devices should be mandatory.

> **Good to Know** 🎓
>
> In May 2015, smartphone owners were urged to be cautious when a wave of ransomware viruses spread to mobile devices. The viruses locked devices and demanded payment to an offshore bank account for an unlock code.

Figure 7.11

Mobile devices can be secured with fingerprint readers, passcodes or passwords, and physical cable locks to restrict access.

Bluetooth Risks

Bluetooth technology, which wirelessly connects and exchanges data between two devices in close proximity, is subject to risk from intrusion by others within range. Bluetooth range can be from 3 to 300 feet, depending on the power class of the device. When using Bluetooth in a public space with many people nearby, a risk exists

Tutorial
What Risks Are Involved in Using Bluetooth?

that someone else can connect to your device and send you a virus or access personal data. Turn Bluetooth on only when needed and turn it off as soon as you are finished with it. Consider installing a Bluetooth firewall app that will secure your device from unwanted intrusions.

Mobile devices carry risks unique to their portable nature. Employers may require employees with mobile devices to abide by a mobile computing policy. A mobile computing policy usually requires employees to take responsible measures to secure notebooks, tablets, or smartphones while away from the office, make frequent backups to a secure site, and password protect all sensitive company documents stored on the device.

To reduce security risks, turn off Bluetooth when using a mobile device in a crowded place.

Security Alert | Be Aware of Shoulder Surfers

If you are viewing sensitive or confidential information on a mobile device, protect your screen from shoulder surfers. Privacy screens for notebooks, tablets, and smartphones prevent shoulder surfers from seeing what is on your screen. Be aware of your surroundings!

Career Connection

Computer Security Experts

Computer security is a top priority for many organizations as they strive to protect against network attacks and cybercrime activities. A 2016 report from Cisco Systems (a network hardware manufacturer) estimates that one million job openings exist for cybersecurity professionals. Security professionals are among the highest paid IT workers. A bachelor's degree in computer science or computer security is generally required for a computer security career. Certifications attract higher salaries, and a wide variety of security certifications are available. For someone starting out in the field, the CompTIA Security+ and the GIAC Security Essentials certification from the Global Information Assurance Certification organization are a good foundation.

Explore Further | Using Public Wi-Fi Wisely

Public Wi-Fi networks are unsecured to make them as convenient to use as possible. What precautions should you take when using a public Wi-Fi network to connect your notebook, tablet, or smartphone?

1. Find and read at least two online articles with tips for using public Wi-Fi networks safely. Choose the five tips you think are the most important.

2. Create a presentation with one slide for each tip that describes what you learned. Include a sixth slide with the URLs of the articles you used.

3. Save the presentation as **PublicWi-Fi-YourName**.

4. Submit the presentation to your instructor in the manner she or he has requested.

Topics Review

Topic	Key Concepts	Key Terms
7.1 Unauthorized Access and Unauthorized Use of Computer Resources	Illegal acts involving a computing device on the Internet is cybercrime.	cybercrime
	Computer security activities are related to protecting hardware, software, and data from loss due to unauthorized access, unauthorized use, theft, natural disaster, or human error.	computer security
		unauthorized access
	Unauthorized access occurs when someone gains entry without permission to a computer through a network.	hacker
		hacking
	A hacker is an individual who accesses a network without permission, while hacking describes activities used to gain unauthorized access to a network.	white hat
		black hat
	A white hat is a hacker who gains entry into a network to pinpoint weaknesses in the network security.	war driving
		piggybacking
	A black hat is a hacker who gains entry into a network with malicious intent.	unauthorized use
		strong password
	War driving occurs when someone drives around with a portable device trying to connect to someone else's unsecured wireless network.	biometric device
		firewall
	Piggybacking refers to connecting to a wireless network without the network owner's permission.	encryption
		Wi-Fi Protected Access (WPA)
	Unauthorized use is performing activities on a computer other than the intended uses.	WPA2
		intrusion detection software
	A strong password is difficult to hack by humans or password detection software programs.	acceptable use policy (AUP)
	Physical entry to rooms with computing equipment at workplaces is secured by locks and biometric devices. A biometric device uses physical characteristics of an individual to authenticate identity.	
	A firewall is hardware, software, or a combination thereof that blocks unauthorized access.	
	Encryption scrambles communications between devices so that the data is unreadable to anyone except the originator and intended recipient of a transmission.	
	Wi-Fi Protected Access (WPA) and WPA2 are the most recent encryption standards used in wireless routers and access points.	
	Organizations may use intrusion detection software that analyzes network traffic for suspicious data to thwart network attacks.	
	An acceptable use policy (AUP) spells out appropriate and inappropriate use of computing equipment in the workplace.	

continued…

Topic	Key Concepts	Key Terms
7.2 Botnets and Denial of Service Attacks	A zombie is a computer controlled by a hacker or cybercriminal without the owner's knowledge.	zombie
	A collection of zombie computers that attack a network is called a *botnet*.	botnet
	A computer becomes a zombie by being infected with software, usually from a virus, that is hidden from the user.	denial of service (DoS) attack
	To prevent a computer from becoming a zombie, scan regularly with up-to-date antivirus software, update the OS regularly, and make sure a firewall is always active.	
	A denial of service (DoS) attack occurs when a botnet attacks a network by sending a constant stream of messages that slow down or completely shut down a server.	
	Organizations use firewalls, intrusion detection software, and antivirus tools to prevent DoS attacks.	
7.3 Malware Infections	Malware refers to any type of malicious software.	malware
	A virus is a form of malware that replicates itself, spreading to other media on the infected computer and to other computers.	virus
	A macro virus is a virus embedded in a document macro; when the user enables the macro, the virus infects the computer.	macro virus
	A drive-by download occurs when the user's computer is infected simply by visiting a compromised website using an out-of-date browser, app, or OS that has a security flaw.	drive-by download
	A worm is a self-replicating program that infects other computers on a network without user action.	worm
	A Trojan horse is a program that appears to the user to be a useful program but which in fact is malware.	Trojan horse
	Rootkit programs provide a back door (a way to bypass security) for a hacker or cybercriminal to control a computer remotely.	rootkit
	Ransomware is a form of malware where the target device is locked or encrypted and a demand for payment is made by the malware creator to provide the owner with an unlock code.	back door
	Antivirus programs detect and remove malware.	ransomware
		antivirus program
7.4 Phishing, Pharming, and Clickjacking Threats	Identity theft occurs when personal information is obtained by a criminal who uses the information for financial gain.	identity theft
	Phishing activities usually occur in messages that appear to be legitimate but are intended to steal personal information by convincing the user to click a link to a phishing website where the user enters personal information.	phishing
	Pharming is where malicious code redirects a URL to a fake web page after a person types a web address at which the unsuspecting user enters personal information.	pharming
	Spoofing techniques alter a sender's email address or a web address so that they appear legitimate.	spoofing
	Clickjacking occurs when a user clicks a phony button, image, or link and is redirected to another website or a virus downloads to the device.	clickjacking

continued…

Topic	Key Concepts	Key Terms
7.5 Information Privacy	Information privacy refers to the rights of individuals to control information that is collected about them.	information privacy
	A cookie is a small text file placed on your hard drive by a web server with information about your user name and the pages you visited.	cookie
	Spyware is software that tracks your activities without your knowledge.	spyware
	Keystroke loggers, or keyloggers, record every keystroke you type and send the data to a cybercriminal.	keystroke logger
	Adware displays pop-up ads on your desktop or at web pages and will sometimes piggyback spyware onto your computer.	adware
	A man-in-the-middle (MITM) attack occurs when a hacker intercepts communications between a user and a website for purposes of capturing personal information.	man-in-the-middle (MITM) attack
	Spam is unsolicited email sent to large groups of people.	spam
	A Twitter bot is software programmed to follow people based on popular keywords and usually results in spam or malware when a user clicks a link in a tweet posted by a bot.	Twitter bot
	A closed padlock next to the Address bar and *https* at the beginning of a website address are signs indicating that the website is a secure website using Transport Layer Security (TLS), which encrypts transmitted data.	Transport Layer Security (TLS)
	Find out the privacy and security policies in effect at cloud-providing websites where you store pictures and documents.	
	Review and change privacy settings at social networks, such as Facebook and Twitter.	
7.6 Mobile Device Security	Mobile malware are viruses designed for mobile devices.	mobile malware
	Android devices are attacked more frequently due to their open source mobile operating system.	
	A smartphone or tablet gets a virus by downloading an infected app, by being connected to an infected computer, from a message attachment, or via a Bluetooth connection.	
	All mobile devices including tablets and smartphones should have mobile security software installed.	
	Mobile devices should be secured with locks, biometrics, or remote wiping and tracking tools in case of loss or theft.	
	Using Bluetooth in a public space leaves you vulnerable; someone else with a Bluetooth device can access your smartphone, tablet, or notebook and send you a virus or steal personal data.	
	Employers may require mobile workers to abide by a mobile computing policy that requires them to take responsible measures to secure their devices.	

 Recheck
Recheck your understanding of the topics covered in this chapter.

 Workbook
Chapter review and assessment resources are available in the *Workbook* ebook.

Buying a New Computing Device

Buying a new notebook, tablet, or smartphone requires an understanding of the technical jargon that often appears in computer ads. An experienced electronics sales associate will help you choose the right device; however, some people like to shop online or find out in advance the features that are important to consider. In this appendix, you will learn to shop for a device that meets your needs using a step-by-step buying process model.

Buying a New PC or Tablet

Are you in the market for a new computer or are you looking to add a second device to supplement a computer you already own? Many people own more than one computing device. Perhaps you have a desktop PC and want a notebook or tablet to use for school. The following pages will guide you through a decision-making process that will help you make an informed purchase. Spending a little time planning your requirements will save time and money and help you avoid making an impulse purchase you may regret.

A section with tips for making a smartphone purchase is included at the end of the appendix. The following steps are geared toward deciding how to buy a personal computer or tablet.

Step 1: Determine Your Maximum Budget

Before you start browsing computer ads, know how much money you can afford to spend. Computers are sold in a wide range of prices, from a few hundred dollars to a few thousand dollars, to suit a variety of budgets. Setting your maximum price will help narrow the search when you are ready to shop.

Start by setting the maximum budget.

Step 2: Decide on a Desktop, Notebook, Ultrabook, or Tablet

Desktop PCs are declining in usage, but nevertheless, some people prefer the stationary system unit that sits on or under a desk with an attached monitor, keyboard, and mouse. If you normally work in one place and have the physical space to accommodate the larger PC, a desktop is a good value. The desktop PCs of today last longer than earlier desktops and are easier to upgrade than most mobile devices. All-in-one PCs pack all the system unit components behind the monitor, which requires less desktop space. Desktop PCs also include a larger screen for easier viewing of content.

You will need to decide between a desktop PC, notebook, ultrabook, convertible laptop, or tablet.

If you are looking for a portable computer for school or work that you can move around the house, that has a full-size keyboard with all the power and capability of a traditional desktop, and that has a medium-size screen, then a notebook or ultrabook is what you need. Which option you choose will depend on how you plan to use it. A notebook computer provides everything a traditional desktop PC provides, in a portable case that you can carry around. Notebooks are available in a wide variety of configurations and screen sizes. The weight of a notebook varies: some smaller units weigh in at 2.5 pounds, but those with a larger screen can top the scales at over 7 pounds. An ultrabook is lighter and slimmer than a notebook, with most models weighing less than 3 pounds. The battery on an ultrabook lasts longer than that in a traditional notebook. If your computing needs are primarily just surfing the web, and sending and receiving email, a low-cost notebook with a small screen, sometimes called a *netbook*, may be for you.

Tablets are smaller and lighter than notebooks. Typically, people buy a tablet as a secondary device, with a desktop or notebook PC serving as their primary device. However, the available options include convertible tablet PCs (with screens that rotate 180 degrees to fold over a keyboard) and tablets supplied with a docking station that includes a full-size keyboard. If you want to use a touchscreen, or a stylus to handwrite notes, a tablet is the way to go.

Step 3: Decide on the Software Applications and Operating System

Computers come with an operating system and some software applications preinstalled, so you may be tempted to skip this step. However, this step is important because it can help you keep within your budget. Watch for systems that preinstall limited trial editions of software applications. These applications usually expire within a short time frame, such as 90 days, or at some point within the first year after purchase. Following expiration, you have to pay a license fee to continue using the software. You need to find out in advance if you will have to set aside money to pay for software applications separately.

Check your school's computer store to see if you can buy software applications at academic pricing, or even get software for free. For example, Microsoft provides free software, such as Microsoft Office, to eligible students at some qualifying schools (see Figure A.1). Some academic licenses have to be purchased through your school to qualify for student discounts; however, increasingly, retailers are able to offer the same pricing upon proof of student registration.

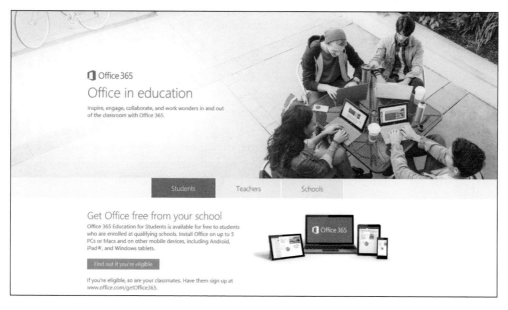

Figure A.1

The Microsoft Education program provides Microsoft software for free to some qualifying schools.

It pays to shop around for the best price on the software application you want to install. Some software publishers offer coupons for web-based purchases, and some retailers can offer attractive pricing when you package the software with your hardware. Look for a software suite that will bundle together multiple applications in one product. These are always a better value than buying individual applications.

Deciding on the software applications you want to use will help you choose the appropriate hardware and OS. All software applications will specify the system requirements for running the software. You will notice that software companies specify minimum and recommended system requirements. Go for the recommended requirements in a new purchase because performance is usually slower at the minimum requirements. Pay particular attention to the specified operating system that is needed to run the application, the amount of RAM, the processor speed, and the disk storage used by the application(s).

Software applications are typically available in a Mac or a Windows-compatible edition. With the popularity of cloud-based software that functions on either platform, deciding between Mac and PC is becoming less dependent on software and more a personal choice and budget issue. Apple PCs are more expensive than Windows-compatible PCs. The Apple iPad and iPhone are also more expensive than Windows-compatible or Android tablets and smartphones.

Apple PCs and mobile devices are generally more expensive than Windows-compatible computers, but fans argue the money is well spent.

Apple fans are fiercely loyal to the brand and will argue that the extra money for Apple is well worth the investment. Ultimately, if you are not partial to either platform or OS family of products, you should try both environments at your school or at a store to determine whether you become a Mac or a PC owner.

Step 4: Compare Hardware Components to Match Software Needs

Table A.1 (page 195) provides an overview of specifications you should check in a typical ad for a Windows-compatible notebook computer. If necessary, review Chapter 3 for more information on any of the hardware components that are listed.

If you can afford to spend more, buy more than you need to meet the recommended requirements. This will ensure you have a computer that will meet your needs into the future. In a nutshell, go for the computer with the fastest processor, most RAM, and largest internal hard disk drive. These systems will typically be packaged with other components that will be adequate for an average computer user working with Microsoft Office desktop applications and the Internet. If you cannot afford to spend more now, look for a computer ad that says the RAM is expandable. This will be a better choice than one that cannot be upgraded or that can accommodate only a limited amount of RAM added later.

Look for the Energy Star logo or something in the ad that says the device is Energy Star qualified. This means the computer will use less energy than one that is not rated.

Look for this logo, which tells you the device is energy efficient.

Examine the width, height, and weight specifications to get an idea of the physical characteristics. Pay particular attention to weight and screen size if you will be carrying the computer around at school in a backpack.

Step 5: Choose Options

If you are purchasing a notebook to use in place of a desktop PC, you may want to add an external monitor, keyboard, and mouse. These peripherals will allow you to design an ergonomically correct workspace at home to avoid the repetitive strain and

Table A.1

Hardware Components Typically Advertised for a Notebook PC

Processor	Intel Core, Atom, AMD, or ARM processors are commonly found in notebooks and tablets. Notebooks and tablets are sold with multiple-core CPUs, usually dual- or quad-core. Look for the amount and type of cache memory (L1, L2, or L3) with the CPU and the highest processor speed (1.5 GHz and higher).
RAM	RAM works with the CPU to give you high-speed performance. The more RAM you have, the better your system will perform. Look for a minimum of 4 GB of RAM on a notebook and 2 GB on a tablet. Check if RAM is expandable in modules that can be added to the device at a later time. A system with a higher level of expandable RAM will last longer.
Screen	A desktop PC will have a larger screen than a notebook or tablet, typically 19 inches or more. A notebook or ultrabook will have a screen size in the range of 15 inches or higher. Tablet screens are smaller, ranging from 9 to 12 inches. Screen size is measured diagonally from corner to corner.
Video Card	In most cases, the video card supplied with a notebook is adequate. If you are going to use your computer for gaming or high-end graphics design, pay attention to the graphics card, video memory, and GPU. Look for higher specifications for these items to achieve faster graphics processing capabilities.
Hard Disk Space	The larger the amount of hard disk storage space you can get, the better. However, keep in mind that you can always buy external hard disk drives to store digital photos, videos, and music files. Many notebooks are now supplied with a 1 TB HDD, but capacity varies. Look for a minimum of 500 GB.
Optical Disc Drives	Some notebooks include a DVD or Blu-ray Disc drive. Ultrabooks do not have optical drives (although you can purchase one as a peripheral). Optical drives are expected to become obsolete in the next few years as more people opt to stream movies and music.
Digital Media Reader	Transferring data from a digital camera or smartphone is easier if the notebook has a digital media card reader. Most notebooks are equipped with a reader or include a slot for one.
Networking Capabilities	Notebooks are equipped with integrated Wi-Fi networking capabilities. Some also come with integrated Bluetooth connectivity. An Ethernet port provides the added capability of plugging in to a wired network using a twisted-pair cable (sometimes called an *RJ-45 connector*). At school, some classrooms, lounges, or libraries may be equipped with network plug-ins that will give you faster Internet access than the wireless network.
Battery Life	Check the battery life to see how long the computer will operate before requiring power from an outlet. Battery life is important if you will be using the notebook away from power outlets for long periods of time.
Ports	Check the number and type of ports that are available on the notebook. The more USB ports the better, although you can buy an inexpensive USB hub if you need to expand the port availability. An HDMI port will allow you to plug in the notebook to a high-definition television screen for watching movies. A video port is also typically included to allow you to plug in an external monitor.
Integrated Web Cam	Most notebooks are equipped with a web cam. If you plan to do video calling, this feature will be important to you.

eye strain that occur from prolonged use of notebooks. Wireless keyboards and mice allow you to adjust your workspace to more comfortable positions.

If you like listening to music or watching movies, you may want to invest in external speakers or high-quality, noise-canceling headphones. A headset with a microphone is desirable if you plan to use voice technology in many applications.

If you need to print at home, consider whether you want a laser or inkjet printer. Compare the cost of toner versus ink and the number of pages you can print before replacing supplies to help you decide on the type of printer. Some computers are bundled with a printer. Make sure the printer included in such a package is one you want; if you would prefer a better quality printer,

Choose the options you want to purchase in addition to the computer.

try to negotiate a discount on it rather than accepting the packaged device. Consider an all-in-one printer that includes scanning and copying capabilities. All-in-one printers are a good value and will use less desk space than multiple devices.

If you are purchasing a computing portable device, think about how you will carry it and buy a well-padded case or backpack. Consider buying a case with wheels if you will be carrying a notebook along with your textbooks at school. For tablets, consider buying a sleeve or case that you can use to protect the screen surface.

Many mobile devices are subject to theft or loss. Consider biometric options such as a fingerprint reader, or tracking software and hardware that will allow you to remotely monitor or wipe the device should it be stolen or lost.

Step 6: Decide Whether to Buy an Extended Warranty

Most computer equipment carries a one-year parts and labor warranty.

Computers come with a limited parts and labor warranty that is typically good for one year. Consider if you want to buy the extended warranty plans that are offered when you buy a new computer. These warranties are priced depending on the value of the device, and some retailers' warranties will fix mishaps not covered by the manufacturer. Decide if you want to spend the money on these plans. Some people believe extended warranties are a waste of money, while others prefer the peace of mind that comes with knowing they are covered for anything that might happen.

If you have a credit card that includes a buyer protection plan, find out if you must make the purchase using the card and check the policy to see if the credit card insurance will cover you for any accidental damage or loss. If you have coverage, you may not need the extra protection from a retailer's extended warranty.

Step 7: Shop Around, Ask About Service, and Check Reviews

Spend some time on the web before deciding what to purchase, comparing two or three devices in the same price range that you can afford. Also compare the pricing at in-store electronics retailers and online e-tailers. Be mindful of shipping costs that you may incur if you buy from a web-based store. Consider creating a spreadsheet to compare a few options side by side.

Make sure to visit your school's computer store. Schools often offer attractive deals from hardware manufacturers that have discounts negotiated for the large school audience. School staff will also be able to help you choose a computer for programs with specialized hardware or software requirements.

If you are comfortable negotiating at an electronics store, you may be able to convince the retailer to upgrade some options for you in a package price. For example, it would not hurt to ask the sales associate to throw in a wireless keyboard or mouse, or a set of speakers, with a new notebook PC.

Make sure to inquire about service options. Ask where warranty work and other repairs are performed. Some stores will do warranty repairs or out-of-warranty repairs onsite, while others have to ship the PC back to the manufacturer. If the retailer ships the computer elsewhere, ask how long a typical repair will take. In some cases, you could be without your PC for more than week if the store ships the repair offsite. Ask who pays for the shipping to and from the repair center. Finally, some stores do not offer any assistance with repairs—avoid these locations if you are not technically savvy or are adverse to risk.

Some people prefer to pay a little more for a computer that they can have serviced at the store of purchase in case of malfunction. You will have to decide how important the repair facility is to you before making a purchase. Be sure to ask all these questions to help you make the choice with which you are most comfortable.

Search the web for reviews of the product you are considering and the retailer from which you want to purchase it. While reviews are not always helpful (many are negative and the positive ones may not be authentic), they do provide insight into the questions you should ask and the issues for which you want to be on the alert.

Compare prices at in-store and online retailers, investigate service options, and read reviews on the web.

Considerations for Buying a Smartphone

Before buying a smartphone, choose the provider with which you want to subscribe, the data plan that will meet your needs, and the features you want in a smartphone. Consider whether the provider you have chosen includes the cost of the smartphone in the contract. Some wireless providers will provide a base model smartphone free of charge or at a discounted price, or an upgraded model at a low price, if you sign up for a specified contract period. Watch for limits, caps, and time-of-use charges that may apply. For example, a plan may advertise unlimited use, but the unlimited use may apply in certain hours only. Note that some tablets may also include 3G or 4G wireless access and will need a data plan from a wireless carrier to take advantage of a cellular network when you are not in range of a Wi-Fi hotspot.

Good to Know

Some people prefer to buy an unlocked smartphone. An unlocked smartphone is not tied to a specific wireless carrier. This means you can buy a month-to-month voice and data plan without being locked into a long-term contract. To activate the phone, you will need to purchase a SIM card (a card you insert into the phone with your phone number, contacts, and call history) from the wireless carrier you choose.

Once you have chosen a data plan, compare the smartphones the carrier offers. Visit a store where you can try out a few smartphone models in advance. You will want to try models with different screen sizes. Larger screens might be nice, but consider how you will carry the smartphone and whether it will fit in your hand, pocket, or purse conveniently. You will want to try out messaging and browsing on different size screens to find the one with which you are comfortable. Input can be touch-based with an onscreen keyboard or you can use a keyboard with trackpad input. Keyboards may slide out or be built in below the screen. Try a few tasks with a touchscreen to make sure you are comfortable with touch input. Some people prefer keyboards over touch-enabled screens; however, you will find more selection among smartphones with touch-enabled screens because they are more popular.

Compare the battery life of various smartphone models. Battery technology is improving and newer batteries last longer, but often battery life does not live up to the advertised specifications. Talk time is the standard by which to base comparisons. Look on the web for reviews that have tested models and provide actual talk time statistics. You may want to inquire about purchasing a second battery if you will often be away from charging stations and think you will use the phone more than the advertised specifications. Another option is to purchase an external battery pack, which can be used with other devices as well as your smartphone.

People use their smartphones to do much more than just make phone calls—to take pictures or record video, play music, and communicate using messaging applications. The apps for performing these tasks need storage space on a memory card. Check the size of the memory card that comes with the smartphone and consider if you will need to buy a larger memory card. Check the compatibility of the memory card with your notebook or other computing devices so that you can easily exchange media files among them.

When acquiring a smartphone, start with a data plan and then try out various smartphones to choose the one that suits you. Consider the screen size, input method, battery life, and memory card options.

Ask if a car charger adapter comes with the smartphone or if you have to buy the car charger separately. This could be a negotiating item if you think you will use a car charger often.

Replacing an Older Device?

When you buy a new device, try to sell your older device, donate it to charity, or trade it in if the seller accepts trade-ins. If you cannot sell, give away, or trade in older electronics, remember to look into disposal options for e-waste that will properly recycle the device. Go to http://CC2.ParadigmCollege.net/EWaste for more information on recycling electronics.

Wireless Networking

A wireless network is the standard for most homes. People prefer a wireless network so that a network cable does not have to be installed from room to room through floors or ceilings in their home. With a wireless network, you can move freely around the house and outside to your yard, with your computing device, and not lose a network connection. You can connect PCs, tablets, smartphones, wearable devices, gaming consoles, smart appliances, and smart TVs. Family members browse the Internet, watch YouTube, and stream movies from any room in the house. In this appendix, you will learn the basic steps for setting up a wireless network and connecting devices to the network in a home. You will also learn how to set up a wireless network on Apple equipment, and how to connect to a public wireless network.

Tutorial

How Do I Set Up
a Wireless Home
Network?

Good to Know 🎓

The term *802.11* refers
to a set of specifications
developed by the
Institute of Electrical and
Electronics Engineers
(IEEE) that tells wireless
devices how to connect
with each other using a
series of access points
and radio frequencies to
transmit data. The letter
or letters after 802.11
(for example, *ac*)
reference the version
of the standard being
used.

Setting Up a Wireless Network at Home

Wi-Fi uses a combination wireless router / wireless access point and radio signals to transmit data within a limited range. The speed you will experience in a wireless network will vary depending on the equipment, the ISP service, the number of people sharing the connection, and the type of bandwidth being used by each connected user. Most wireless routers in use are either wireless ac (802.11ac) routers, or wireless n (802.11n) routers. A wireless ac router can operate approximately three times faster than a wireless n router, with ac routers tested in real world environments maintaining a speed of just under 1 Gbps. While this speed sounds lightning fast, bear in mind that the equipment can only deliver the Internet speed for which you have subscribed (see Step 1). You also need to have devices that are compatible with the wireless router to take advantage of newer technology.

Even with a wireless network, some homes will have a desktop PC that is connected by plugging in a network cable to the wireless router. The following steps describe the general process for setting up a wireless network. Different routers provide slightly different software interfaces; however, the general steps will be the same.

A modem provides Internet access. A wireless router allows you to share that access among multiple devices. Newer devices combine a modem and router into one unit.

Step 1: Subscribe to High-Speed Internet Service with an ISP

As you learned in Topic 2.2 in Chapter 2, to connect to the Internet, you need an account with an Internet service provider (ISP). Contact a telephone company, cable company, or dedicated Internet service company for high-speed Internet access. Each provider will offer different pricing levels that vary according to the speed, with faster speeds costing more per month than slower speeds.

A telephone company will provide you with a DSL modem, and a cable company will provide you with a cable modem. Newer modems provided by ISPs are a combination wireless router and modem in one piece of equipment called a *modem router*. Some installations may require two pieces of equipment: a DSL or cable modem, plus an additional wireless router. To proceed to Step 2, you need the ISP service activated, as well as a DSL or cable modem router, or a modem plus wireless router. If your ISP does not provide a wireless router, you can buy one at an electronics store. Brand names for commonly used wireless routers are Linksys, D-Link, and Cisco.

Your ISP may also provide instruction documentation when you subscribe for service

A modem router or cable modem provide high-speed Internet access.

and may give you a USB flash drive or DVD that automates the setup process if the company's technician does not go to your residence to do an on-site installation. New subscribers generally have a technician visit their home to set up the service and install and configure the equipment. Subscribers with existing service who are upgrading a router or modem will generally do the installation themselves, possibly with telephone assistance from the ISP. If the documentation from your ISP contains instructions that vary from the steps below, complete the steps according to the instructions from the ISP.

Step 2: Connect the Networking Hardware Equipment

Connect one end of a coaxial cable (cable modem) or twisted-pair cable (DSL modem) to the modem and the other end to the cable or telephone line coming into your house. Plug the power adapter into the modem and into a power outlet. You should see lights illuminate on the front of the modem, indicating power and connectivity are live.

Next, connect the modem to the wireless router if you need a standalone router (if your ISP did not provide you with a combination modem router). To do this, plug one end of a network cable into the back of the modem and the other end into the back of the wireless router. Plug the power adapter into the wireless router and into a power outlet. You should also see lights illuminate on the front of the standalone router.

If you have a desktop PC in the same room as your networking equipment, you can connect the PC to the integrated modem router or standalone router by plugging one end of a network cable into the PC network port and the other end into the back of the modem router or standalone router. This allows the PC to use a wired connection to the router, while the remaining devices in your home will use a wireless connection.

Connect a cable or DSL modem to a wireless router using a network cable.

Once the networking equipment is connected and has power, you can move on to Step 3.

Step 3: Configure the Wireless Router

Integrated modem routers or standalone routers may come with an installation CD, DVD, or USB flash drive that walks you through the steps to set up the router, or you may be instructed to go to a website to configure the router. One computer will need to be plugged into the wireless router while you configure it. After this step, you can unplug the PC from the router and connect wirelessly afterward.

Start with the computer connected to the router through the Ethernet port and the configuration medium installed or website open in your browser (Figure B.1, page 202). Proceed by following the instructions that appear in the setup program. The software interface is user-friendly, and prompts assist you at each step. Generally, you need to do three tasks: assign the router a name (called the *service set identifier [SSID]*) and security key, change the administrative password for the router, and choose the security standard you want to use.

Figure B.1

Insert the CD, DVD, or USB flash drive into a PC to start the router setup program (left), or open a browser window and type in the URL given to you by the ISP (right).

If you did not receive an installation medium with a preprogrammed setup process, look for instructions that came with the equipment that provide a URL or IP address to configure the router. Open a browser window and type the URL or IP address to start the software interface as shown in the image in Figure B.1. Note that the software interface for each router will vary. If in doubt about how to proceed, call the technical support assistance telephone number given to you.

Wireless routers come with a default user name and password—usually *admin* for both user name and password, or *admin* and *password*. Log on to the router device and proceed to change the settings as needed.

When giving the router a new name, try not to use an obvious name that will identify you with the router. For example, do not use your name or your address. If you use an obscure name, then when someone is within range of your router, they will not associate the network name with you and try to break into your Internet access (this can help you avoid situations such as a neighbor trying to piggyback your connection). A good idea is to prevent the router from broadcasting the router SSID. Although free public Wi-Fi networks, such as those at airports, coffee shops, and libraries, use a recognizable name to provide unsecured network access to everyone who is within range, home users should choose a name that is not easily associated with the location. Also assign a security key that your neighbors or anyone who knows you would not be able to guess.

Wireless routers may include a CD, DVD, or USB that automates the setup process. If none of these are provided, look on the bottom of the router for the address to type into a browser window.

Change the default administrator password to a strong password known only to you. The administrative password will be needed if you ever want to change the router settings in the future. If necessary, write down the user name and password for administering the router and store it in a secure location.

Activate the security standard for the router, preferably using Wi-Fi Protected Access WPA2. Some older devices may not support WPA2; in that case, use WPA. Avoid using the less secure WEP standard. WPA2 secures your wireless network with encryption. People will not be able to connect to the wireless router unless they know the security key, and data transmitted across the wireless network will be encrypted.

If you used a notebook PC to configure the wireless router, you can unplug it when finished and proceed to connect each wireless device to the router as described in Step 4. You can leave a desktop PC plugged into the router if the desktop PC does not have a wireless network adapter or you do not want to use it wirelessly.

Step 4: Connect Individual Devices to the Wireless Router

Notebooks, tablets, wearable devices, and smartphones come equipped with a built-in wireless interface card, called a *network adapter*. Generally, the wireless network adapter turns on by default when the device is powered on. For smartphones and some tablets, you may need to turn on Wi-Fi connectivity.

If a PC or other computing device does not have a built-in wireless interface card, you can purchase a network adapter for wireless networking. For a desktop PC, buy a USB wireless network adapter; for a notebook PC, buy a wireless network card adapter. A tip for ensuring a smooth setup process is to buy a wireless network adapter made by the same manufacturer as your wireless router.

For each device you want to connect to the wireless router, follow the steps similar to those illustrated in Figure B.2.

Connect a television, gaming console, or other smart device by following instructions provided by the device manufacturer. In most cases, you have two options. One is to use a push button on the router to instruct the device to automatically detect the router. The other option is to use a remote control to enter the device name and security key in an on-screen menu on the appliance.

Figure B.2

There are two steps to connecting to a wireless router manually in Windows 10.

Setting Up a Wireless Network on Apple Equipment

To set up a wireless network with Apple computers, you will need a Wi-Fi router, which Apple calls an AirPort. AirPort Express is the name of Apple's 802.11n router, and Airport Extreme is the name of Apple's 802.11ac router. Another device, called AirPort Time Capsule, combines an 802.11ac router with up to 3 TB of storage for backing up data in one device. Plug the Airport Express, Airport Extreme, or Time Capsule device into the high-speed cable or DSL modem from your ISP and then follow the instructions that appear in the AirPort Utility program that appears on your computer or iOS device.

Connecting to a Public Wireless Hotspot

Follow the steps to manually connect to a public wireless hotspot shown in Figure B.2 on page 203. The network name should be obvious in the list of available networks; however, if necessary you can ask a staff person (such as a store clerk, hotel clerk, or airport worker) for the network name and password. Exercise caution when using a public Wi-Fi hotspot, and do not transmit personal or confidential data, as public networks are not secured with encryption and are at risk of interception by hackers. Never perform financial transactions using a public Wi-Fi hotspot. If you must check email or sign in to a social network in a public Wi-Fi hotspot, do so with awareness of your surroundings and avoid entering confidential information in an email or post. If you frequently sign in to email or social networks using public Wi-Fi networks, consider having a different user name and password for these services than the ones you use for other online activities—especially banking or online shopping accounts.

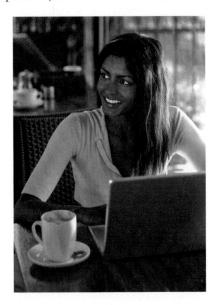

The Future of Wireless Networking

Wireless networking is becoming ubiquitous. More home devices are becoming Internet-enabled—even beyond smart appliances and televisions. The Internet of Things is expected to bring increasingly more connected objects into our day-to-day activities. As you move into this more connected future, it will become even more important to be diligent with wireless network security to ensure that your personal data is not subjected to unwanted access. If you change to a new modem or router, remember to use an SSID that is not easily associated with you or your home or disable the broadcast of the SSID. Also be sure to always use a strong password for both the network and the router administration.

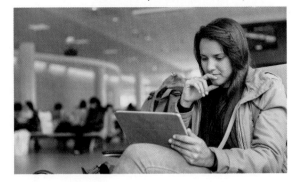

Glossary/Index

P

packaged software traditional desktop software that can be purchased at a retail store, from an e-commerce website, or directly from the software publisher, 134

Panasonic Firefox OS, 98

parallel processing a computer configuration that involves having multiple microprocessor chips or a multicore processor to execute multiple instructions simultaneously, 65

passwords
    criteria for strong, 171
    protection for mobile devices, 96

PayPal, 54

peer-to-peer (P2P) file sharing a form of file sharing facilitated by a website at which users exchange files directly with one another over the Internet, 154

pen drive, 81

peripheral hardware used for input, output, connectivity, or storage that you plug in or connect to your computer wirelessly, 63
    operating system configuring, 90
    options and buying new computer, 194, 196

personal computer (PC) a computer in which the input, processing, storage, and output are self-contained, 4
    buying a new, 192–197

personal finance software programs used to keep track of a checking or savings account, investments, or other personal financial information, 126

personal information management (PIM) application a software program that helps you organize messages, schedules, contacts, and tasks, 118

petaflop a measurement used in scientific calculations that represents a quadrillion floating point operations per second, 9

PewDiePie, 158

phablet means the combination of a *phone* and *tablet* and describes a smartphone with a screen larger than 5.25 inches but not as large as a typical tablet, 6

pharming a scam in which an individual is tricked into typing in personal information at a phony website that appears to be the real website requested by the individual, 181

phishing activities that appear to be initiated by a legitimate organization in an attempt to obtain personal information that can be used in fraud, theft, or identity theft, 180

Photobucket, 155

photo editing software programs used to edit pictures and add special effects and text to photos taken with a digital camera, 122

photo printer an output device that connects directly to a digital camera to print high-quality photos on photo paper using inkjet technology, 74

photos
    mobile apps for sharing, 155, 157
    websites for sharing, 155

Picasa, 155

piggybacking connecting to someone else's wireless network without the network owner's knowledge or consent, 171

Pinterest a website with virtual pinboards on which people pin pictures of things they have seen on the Internet that they like and want to share using the Pin It button, 151

pixel a square with red, green, and blue color values that represent each color needed to form an image. Millions of pixels make up the image shown on a screen, 73

plasma a flat-panel technology that provides truer color representation but is expected to become obsolete by the improved technology in LEDs, 72

platter, 80

player a software program that allows the browser to display enhanced content that it cannot display on its own. Also called add-on or plug-in, 52
    installing tips, 52–53
    popular, 53
    updates, 53

plotter an output device that moves one or more pens across the surface of the paper to produce a drawing, 74

plug and play OS technology in which the OS searches a newly plugged-in device for the driver, loads it automatically, and displays a message when the device is ready to use. See also *driver,* 90

plug-in a software program that allows the browser to display enhanced content that it cannot display on its own. Also called *add-on* or *player,* 52
    installing tips, 52–53
    popular, 53
    updates, 53

podcast an audio or video file that is usually a part of a series and is streamed or downloaded to your computer or mobile device, 154

podcatcher a software program that automatically downloads new podcasts for which the user has subscribed to a computer or mobile device, 154

Popurls, 47

portable media player a device on which to play music, watch videos, view photos, play games, and/or read electronic books, 6

port a connector located at the back, side, or front of a computer or mobile device that is used to plug in external devices, 66–67
    dock port, 68
    specification when buying computer, 195

posture-related injuries, 20

potentially unwanted program (PUP), 177

presentation application software used to create slides for an electronic slideshow that may be projected on a screen or displayed at a self-running kiosk, 116

printers
    options and buying new computer, 196
    types of, 74–75

Priv, 97

privacy issues
    awareness of shoulder surfers, 187
    cookies, 182
    data privacy in cloud, 184–185
    social network privacy setting, 149
    spam, 183
    spyware, 183
    ways to protect personal information, 184

processing one of the four progressions in the information processing cycle in which data is manipulated or otherwise acted upon by the central processing unit, 13
    in information processing cycle, 13

processor, 195

productivity software, 114
    mobile apps for, 139
    for workplace, 114–121

productivity suite programs used in the workplace that includes word processing, spreadsheets, presentations, and database management. Also known as *software suite,* 114

ProjectLibre, 119, 120

project management application a software program used to enter all the tasks needed to get a project done, establish time frames, assign resources, and allocate budget money to each task, 119–120

protocol a set of rules that defines how data is exchanged between two devices, 76

Q

QR (Quick Response) code a type of bar code that looks like a matrix of black square dots and directs the device (usually a smartphone) to display a website, 69

QuarkXPress, 123

QuickBooks, 119

Quicken, 127

QuickTime, 53

Quora, 160

R

radio frequency identification (RFID) reader a device that scans an embedded RFID tag (a chip with an antenna) to identify an object, 69–70

random access memory (RAM) temporary storage for instructions and data that is cleared when power to the computer is lost, 14
    on motherboard, 66
    specification when buying computer, 195

ransomware a type of malware that locks or restricts access to a device, and the malware creator demands a ransom payment in exchange for unlocking the device or providing the unlock code, 178

raw data characters that are typed or otherwise entered into a computer, 12

Rdio, 156

read-only memory (ROM) memory built on the motherboard that is used for storing computer instructions that do not change, 66

Really Simple Syndication (RSS) a specification used by content aggregators to distribute updates to subscribers. See also *Atom,* 46

Real Player, 53

reddit a social networking website where registered members post content, which other members vote up or down to create a submission score. The score determines the position of the entry on the page, 148

redditors, 148

Red Hat, 94

reference software programs that use multimedia tools to provide rich content information in encyclopedias, dictionaries, translation guides, atlases, and other reference resources, 129

repetitive-strain injury (RSI) an injury or disorder of the joints, nerves, muscles, ligaments, or tendons, 20
    prevention strategies for, 21
    symptoms of, 20

Windows Embedded a family of OSs based on Windows that are used to present an interface and manage input, output, and resources for devices or appliances that have an embedded processor, 98

wired connectivity, network adapters for, 76

wireless connectivity, network adapters for, 76–77

wireless ExpressCard an adapter that plugs into a narrow slot on a notebook or other mobile device to provide wireless network connectivity, 77

wireless interface card built-in wireless adapter that allows you to connect to a network using wireless technology, 32

wireless networks

    benefits of, 199

    connecting to public wireless hotspot, 204

    equipment for, 200

    future of, 204

    securing, 172–173

    setting up at home, 200–203

    setting up on Apple equipment, 204

    as target for hackers, 170–171

wireless router, 200–203

WordPress a blog hosting website that uses the WordPress open source blogging software, 158

word processing application software used to create documents containing mostly text, 114–115

workplace

    ergonomically correct workspace, 21

    productivity applications for, 114–121

World of Warcraft (WoW), 128

World Wide Web the global collection of electronic documents circulated on the Internet in the form of web pages. Also called *web*, 29

worm a self-replicating program that requires no user action to copy itself to another computer on a network; a computer becomes infected simply by connecting to an infected network, 177

WPA2, 172–173

Wrike, 119

Y

Yahoo!, 44

Yik Yak, 148

Yosemite, 93

YouTube the most popular video sharing website owned by Google, 123, 154, 156

Z

Zoho, 114, 130–131

zombie a computer that is connected to the Internet and is controlled by a hacker or other cybercriminal without the owner's knowledge, 174